W9-ACA-978

DIGGING THE AFRICANIST PRESENCE IN AMERICAN PERFORMANCE

For Eliza, Amel, and Sky
(my mother, daughter, and granddaughter):
Yesterday, Today, and Tomorrow

DIGGING THE AFRICANIST PRESENCE IN AMERICAN PERFORMANCE

Dance and Other Contexts

Brenda Dixon Gottschild

Westport, Connecticut
London

The Library of Congress has cataloged the hardcover edition as follows:

Gottschild, Brenda Dixon.
    Digging the Africanist presence in American performance : dance
and other contexts / Brenda Dixon Gottschild.
        p. cm.—(Contributions in Afro-American and African
studies, ISSN 0069–9624 ; no. 179)
    Includes bibliographical references and index.
    ISBN 0–313–29684–7 (alk. paper)
    1. Afro-Americans in the performing arts.   2. Afro-American dance.
I. Title.   II. Series.
PN1590.B53G68   1996
791′.08996073—dc20   95–20558

British Library Cataloguing in Publication Data is available.

A hardcover edition of *Digging the Africanist Presence in American Performance*
is available from Greenwood Press, an imprint of Greenwood Publishing
Group, Inc. (Contributions in Afro-American and African Studies, Number 179;
ISBN 0–313–29684–7).

Library of Congress Catalog Card Number: 95–20558
ISSN: 0–275–96373–X (pbk.)

First published in 1996

Praeger Publishers, 88 Post Road West, Westport, CT 06881
An imprint of Greenwood Publishing Group, Inc.

Printed in the United States of America

The paper used in this book complies with the
Permanent Paper Standard issued by the National
Information Standards Organization (Z39.48–1984).

10 9 8 7 6 5 4 3 2 1

$$\begin{array}{r} 59 \\ -47 \\ \hline 12 \end{array}$$

CONTENTS

ILLUSTRATIONS

ACKNOWLEDGMENTS

Many thanks to those colleagues who read parts of this manuscript in its various stages and whose comments, critical and encouraging, helped fuel my fire: Yvonne Daniel, Sterling Stuckey, Lawrence Levine, Neil Hornick, and, early on, David Gere and Nicole Plett. Thanks also to my friend and colleague, Vèvè Clark, for her valued intellectual and spiritual support, and to Nina Pearlstein and Andrea Mastor, my editors.

I am grateful to the Rockefeller Foundation Bellagio Conference and Study Center for a much-needed writing retreat; to Temple University for the summer research fellowship, grant-in-aid, and research leave, which gave me the time and license to complete this work; and to the Pennsylvania Council on the Arts for funds that helped facilitate the completion of an earlier, abbreviated version of Chapter 5.

My doctoral students have been wonderful in allowing me to use my seminars as a laboratory for exploring ideas and in offering themselves as sounding boards and dialogic partners. Particular thanks go to Meira Weinzweig-Goldberg and Julie Kerr-Berry, who were with me, directly and indirectly, as I began the odyssey that resulted in this book.

Thanks to the very helpful staff of the Dance Collection, New York Public Library at Lincoln Center, and especially to Monica Moseley for her good leads; and to all those who granted permission to use the illustrations included herein. A shout goes out to Tony Anderson for his indispensable help in preparing the camera-ready copy.

I thank my siblings, especially Christine and George, for believing in me; and my husband, Hellmut, for challenging me in his chosen role of devil's advocate, while always providing me with a ground and base of unconditional love and support; and thank God that this work is done!

INTRODUCTION

My aim in this work is to reach underground and excavate the subtextual Africanist components, correspondences, influences — presences, if you will — that are essentials in defining and shaping Euro-American endeavor in the United States. I will examine these elements in concert dance forms, daily life, and popular performance arenas from minstrelsy to hip hop. Issues of power and agency, as framed by ongoing racialized disparity, enter the discussion. I utilize performance studies methodologies as my research tools: namely, observation, documentation, and analysis of live and taped performance; oral interviews and conversations; and critique of scholarly and popular texts on dance and culture. Chapters 1, 2, and 3 examine Africanist aesthetic principles, their manifestation in European American popular culture and lifestyles, and their function as one of the sources of modernism and postmodernism in the visual arts. Chapter 4 is a discussion of these resonances as an integral component in the undergirding foundations and assumptions of postmodern dance, with references to its predecessor, modern dance. In Chapter 5 I investigate the Africanist presence in George Balanchine's Americanization of ballet. Chapter 6 is a reexamination of minstrelsy — that old repository of skewed economic, psychological, and aesthetic relationships between blacks and whites. The final chapter focuses on the sociopolitical and cultural issues of power and empowerment that arise in the contemporary performance arena, on stage and in life, as ethnicities clash in acknowledgment or denial of their differences. Hip hop culture enters the discussion due to its central role in the contemporary discourse on hegemony and privilege.

The term "Africanist" is used by contemporary African American scholars such as Joseph Holloway and Toni Morrison (and, in an earlier

generation, by anthropologist Melville Herskovits).[1] I use it here to signify African and African American resonances and presences, trends,
and phenomena. It indicates the African influence, past and present, and
those forms and forces that arose as products of the African diaspora,
including traditions and genres such as blues, jazz, rhythm and blues,
and hip hop. It denotes the considerable impact of African and African
American culture on modern arts and letters; the wealth of African-based
American dance forms that proliferate from ballroom and nightclub
floors to popular and concert stages; and, finally, the pervasive African-
rooted presence in everyday American lifestyles—from walking, talking,
hairdos, and food preparation to acting "hip." In sum, the term denotes
concepts and practices that exist in Africa and the African diaspora and
have their sources in concepts or practices from Africa.   In turn,
"Europeanist" is used to denote concepts and practices in Europe and the
Americas that have their tap roots in concepts and practices from
Europe. Although these two massive cultural constellations—European
and African—are fused and interwoven in many aspects, they also manifest distinct, discrete, and somewhat opposing characteristics and lend
themselves to discussion as binary opposites, if not separate streams.

Some readers may find the language of the discourse that follows a
little dense and layered. It is dictated by and reflects the complexity,
convolutions, and dimensions of the area of study. I have tried to avoid
misrepresentation and reduction of the subject matter. Instead, I hope
that in mirroring its intricacy I have made it visible. As I write this work,
I assume the dual roles of cultural critic and dance historian. Throughout, I turn an Africanist eye on American performance and serve as the
conduit for bringing together theories from different disciplines, con-
necting and focusing them through my vision as the performance studies
scholar-as-archeologist, digging—and "digging"—the Africanist presence in our culture. I am not the first to take up these issues. I see myself
not as the creator of virgin theory but the instigator of a fresh spin on
what is already out there—a patchwork quiltmaker in culture theory.
Yet, some of my "takes" have been firsts, and at least one of them—the
discourse on Africanisms in the work of George Balanchine—has subsequently been picked up in the work of other dance writers.

My background and preparation for this work began long before I
became a writer. My intellectual and philosophical perspectives are
rooted secondarily in the European tradition of my formal education but
primarily in the Southern Baptist tradition, which has spawned generations of African Americans who pledge allegiance to "the life of the
mind" and "the struggle for freedom" (West in hooks and West 1991, 30).
Bernice Reagon says that there is sweetness in struggle, that being a
fighting warrior artist is a way to safeguard one's sanity (1992). I thank

her for naming our mission. As an African American raised in the borough of Manhattan (a longtime seat of Creolized culture), educated and employed in European American universities, and having performed with European American modern dance and experimental theater groups stateside and abroad, I live equally in black and white worlds, as do many African Americans. With a firm foundation in both (and an understanding of the historical intertextuality between them), I base my research and conclusions on theoretical investigation tempered and tested by years of practical experience.[2] I have written dance and theater reviews and scholarly articles for two decades; attended innumerable dance, music, theater, and visual arts events; presented my research at scholarly convocations and public lectures; and conducted interviews and held conversations with performers, students, scholars, and lay people. My approach is, if you will, a Creolized one, since "traditional scientific method can't tell you where you ought to go, unless where you ought to go is a continuation of where you were going in the past" (Asante 1987, 114).[3]

The postmodern choreographer Trisha Brown states in the film "Beyond The Mainstream" (1980) that her work is "silky, daring, kinesthetic," sometimes "slipping off the air" and then returning to something safe and predictable. As an ex-performer balancing my act between modernism and postmodernism—and as an African American scholar who is also a scholar who is African American—I recognize a bit of Brown's approach in my own choreography for the page, as I slip on or off risky ideas and return to metaphorically toe or stomp the line with a bare, black foot. . . .

NOTES

1. See Morrison (1992) and Holloway (1990). Herskovits used the term in an earlier generation (1958) in the anthropological sense or, as Sterling Stuckey pointed out (correspondence, March, 1995), in a way that suggested "vestigial remains," or "survivals"—a usage that "falls short of conveying a sense of process." My usage is intended to designate the vitality and energy of a lively aesthetic that is characterized by the privileging of process or experience over product or thingness. Morrison uses the term "Africanist presence," which I have adopted.

2. To be clear, the terms "African," and "European"—and, for that matter, "Asian," "Latino," "Native American," and "Oceanic"—are grand, generalized markers indicating many different cultures and representing a complex variety of aesthetic, social, political, and religious configurations. I cite European and African, knowing full well that Asian, Latino, Native American, and Oceanic must also be accounted for in the American equation but knowing also that the nitty-gritty chasm in the United States runs along the black-white fault line, with all peoples of color heretofore obliged to buy into one "side" or the other.

3.   Quoting Robert Pirsig, *Zen and the Art of Motorcycle Maintenance*, New York: Bantam Books, 1972, 275.

1

UP FROM UNDER: THE AFRICANIST PRESENCE

Although many other massive movements of peoples have occurred analogous to the confrontation of Europeans and Africans in the New World, no clear statement exists of the variables that operate in such situations. Instead, a casual, anecdotal approach has been taken in which the encounter is seen from the viewpoint of the politically or economically superordinate people as against the subordinate, with the assumption that such subordination leads to cultural as well as political and economic dominance. *No case undercuts this model of acculturation so clearly as that of Afro-American peoples, because many of the most basic features of plantation and modern New World life have been obviously influenced by Afro-American cultural practices.*

John F. Szwed and Roger D. Abrahams 1977, 65; emphasis added

In a modern dance film, "Dance: Four Pioneers," which is screened in college dance department classrooms across the nation, the narrator states that the contributions of Doris Humphrey, Charles Weidman, Hanya Holm, and Martha Graham are felt in American dance from Broadway to the concert stage. Just as those venues are infused with the work of the "four pioneers," so also they are steeped in Africanist influences. As dance critic Deborah Jowitt wrote, "There are looks in the air that dancers absorb willy nilly — the common movement currency of our day, so much a part of the creative framework that they're taken for granted, especially by those born to them" (1987, 3). Jowitt was referring to imitators of Trisha Brown, a popular post-Merce Cunningham, postmodern choreographer, but her statement applies only too well to the subject at hand. The Africanist presence in American culture has shaped a New World legacy that sets American culture apart from that of Western Europe. It is a potent, vital force that plays a significant role in defining the American aesthetic. At the same time, it has suffered from sins of commission and omission; it has been "invisibilized," to coin a new word. Racial segregation and discrimination are the culprits in the systematic denial and exploitation of this powerful influence. We even doubt that we should look at it, in the context of our everyday lives. For example, in the mid-1980s a student in a course I teach, "Black Performance from Africa to the Americas," came up to me at the end of the first session and asked, "Should I take this class—I mean, since I'm white?" I looked at her and said, "Honey, you're taking it right now; you've been taking it all your life!"

It is improbable that the question would be posed today, now that the buzzword "multiculturalism" is bandied about in classrooms and curriculum meetings nationwide. But, as we hover on the brink of a new century, how far have we advanced in our willingness to acknowledge, assess, respect, and embrace the contributions of African-based cultures that make America the particular experience that it is? The student who asked me that question is not unique. As Americans—African, Native American, European, Latino, Asian, Oceanic—we are all part of that course, alone or together, whether we signed up for it or not, whether we like it or not. Some of us don't know it. Some do, but deny it.

My purpose here is not to valorize Africanisms by comparing them with Europeanist phenomena, but to show that the latter are dependent upon the former, and that, overtly and subliminally, these invisibilized influences significantly shape European American experience. A school of contemporary scholars, taking their lead from anthropologist Melville Herskovits, have examined Africanisms in African American culture. (It was Herskovits who advised Katherine Dunham to combine her dancer-choreographer persona with her anthropologist-scholar side and research Africanisms in Caribbean dance forms. He gave similar inspiration to folklorist Roger Abrahams in encouraging him to seek out African retentions in urban Philadelphia speech patterns; see Abrahams 1991.) Their focus is the African/African American connection. My attempt here is to take the next logical step and investigate the African American/European American connection, utilizing an Africanist perspective as my guide.

Influences, presences, correspondences, correlatives, cross-pollinations, and borrowings are part of the history of humankind. Art historians and scholars are concerned with distinguishing among these concepts to ascertain the degree and category of penetration and exchange. They designate two generic categories of borrowing: direct influences and broader affinities. Both exemplify the structuralist-poststructuralist principle of intertextuality. This theory (developed and utilized by Roland Barthes, Julia Kristeva, Mikhail Bakhtin, Jacques Derrida, and others) can be summed up in a phrase that is reductive and rather pat, but bears repeating: All texts are intertexts. That is, forces, trends, languages, movements, modes—texts, in other words—of previous and contemporary societies influence us, live within and around us, and form the threads through which we weave our "new" patterns. They are the anonymous, unauthored codes of the culture. The first implication is that there really is nothing new under the sun, only variations on prior remnants, formulas, and patterns that are assimilated and reconfigured in the present moment. Our American culture, like every culture, is a panoply of quotations from a wide spectrum of past and present conditioning forces. Two additional implications ensue: First, the multitudinous sources, anonymous and unauthored, of any given set of texts are so thoroughly interwoven that their origins are difficult, if not impossible, to sort out. Second, the fusion process is unconscious and automatic, not dissimilar to Jowitt's "looks in the air."

Both perspectives—Jowitt's and the poststructuralist—acknowledge that there are forces that rub up against other forces, and that the process is largely subliminal. I agree, without losing sight of the fact that there are other cultural borrowings that are calculated and intentional. In terms of the Africanist aesthetic in American culture, I disagree with the origins part of the intertextual argument. Although we do not need to and cannot reduce the intertextuality of the African American/European American equation to a laundry list of sources and influences, we desperately need to cut through the convoluted web of racism that denies acknowledgment of the Africanist part of the whole. Jowitt detected "Trisha Brownisms" as a particular, intertextual thread in postmodern dance; similarly, I detect the Africanist as a particular, pervasive presence that touches almost every aspect of American life. The peculiar binary relationship between black and white cultures in the Americas, fused but also separated, demands a reconfiguration of the discourse on intertextuality. Separate strands are indeed identifiable, and that is what I hope to show. In fact, to discern Trisha Brownisms or Africanisms in American culture expands, rather than refutes, intertextuality. The impact of the Africanist presence has come up from under in the current or postmodern era, but it is really nothing new. These influences have existed in European American life and culture since Africans and Europeans together set foot on American shores. Plantation-era contacts between the two groups forged and shaped a unique, Creolized, Afro-Euro-American culture. Africanist characteristics frequently stand out on the cultural landscape as markedly different from traditional Europeanist attributes. More fitting for qualitative than quantitative analysis, Africanisms shape processes or the way that something is done, not simply the product or the fact that it is done. Concomitantly, a theory of Africanisms parallels a theory of intertextuality, which seeks to deal with the how or the process-phenomenon of the living text, rather than the text as product.

The African-European paradigm is the bottom line of American culture that greets and grounds every newly arrived immigrant, regardless of ethnicity and political, social, religious, or economic persuasion. (Native American presences and peoples are implied in this mix, but in a different degree, due to their specific history of enslavement and decimation. That is another story for another book.) Of course, American culture includes important, significant influences from many other cultures as well. But it is rooted in and defined by the pervasive cultural manifestations of peoples of (Central and West) African and European lineage. The cultural constructs of these broad but divergent groupings form the matrix, the scaffolding of American culture. Asian peoples from the many ethnicities represented by that continent and sub-continent are forced, gently or otherwise, to buy into this Afro-Euro polarity. As one writer said, people of color in America "spend too much energy understanding our lives in relation to whiteness" (Martinez 1994, 57). Every new wave of immigrants, be they from Europe or Asia, are automatic inheritors of both Africanisms and the anti-black racism that pervade American society and that are ineluctably assumed by newcomers in their process of Americanization. Similarly, every immigrant of African descent, regardless of ethnocultural background, is likely to be considered part of the black American underclass and is subject to racial segregation and discrimination solely on the basis of skin color. African immigrants are treated as African Americans for reasons of restriction, not in acknowledgment and celebration of the rich continuities that exist between African and African American traditions. Stories of the black business executive mowing his front lawn who is mistaken for the gardener, or the female African American party guest who is asked to bring another drink, are told every day, hundreds of times and in hundreds of variations. It may very well be true that "African Americans experience racism as such and that the suffering of other people of color results from national minority [status] rather than racial oppression" (paraphrased in Martinez 1994, 58).

The African presence in the New World has always posed questions for the dominant culture, not because it is a negligible quotient but precisely because of its potency. American society is permeated by Africanist attitudes, forms, and phenomena, from African agrarian practices, which were basic to the success of plantation agriculture, to such African American specifics as potato chips, peanut butter, revival meetings, and the Charleston. In spite of trivialization, concealment, or repression, cultural information is intertextual, not linear. Exchange and adaptation are not a matter of jewels of wisdom from the dominant culture wafting down from places of power to enlighten the disenfranchized. Rather, cross-pollination is the closer model, and Creolization is the name of the game. But what is the game, and how is it played? The significant points are: What is the text? Who is doing the documentation? From whose perspective? By whose criteria? And what is being recorded? When the dominant culture oversees these processes, the results are almost predictable. If language is the exercise of power, and the act of naming is an act of empowerment, then what is not named, or misnamed, becomes an impotent backdrop for someone else's story. How else can one explain the focus of Hollywood films such as "Mississippi Burning," "Cry, Freedom," "Glory," or "Dances With Wolves?" In each case the thrust of the historical moment was skewed to highlight the dominant-culture male. The African or Native American perspective was represented as a byproduct of the white hero's coming of age. Historian Mary Helen Washington addressed this issue in a discussion about the television series, "I'll Fly Away," which is set in Mississippi at the beginning of the Civil Rights era and focuses on a European American family and their African American maid, Lily:

As strong and appealing as Lily is, I have continued to feel uneasy about the intent of this show, especially its focus on whites and its relegating black characters to the background. . . . Isn't it ironic that black people, who produced, directed, cast and starred in the original Civil Rights Movement, have become minor players in its dramatic reenactment? (Washington 1992, 35)

Displacement of ownership by the television and film industries is the tip of the iceberg, beneath whose cold waters lurk grosser magnitudes of denial.

Parallels exist in other cultural examples. A contemporary school of historical theory in France and Germany takes pains to exclude Jewish contributions from national memory in what stands as a signal example of how history is written and rewritten from the dominant perspective. In the eyes of contemporary historians Robert Faurisson and Michael Sturmer and philosopher Ernst Nolte, the Jewish Holocaust is either a fiction or an overblown historical footnote. Historian Pierre Nora omits the Dreyfus Affair, a key incident in modern French history, from his *lieux de mémoire*, a late 1980s nationally popular catalog of important events in French history.[1] Walter Rathenau, a German Jewish politician who was assassinated in the early 1920s, had this to say about growing up Jewish in pre-Nazi Germany: "Some time in the youth of every German Jew a moment comes when he realizes he is a second-class citizen" (quoted in Heilbut 1983, 10).

African Americans experience a similar feeling about growing up in the United States. It is extraordinary that the cultural legacy of these "second-class citizens," Jewish or African, exerted such a significant influence on the cultures of their oppressors. In South Africa oppression was so severe that the subjugated population was relegated to "homelands" — a witless irony in terminology — that were segregated from the dominant culture so as to invisibilize and marginalize this indigenous influence. For African and Jewish peoples these facts of history are our facts of life, and the memory of history is synonymous with the "memory of suffering."[2] Attempts to eradicate memory act as a roadblock to empowerment, perpetuate a language of silence, enforce a politic of denial, and reinforce past suffering into the present. Toni Morrison was right on the mark with her novel *Beloved*, which is all about this anguished historicity, and with her incisive comments in a magazine interview, "The Pain of Being Black," which poignantly discussed the permanence of American racism (Morrison 1989, 120–22). Unlike Germany after Hitler, the white American South was never humbled and brought to its knees for its institutionalized racism. On the contrary, black American suffering has been sugared over by the white American romance with the antebellum South, epitomized in works like *Gone With The Wind* and the idealization of the "Southern belle."[3] Slavery remains an unhealed and unacknowledged wound on the collective American body, and the black-white playing field remains uneven; in fact, it is a battleground.

It is interesting how Otherness defines itself in different times. Fifty or so years ago, blacks were expected to step off the sidewalk when crossing paths with whites. Now, it is often the case that white people cross over to the other side of the street when encountering young black men. The superiority syndrome thus shows its flip side of fear.

Were we to do justice to this fertile Africanist presence, we might begin with a reversal. What if we were to stand on our heads and assume that our American culture is African-rooted, so that the European elements could be regarded from an Africanist perspective? Revisionist thinking is basic to my investigation of American concert dance.[4] It is also the driving force behind dance anthropologist Joann Kealiinohomoku's signature essay, "An Anthropologist Looks at Ballet as a Form of Ethnic Dance" (1983, 24–33). The title implies an about-face. Feminist writer Jill Johnston suggests gender turnarounds as a way of unveiling the underlying sexual politics in performance (1991, 2). Toni Morrison's *Playing in the Dark: Whiteness and the Literary Imagination* (1992) examines the utter dependence of European American literature on the African American presence in order to define itself. Historian Eric Foner's Afrocentric perspective on the American Revolution reveals not a victory for liberation and equality but an upheaval that engendered deteriorating conditions for African Americans and strengthened the institution of slavery (1990). Florida State University psychologist Naim Akbar offered the following example to explain the difference between an Afrocentric and a Eurocentric perspective: from a Eurocentric perspective, Europe is the Old World and America the New World; from an Afrocentric perspective, Africa is the Old World and Europe is the New World (1990). An Afrocentric perspective on the origins of Greek culture, known by scholars as the Ancient Model, considers the Egyptian and Semitic origins of ancient Greece; the Eurocentric, or Aryan, model minimized those influences in an effort to establish a "pure" Greece worthy to sire European culture (Bernal quoted in Morrison 1989, 7). These random examples show the multiplicity of revisionist approaches in contemporary historiography and cultural studies.

Reconceiving the traditional canon can also be described in visual terms. In sketch classes, students occasionally are assigned a reversal exercise that can stand as a metaphor for our scholarly reassessments. They must make a drawing that depicts only the negative spaces, the areas in and around the subject. The exercise shows, by the experiential process and its result, that subject-object and foreground-background are interdependent constructs. The dichotomy between subject and object blends into a dialogic relationship when seen from this amended perspective. Like photographers, scholars are beginning to see that the negative contains the positive, and the two are interrelated and inseparable. In our United States, European culture has assumed the role of the positive foreground, and Africanist culture is assigned the negative space, if any space at all. But, truth to tell, the two are conjugated, and the European heritage is no greater than the African influence in shaping American culture. As one writer stated, "looking for the roots of blues for a white [American] person is looking through your own roots" (Davis, quoted in Gonzales 1995, 25). Indeed, Americans black and white inherit the Africanist aesthetic.

By reexamining our perspective we can revise our understanding of performance values basic to each aesthetic approach. African-based cultural forms and practices in the Americas can be traced to Central and West African traditions and have signposts that differentiate them from European-based forms and practices. True, American culture is a fusion of African and European elements, but it is possible to tease apart some of the component strands and designate them as recognizably or predominantly African or European. Such an analysis is possible because European and African aesthetic principles differ markedly and occasionally represent opposing perspectives. For example, the diatonic scale of traditional European orchestral music is based upon a principle of melodic and tonal resolution structured around seven basic notes. In contrast, African music is chromatic and polyphonic and, not unlike classical Indian music, characterized by microtonal shadings. Another example lies in African "dilemma" tales that illustrate a principle of contrariety, open endedness, or living with opposition, without the necessity of resolution or closure. These are stories that end with a question or call for a discussion, rather than a solution. They stand as a challenge to the linear concept of beginning-middle-end, or even the necessity of a happy ending. The Africanist aesthetic values repetition or, more precisely, repetition-as-intensification. To the Europeanist ear, the reprises may seem monotonous and superfluous; in the Africanist perspective each repeat is different than the one that went before, is shaped by the one that went before, and predicates the one that will follow. The repetition principle exemplifies the transcendent power of the Africanist worldview, for there is much repetition in traditional, quotidian African life: pounding grain, seeding ground, kneading bread, reaping the crop. In transferring repetition from the chores of daily life to the realm of creative expression, the Africanist aesthetic transforms the prosaic into the sublime and makes a spiritual and conceptual connection between the two. It is in the African-Asian-inflected postmodern era that repetition, in a Europeanist context, resonates as a value rather than a demerit.

In traditional European dance aesthetics, the torso must be held upright for correct, classic form; the erect spine is the center—the hierarchical ruler—from which all movement is generated. It functions as a single unit. The straight, uninflected torso indicates elegance or royalty and acts as the absolute monarch, dominating the dancing body. This vertically aligned spine is the first principle of Europeanist dance, with arm and leg movements emanating from it and returning to it. The ballet canon is organized around this center. In fact, this structural principle is a microcosm of the post-Renaissance, colonialist world view. Like the straight, centered spine of its dancing body, Europe posited itself as the center of the world, with everything else controlled and defined by it.

Africanist dance idioms show a democratic equality of body parts. The spine is just one of many possible movement centers; it rarely remains static. The Africanist dancing body is polycentric. One part of the body is played against another, and movements may simultaneously originate from more than one focal point (the head and the pelvis, for example). It is also polyrhythmic (different body parts moving to two or more rhythms simultaneously), and privileges flexible, bent-legged postures that reaffirm contact with the earth (sometimes called a "get-down" stance). The component and auxiliary parts of the torso—shoulders, chest, rib cage, waist, pelvis—can be independently moved or articulated in different directions (forward, backward, sideward, or in circles) and in different rhythms. From an Africanist perspective, a pulled-up, aligned stance and static carriage indicate sterility and inflexibility, and the performer is encouraged to "dance with bended knees, lest you be taken for a corpse" (Thompson 1974, 9-10). In the classical Europeanist view, the movement exists to produce the (finished) work; in the Africanist view, the work exists to produce the movement. As assessed by Africanist aesthetic criteria, the Europeanist dancing body is rigid, aloof, cold, and one-dimensional. By Europeanist standards, the Africanist dancing body is vulgar, comic, uncontrolled, undisciplined, and, most of all, promiscuous. The presumption of promiscuity is allied with and leads directly to the sexually licentious stereotypes that the Europeanist perspective attributes to Africanist dance and, by extension, African peoples.

The origin of conflict here is the clash between Europeanist and Africanist views regarding the relationship of body/mind/spirit, and it merits some discussion. On the one hand, Africanist religions are geocentric (earth-centered) and based on the beneficence of polytheistic forces, or attributes, whose identifying characteristics represent particular facets of the human personality.[5] Deities make contact with humans when they are embodied by their followers in danced ceremonies.[6] Thus, dance and the dancing body are manifestations of the mind-spirit. On the other hand, Christian (particularly Protestant) thought separates mind-spirit from body; the body is regarded as the site of original sin and must be controlled in order for the spirit to be ascendant, or even for daily work to be accomplished efficiently. The Christian philosophy and its theocentric (God-centered) practice is predicated upon a paternalistic, monotheistic belief system (as the Native Americans characterized it, worship of the "great white father") wherein the deity does not physically enter the human body but resides above it in an ethereal, heavenly paradise. This separation and hierarchy is replicated in the separation of mind from body, with the former the master of the latter — just as the supreme deity is master of the human entity. Thus, those peoples whose traditions invite and celebrate embodied deities are in direct opposition to the Christian, particularly Protestant, ethic of body/mind/spirit separation. Specifically, black bodies become the target and screen upon which the dominant culture projects its collective fantasies — the ideals of a nation built on an ethic of somatic denial that designates African peoples as its hated or loved "primitives," the trope of its frustrations.[7]

These few examples, generalized as they are, will help lead us to the specifics of the Africanist aesthetic, its far-reaching presence and unacknowledged potency in American life. In spite of the politics of exclusion, Africanisms are inextricably dreadlocked into the weave of the American fabric and, like that hairdo, cannot be undone without cutting off both black and white strands at the root and diminishing the potential quality of life for us all. Let us examine some important characteristics of the Africanist aesthetic as they are played out in performance.

NOTES

1.   See Kramer (1987). Alfred Dreyfus (1859–1935) was a Jewish captain in the French army who was framed, tried, and convicted as a traitor (1894) by military court martial in spite of his protests of innocence at a time when the French military was infused with anti-Semitism. Despite clear, new evidence that pointed to high-ranking French officers as the actual perpetrators (1898), a second court martial reindicted Dreyfus. He was finally exonerated by presidential pardon and a supreme court of appeals decision (1906). This extended affair attracted world attention, involved the protest of writer Émile Zola, and coalesced and empowered the French left wing.

2.   For a discussion of "memory of suffering" in another context, see Welch (1985, 35–46).

3.   Major issues that beg examination include the cult of the "Lost Cause," largely the construct of white Southern women; the force of those racist white Northerners who disregarded the failures of Reconstruction and, equally, ignored the significant black contribution to the Union's cause; and the oppositional icons of "mammy" and "belle." All have evidenced an enduring national appeal. See Clinton (1995).

4.   That is, ballet, modern, and postmodern dance, performed in concert halls, lofts, or alternative, experimental spaces and considered "dance as art" by the establishment's connoisseurs of taste, as opposed to the popular entertainment and vernacular dances of the culture.

The terms "revise," "revision," and "revisionist" are used in their currently coined designations, as in "revising the canon," and indicate reassessment, reappraisal, or reevaluation of traditionally sanctioned viewpoints.

5.   African religions have generally eluded Europeanist comprehension. The deities are not objects (trees, rocks), animals (snakes), or people (although people, as ancestors and heroes, may become deities). Instead, they are the attitudinal aspects or driving forces—the sub-inter-super-texts—that shape people, animals, or things. They are processes, not products. The error lies in attempts to define the Africanist through a Europeanist terminology and frame of reference.

6.   I consciously use the term "embodied" rather than "possessed." The process is learned and culturally conditioned and is characterized by heightened control and a deepened level of perception. The intelligent, quasi-omniscient spirit-force is embodied in the practitioner. The word "possession" designates an Africanist experience in Europeanist terminology. It is biased toward the European perspective, which could see only chaos and confusion in witnessing the powerful, rhythmic movement and physical transformation brought on by danced religions.

7.   I use the word "trope" to mean a constellation of images and ideas that takes on a meaning and implication beyond its literal designation and carries the force of a cultural imperative.

2

First Premises of an Africanist Aesthetic

What are some of the signposts of the Africanist aesthetic, and how is it manifested in European American culture? In word, text, performing and visual arts, and everyday life, it is a standard that values process. How a thing is done — the movement of the action — is as important as getting it done, the static fact of the result or product. Even language (the written and, especially, the spoken word) is conceived as a mobile concept, a shaker and mover, with the power to effect change. Honoring this tradition, Paul Carter Harrison uses the Bantu term, *Nommo* (which can be roughly translated as "the power of the word"), for the title of his book on African American drama and its cathartic, catalyzing effect (1972). Words are verbal movement, and the gesture is a physical manifestation of *Nommo*.

Physical and verbal movement — thus, traditional West African gods are dancing deities in danced religions. Each one has its own chants, rhythms, gestures, and steps. These sacred principles were brought to the New World in Middle Passage[1] and through them African Americans changed the face, shape, and sound of Christianity. As Africanist scholar Sheila Walker has pointed out, the existence of these danced religions is an acknowledgment that the universe is a dynamic process-in-motion, not a static entity (1993).

Physical and verbal movement — according to sociolinguist Thomas Kochman, action words are positive-value indicators in the African American vocabulary ("swinging," "dig," "bopping," "jamming," and so on), while unfavorable words are likely to indicate passivity or immobility ("square," "lame," "stiff," "a drag," "hung up," "put down," "strung out," "busted," and so on) (1972, 160–69). These words and phrases are fat with irony, multiple meanings, and innuendo, three interrelated attributes of the Africanist aesthetic that have been worked, reworked, and brought into high relief because of the need of diasporan African peoples to simultaneously conceal and reveal, disguise and display themselves in alien, if not hostile, New World environments.

Similarly, in Africanist visual arts, motion concepts are privileged to such a degree that art historian and Africanist Robert Farris Thompson can justifiably speak of "African art in motion." In his book of the same title he identified a constellation of essential attributes in West African aesthetics that he termed "canons of fine form" (1974, 5–45). Due to geographical and chronological continuities and retentions, these characteristics persist, even in diasporan Africanist cultures. Middle Passage and subsequent wrenching experiences of the African diaspora stripped African peoples of their societal organization, but not of their cultural systems.[1] They were desocietized but not decultured, to borrow the terminology of folklorists John Szwed and Roger Abrahams (1977, 66). The overriding principle of Thompson's canons is that of balance, coolness, or "the aesthetic of the cool." It is "an all-embracing, positive attribute which combines notions of composure, silence, vitality, healing and social purification" (1974, 43).

A good way to understand the Africanist aesthetic is to isolate specific aspects of that principle for the purposes of discussion, apply them to a specific Africanist example, and discuss that example in light of the Europeanist aesthetic. Thompson, Susan Vogel and Kariamu Welsh Asante, among others, have investigated the Africanist aesthetic and described its primary characteristics.[2] Borrowing from these sources, I have designated five Africanist elements that occur in many forms of European American concert dance, including ballet. It is important to note that these traits work together and are separated and categorized only for the sake of discussion. They indicate processes, tendencies, and attitudes; they are "intratextual," so to speak, and do not appear as separate entities in practice. To show their interactive nature, I use the dance routine of Earl "Snake Hips" Tucker to illustrate each attribute. An African American novelty dancer who attained enormous popularity in the Swing Era of the 1920s and 1930s, Tucker's cabaret routine clearly demonstrates Africanist principles, as described in Marshall and Jean Stearns' book, *Jazz Dance* (1979, 236–38). Other Africanist dances could have served as my example, for they share subtextual characteristics with Tucker's dance, even though their form and function may differ considerably.

Ballet, the academic dance form of Europe, offers the most dramatic contrast to Africanist dance aesthetics. It has been regarded as the repository of European values and is characterized by aesthetician Rayner Heppenstall as a reflection of "what is thought most significant in the culture of the West. . . one epitome of the total history of the West" (quoted in Cohen 1982, 131). For these reasons, I use ballet as the quintessential European referent in elucidating the five principles that follow.

EMBRACING THE CONFLICT

In a broad sense, the Africanist aesthetic can be understood as a precept of contrariety, or an encounter of opposites. The conflict inherent in and implied by difference, discord, and irregularity is encompassed, rather than erased or necessarily resolved. That this principle is basic to the Africanist world view is manifested in the importance of the crossroads as a symbol in Africanist cultures worldwide. The crossroads is the locus of the "coincidence of opposites" (Deren 1991, 100n). Thus, Africanist art forms deal in paradox as a matter of course, with irony following close behind. Contrariety is expressed in African dilemma tales, in music or vocal work that sounds cacophonous or grating to the untrained ear, and in dance that seems unsophisticated to eyes schooled in a different aesthetic. This principle is reflected in the others and they, in turn, are reflected in it. Embracing the conflict is embedded in the final principle, the aesthetic of the cool, since coolness results from the juxtaposition of detachment with intensity. Both precepts—and all the other aesthetic principles—are manifested as simultaneously ludic and tragic (frequently even self-mockingly so, as in the blues), in an attitude and style that is uncharacteristic of Europeanist endeavor. These opposites would be difficult to pair and to leave unresolved in European academic aesthetics, but there is room for their encounter in Africanist aesthetics, "academic" or otherwise. A routine performed by Tucker in Harlem nightclubs such as Connie's Inn and the Cotton Club demonstrates this concept:

> Tucker had at the same time a disengaged and a menacing air, like a sleeping volcano. . . .
> When Snake Hips slithered on stage, the audience quieted down immediately. Nobody snickered at him, in spite of the mounting tension, no matter how nervous or embarrassed one might be. The glaring eyes burning in the pockmarked face looked directly at and through the audience, with dreamy and impartial hostility. Snake Hips seemed to be coiled, ready to strike.
> Tucker's act usually consisted of five parts. He came slipping on with a sliding, forward step and just a hint of hip movement. The combination was part of a routine known in Harlem as Spanking the Baby, and in a strange but logical fashion, established the theme of his dance. Using shock tactics, he then went directly into the basic Snake Hips movements, which he paced superbly, starting out innocently enough, with one knee crossing over behind the other, while the toe of one foot touched the arch of the other. At first, it looked simultaneously pigeon-toed and knock-kneed. (Stearns and Stearns 1979, 236)

The conflicts are paired opposites: awkward and smooth, detached and threatening, innocent and seductive. Perhaps the most significant conflict resides in the routine's deep subtext, in the ironic playing out of power postures by the otherwise disenfranchised black, male (dancing) body.

POLYCENTRISM/POLYRHYTHM

From the Africanist standpoint, movement may emanate from any part of the body, and two or more centers may operate simultaneously. Polycentrism runs counter to academic European aesthetics, where the ideal is to initiate movement from one locus — the nobly lifted, upper center of the aligned torso, well above the pelvis. Africanist movement is also polyrhythmic. For example, the feet may maintain one rhythm while the arms, head, or torso dance to different drums. This democracy of body parts stands in sharp contrast to the erect body dictated by the straight, centered spine. Again, we turn to "Snake Hips" in *Jazz Dance*:

The fact that the pelvis and the whole torso were becoming increasingly in-volved in the movement was unavoidably clear. As he progressed, Tucker's footwork became flatter, rooted more firmly to the floor, while his hips described wider and wider circles, until he seemed to be throwing his hips alternately out of joint to the melodic accents of the music. (236)

From a "get-down" posture that centers the movement in the legs and feet, Tucker adds the pelvis as another center, illustrating polycen-trism. On top of the crossover step, described above, he interpolates a pelvic rhythm, exemplifying the simplest level of polyrhythm. To repeat, these are interactive principles. Embracing contrasted rhythms, coupled with a shifting center, demonstrate the next characteristic, high-affect juxtaposition.

HIGH-AFFECT JUXTAPOSITION

Mood, attitude, or movement breaks that omit the transitions and connective links valued in the European academic aesthetic are the key-note of this principle. For example, a driving mood may overlap and coexist with a light and humorous tone, or imitative and abstract move-ments may be juxtaposed. The result may be surprise, irony, comedy, innuendo, double entendre, and, finally, exhilaration. All traditions use contrast in the arts, but Africanist high-affect juxtaposition is heightened beyond the contrast that is within the range of accepted standards in the Europeanist academic canon. In those terms, Africanist contrasts may be considered naive and extreme, poorly paced, flashy and loud, lowly and ludicrous, or just plain bad taste. On the one hand, I recall the complaint by the young Anatole Broyard (1950, 56) about the "inauthenticity" of a black jazz singer who moved without transition from singing the ballad "Strange Fruit" to crooning a love song: "A moment ago a lynching, and now a supplication to his 'baby,' — all in the same universe of discourse, all in a day's work. *A real American juxtaposition*" (emphasis added). Indeed, it is a real *African* American juxtaposition, and one that Broyard found rather disturbing. On the other hand, dance writer and enthusiast Arnold Haskell saw beyond the Europeanist aesthetic and gave an Africanist-based reading to these juxtapositions when he wrote, in the 1920s, that African Americans "blend the impossible and create beauty" (1977, 204). "Snake Hips" demonstrates this principle, in part, through his choice of costume, a sequined girdle supporting a seductive tassel:

Then followed a pantomime to a Charleston rhythm: Tucker clapped four times and waved twice with each hand in turn, holding the elbow of the waving hand and rocking slightly with the beat. The over-all effect was suddenly childish, effeminate, and perhaps tongue-in-cheek. The next movement was known among dancers as the Belly Roll, and consisted of a series of waves rolling from pelvis to chest—a standard part of a Shake dancer's routine, which Tucker varied by coming to a stop, transfixing the audience with a baleful, hypnotic stare, and twirling his long tassel in time with the music. (236–7)

Tucker shifts unpredictably from childish and effeminate to challenging and "macho" movements, disregarding Europeanist standards for consistency in characterization. In addition, with no preparation or transition, he changes from light, almost cheerleader-like hand and arm gestures to weighted, sensual undulations centered in the lower torso. A third high-affect juxtaposition occurs with the "break," described above. Tucker cuts off the movement in the middle of a Belly Roll, comes to a break, or full stop, and shifts the mood and rhythm of his intricately structured routine.

EPHEBISM

Emanating from the ancient Greek word for youth (*ephebe*), this principle encompasses attributes such as power, vitality, flexibility, drive, and attack. Attack implies speed, sharpness, and force. Intensity is also a characteristic of ephebism, but it is a kinesthetic intensity that recognizes feeling as sensation, rather than emotion. Thompson (1974, 7) describes it as "the phrasing of every note and step with consummate vitality," with response to rhythm and a sense of swing as inherent attributes. The torso is flexible and articulate: "The concept of vital aliveness leads to the interpretation of the parts of the body as independent instruments of percussive force" (9). Old people dancing with youthful vitality are valued examples of ephebism in Africanist cultures. Moving with suppleness and flexibility is more important than maintaining torso alignment. Rhythmic speed, sharpness (as in sudden or abrupt changes in dynamics), force, and attack, meanwhile, are comparatively muted concepts in the classical European ballet tradition and are dictated and circumscribed by the requisites of the ballet form. Conversely, Africanist ephebic energy takes lead and primacy over form. (Choreographer George Balanchine's Americanization of ballet offers an Afro-Euro-American sense of speed and timing that sets it apart from traditional European ballet.) The percussive force of independent body parts, with rhythm as a principal value, is not part of the European ballet aesthetic:

Tucker raised his right arm to his eyes, at first as if embarrassed (a feeling that many in the audience shared), and then, as if racked with sobs, he went into the Tremble, which shook him savagely and rapidly from head to foot. As he turned his back to the audience to display the overall trembling more effectively, Tucker looked like a murderously naughty boy. (237)

Tucker's Tremble is an excellent example of ephebism. This movement articulates the separated segments of the torso, one against the other, in a broken yet continuous movement sequence. It can only be accomplished with a totally flexible torso which will allow the tremor-like reverberations to ripple non-stop through the body. The movement is also percussive, forceful, and intense in its attack. It racks his body. An additional fillip of ephebism is demonstrated in Tucker's "naughty boy" self-presentation.

THE AESTHETIC OF THE COOL

As Thompson so eloquently explains, this characteristic is all-embracing. It lives in the other concepts, and they reside in it. It is an attitude (in the sense that African Americans use that word) that combines composure with vitality. Its prime components are aesthetic visibility and lucidity (dancing the movements with clarity, presenting the self with clarity), and luminosity, or brilliance. The picture is completed by facial composure, the actualized "mask of the cool." "The cool" contains all of the other principles. It is seen in the asymmetrical walk of African American males, which shows an attitude of carelessness cultivated with a calculated aesthetic clarity. It resides in the disinterested (in the philosophical sense, as opposed to uninterested), detached, mask-like face of the drummer or dancer whose body and energy may be working fast, hard, and hot, but whose face remains cool. Conversely, it may also be expressed as a brilliant smile, a laugh, a grimace, a verbal expression that seems to come out of nowhere to break, intercept, or punctuate the established mood by momentarily displaying its opposite and, thus, mediating a balance. It is through such oppositions, asymmetries, and radical juxtapositions that the cool aesthetic manifests luminosity or brilliance. From them emanate an Africanist understanding and interpretation of concepts such as line and form. The aloofness, *sangfroid*, and detachment of some styles of European academic dance are one kind of cool, but they represent a completely different principle from the Africanist cool. The European attitude suggests centeredness, control, linearity, directness; the Africanist mode suggests asymmetricality (that plays with falling off center), looseness (implying flexibility and vitality), and indirectness of approach. "Hot," its opposite, is the indispensable complement of the Africanist cool. Hot illuminates cool; cool illuminates hot. It is in the embracing of these opposites, in being and playing the paradoxes, from inside-out and outside-in, and in their high-affect juxtaposition that the aesthetic of the cool exists. This precept, the essence of all of the other principles, can be characterized as "soul force," which Gay and Baber describe as "energy, . . . fiber, . . . spirit and flair" (1987, 11). As Lerone Bennett stated in speaking of the concept of "soul," so also can it be said about the cool: "It is, above all, of the *spirit* rather than the letter" (quoted in Gay and Baber, 11).

Throughout Tucker's routine he strikes a balance between the sexual heat implied in his pelvic movements and the cool (or "disengaged" yet "menacing") attitude of his face. The sinister and the seductive are also juggled and balanced. Luminosity and brilliance come through in his direct relationship to the audience and the choreography, and visibility is demonstrated in the fact that he dances not as a character but presents heightened aspects of himself. He manipulates the interface between character and self and is the watcher as well as the watched, playing at seduction while also seducing, all the while shading his routine with innuendo. (This presentation of self as character is a forerunner of and intertextual model for the self-reflexive performance theater of our own postmodern era.) These are valued traits in the Africanist aesthetic landscape and, in their interactive totality, manifest the cool.

The Africanist aesthetic goes beyond Europeanist thinking about form and content. It has had a profound influence on postmodernism because of its ability to communicate in the subjunctive (rather than the indicative or declarative) mood and, thus, to privilege process over product—the doing, not the done, or, as performance theorist Richard Schechner states, *getting* there, rather than getting *there* (1973, 131). Schechner's examination of postmodern performance (1982, 95-106) suggests the following contrastive look at Europeanist and Africanist traditions as paired opposites: linear focus against a multiplicity of signals;

narrative form against self-referential clusters of information; upward progression (toward resolution) against circularity (including repetition); cause-effect against continua; and, finally, product against process. Experimental theater and postmodern dance constructed their identities around a return to the subjunctive, the experiential-experimental mode, in contrast to the Europeanist post-Renaissance, "high" art perspective that privileges product (the dance) over process (dancing). An interesting anecdote highlights the difference:

"Revelations" [Alvin Ailey's most famous choreography] has never been notated or copyrighted. Its survival and its aesthetic integrity are entirely a matter of the oral tradition linking the generations of dancers who have performed it. Only one other company—a small group in Mexico—has ever been given permission to stage the work. By way of explanation, Dudley Williams, an Ailey dancer since 1964, said, "It's very personal to us. Why would you *want* to do it?" The costume designer, Ves Harper, said, "'Revelations' was the result of a kind of intellectual process which produced a behavior pattern that was not necessarily intellectual." He added, "I'm not sure that it can be taught. It has to be lived." (n.a., *New Yorker* 1992, 5)

In an era when the American concert dance world is obsessed with documentation, preservation, and reconstruction of American modern dance "classics," this statement stands out like a voice from another planet. It is, actually, a highly informed voice from another aesthetic, a descendent of the same process-oriented perspective that created homes out of mud and water and paintings in the sand. "Revelations" is a wonderful example of fusion between Africanist and Europeanist movement vocabularies and was made to be performed on proscenium concert stages. One could counter that the Europeanist-inflected conventions inherent in the dance make it an excellent candidate for notation. However, the intent and attitude (that of a "lived experience," so to speak) expressed in the *New Yorker* extract oblige us to regard and value equally the Africanist roots of the work—a necessity if its integrity is to be maintained.

In a 1979 Sunday *New York Times* feature article, George Balanchine, the Americanizer of ballet, stated something about reviving dances that is in a slightly different vein but nevertheless complements the Ailey company statements:

I want to make new ballets. I'm not interested in reviving my works. If you made a borscht, you'd use fresh ingredients. If you were asked to write a book twice, you'd use new words. People say, what about posterity? What do you preserve, I ask? A tape? What counts is now. . . . Choreography is like cooking or gardening, not like painting, because painting stays. Dancing disintegrates, like a garden. It's life. I'm connected to what is part of life. (Hodgson 1979, D17)

(1992).

According to Cornel West:

> And the fact that when you look closely at jazz, or the blues, for example, we see a sense of the tragic, a profound sense of the tragic linked to human agency. So that it does not wallow in a cynicism or a paralyzing pessimism, but it also is realistic enough not to project excessive utopia. It's a matter of responding in an improvisational, undogmatic, creative way to circumstances, in such a way that people still survive and thrive. This is a great tradition intellectually, in fact, it has had tremendous impact on the way in which Americans as a whole respond to the human condition, respond to their circumstances. (hooks and West 1991, 34)

This talent for balancing the ludic and the tragic (which was placed in high relief during the era of blackface minstrelsy, and will be discussed in Chapter 6) will be modified and finessed by European Americans to fit their aesthetic needs as they utilize the Africanist aesthetic in forms ranging from American ballet to mainstream pop music. No longer can we afford to address European and Asian sources of modern and postmodern performance without also acknowledging this forceful, substantial Africanist presence.

These five premises will serve as the orientation and reference point for discussion in the chapters that follow.

NOTES

1. The term, Middle Passage, formally denotes the longest part of the Atlantic Ocean journey traveled by slave ships and their human cargo. In current usage, it means the journey traveled by Africans from freedom to slavery.
2. See Thompson (1974); Vogel (1986); and Welsh Asante (1986). For a more general discussion of Africanisms in America, see also Gay and Baber (1987); and Pasteur and Toldson (1982).

3

DON'T TAKE AWAY MY PICASSO: CULTURAL BORROWING AND THE AFRO-EURO-AMERICAN TRIANGLE

> The reason that HooDoo isn't given the credit it deserves in influencing American Culture is because the students of that culture both "overground" and "underground" are uptight closet Jehovah revisionists. They would assert the American and East Indian and Chinese thing before they would the Black thing. Their spiritual leaders Ezra Pound and T. S. Eliot hated Africa and "Darkies." In Theodore Roszak's book—*The Making Of A Counter Culture*—there is barely any mention of the Black influence on this culture even though its members dress like Blacks talk like Blacks walk like Blacks, gesture like Blacks wear Afros and indulge in Black music and dance (Neo-HooDoo).
>
> Ishmael Reed 1988, 20–21

Although it is possible to distinguish between Africanist- and Europeanist-derived threads of American culture and, although my aim in this work is to shed light on the Africanist part of the equation, may I reiterate that these phenomena are both separate and fused. Indeed, ours is a culture that is in an ongoing, contradictory process of Creolization-cum-segregation, a situation that is an extension of the European colonialism that brought Africans and Europeans to the Americas in the first place. In this chapter I give a thumbnail illustration, by way of selected examples, of the Africanist ingredient in the lives of particular white Americans, in the course of particular kinds of performance, and in our historical European roots.

LIFESTYLES/SONG STYLES

The American dancing body has functioned as a repository for Africanisms, both by design (for example, in minstrelsy) and by accident.

Conversations and discussions with my white students and colleagues reveal the reality of the Africanist presence in their world. Take, for example, a chat I had some years ago with an accomplished European American tap dancer and teacher who completed her doctorate in dance at Temple University.[1] Cheryl Willis was raised in the uniquely blended black-white-Creole-Cajun culture of New Orleans. One of her Philadelphia students, African American, quipped that Willis was born the wrong color because she moved like an African American. This statement rekindled the memory of a similar comment she had received as a child; a family member had said that she moved like an African American male. In analyzing the two statements, and with years of technical movement experience in between, this woman realized that in childhood she had unwittingly picked up the full-body articulation characteristic of African American males (which her relatives recognized as Africanist because of the many public opportunities for black and white cultures to rub shoulders in New Orleans). Her acquired penchant for Africanist movement style predated — and, perhaps unconsciously, dictated — her tap dance studies. (According to Willis, in the New Orleans of her childhood, African American male, full-body movement was the polar opposite of "proper" European American, female movement, which was confined to a rather genteel swaying of the upper torso from side to side.) She was not formally trained as a child to move like an African American, male or female, and she had not consciously learned the trait. She grew up with a language of codified movement patterns and body attitudes, some of which were Africanist and had become public domain but could still be labeled as black body style. It was a choice that was in the air, and she unconsciously embraced it.

Other experiences are acquired deliberately. Allan Jabbour, folklorist, and Ernest Smith, film collector of African American vaudeville short subjects, both described their experiences in going to African American areas of the cities in which they grew up (Jabbour in Miami, Smith in Pittsburgh) to copy the latest "Lindy" steps. Not only were African American youth the originators of the newest turns on the dance floor, but they were also the kids who lived on the edge, literally and figuratively. They represented, as Jabbour commented, a world that was "naughtily illegal."[2] That phrase, and other descriptors such as dangerous, illicit, "in," or "hip," symbolize a prevalent Europeanist perspective on Africanist culture. The African American lifestyle that embraces the hot and the cool satisfies the rebellious needs of European American adolescence in flight from the Protestant ethic.

In another vein, in a conversation with me about his days in the army, Lawrence Sullivan, professor and dance writer, mentioned the unique qualities of his regiment. The outfit was a racially integrated group of inductees from Manhattan. Sullivan commented that the way in which the African American recruits performed their "shape up," by inserting a syncopated bounce in their "hup–2–3–4" so that it was more akin to "hu – up–2–3–4," "nearly drove the drill instructors crazy."[3] Inflecting the dominant culture's style by marching to a different beat meant that the recruits slipped a bit of their heritage into military routine and provided a new opening for the flow of information between African American and European American culture. Witness today's marching bands in contemporary parades and sports events to see the impact of Africanist, syncopated rhythmic invention on changing the face of military spectacle in the United States. Then, witness this influence exported to Europe, as in the parades for the bicentennial of the French Revolution, where the *pièce de résistance* was the performance by the Grambling College Marching Band, bringing up the rear. (Grambling is a historically African American institution.)

What is going on, and what does it mean? Africanisms are not a choice but an imperative that come to us through the culture. Unlike modern and postmodern decisions to appropriate imported elements from Zen Buddhism, yoga, T'ai Chi, Qi-Gong, or other Asian disciplines, the Africanist presence comes to Americans from home base, from the inside. Like electricity through the wires, we draw from it all the time, but few of us are aware of its source. It is marrow in the bones of our culture or, as Toni Morrison writes, "unspeakable things unspoken" (1989).

As Ishmael Reed so bluntly points out, deception and sublimation are put to hard labor to invisibilize this influence in a society that is fertilized by its presence. A statement by African American filmmaker Marlon Riggs stands as a personal testament: "When nobody speaks your name, or even knows it, you, knowing it, must be the first to speak it. When the existing history and culture do not acknowledge and address you – do not see or talk to you – you must write a new history, shape a new culture, that will" (1991, 14). Riggs was addressing the dilemma of being both African American and gay. Misnaming and nonnaming not only contribute to cultural inequality, but are also a matter of oil, gold, diamonds, minerals, and dollars. With the end of the millennium comes talk about multicultural this and that, and cultural sources are beginning to be acknowledged. However, the living members of these cultures still are systematically cut off from the symbolic rewards and economic profits of their inventions.

It is worth our while to examine how denial and appropriation serve the purpose of economic gain. A legendary example is Elvis Presley's "cover" of "Hound Dog," a down-home, rhythm-and-blues song originally recorded, for marketing in the black community, by a raspy-voiced

African American woman known as "Big Mama" Thornton.[4] Cover records such as Presley's, and stylistic steals made by the lineage of "black" white performers from Presley to rock star Joe Cocker and rapper Vanilla Ice, are part of the sanctioned, systemic borrowing that Americans have come to accept. European Americans have taken on the look, sound, phrasing, and body language of their African American mentors. Whether song styles or lifestyles are the targets, appropriation is commonplace in popular culture. One route is outright theft. A less blatant path is the circuitous, unconscious process in which the Africanist aesthetic is picked up from the air we breathe. Then there is a vast middle ground.

According to music scholar Samuel A. Floyd, Jr., "it's possible to switch on the television set, leave the room for a moment, hear Afro-American music accompanying a commercial, sit-com, or religious program, return to the TV, and see only white people playing and singing — 'no black people anywhere'" (paraphrased and quoted in Paul 1987, 6). According to an article in the London *Observer* discussing the impact of Josephine Baker on the Paris of 1925, "We are so accustomed to hearing jazz and American-influenced popular music — the sound of the twentieth century — that our ears cannot imagine a world of sound without the freedom of syncopated jazz" — and that's in London, mind you (O'Connor 1986, 20).

Jazz and jazz presences are the least common denominator of the Africanist aesthetic, infiltrating and shaping cultural forms on both sides of the Atlantic. French modernist composer Darius Milhaud, who freely used jazz motifs in his work (most notably in "La Création du Monde," 1922–23), advised his students in California (one of whom was Dave Brubeck) to orchestrate their fugues for jazz instrumentation, if they so desired: "If you want to express America you must have some jazz in your compositions. Never give up jazz, you have so much freedom" (quoted in Zwerin 1994, 20).[5] The jazz-Africanist aesthetic has been pointed out as a conditioning factor in the Art Deco architecture of 1920s America: "Within its range of new expression were merged the patterning, color and geometry of Egyptian and Aztec cultures; the probing of density and multiple images of Cubism; the dynamism and syncopated rhythms of jazz" (Cerwinske 1981, 10). Dynamism, speed, vitality, and syncopated rhythms — these qualities derive, in great part, from the Africanist influence in America.   As these writers suggest, that presence reaches out and embraces its surroundings in many ways.

Here are some cultural flashpoints. In many instances African-inspired beauty standards have provided "exotic" fodder for mainstream consumption. Where and how did 1970s Hollywood starlet Bo Derek get the idea for long, skinny, beaded braids, for example? Other Africanist hairdos such as cornrows, wrapped strands, and dreadlocks have all been adopted by white Americans. It is worth mentioning that the European American frizzy perm of the 1970s came on the heels of the African American "Afro" of the 1960s. (Africanist innovation, as co-opted by European Americans, does not mean that African Americans are accepted in the white world; on the contrary, it may assure exclusion, since the Bo Dereks and Elvis Presleys need to be perceived as originals.) For years the body language of professional sports has been spliced with Africanist touches. "High-fives," butt slaps, and hip jostlings—hardly a game of competitive sports is complete without the exchange on the field of black exclamation points. The oversized overalls of African American prison inmates caught the fancy of black hip hop culture, were picked up by white American youth, and subsequently inflected styles in the high fashion industry. Many more examples such as these clutter the media.

To return to music and Elvis Presley, according to popular legend the promoter who mused, "If I could find a white man who had the Negro sound and the Negro feel I could make a billion dollars," was Sam Phillips, who became Presley's manager (quoted in Watrous, 1990, 34). A revealing old photograph of Presley and black soul singer Jackie Wilson can open this brief discussion of the black white man (Robinson 1980, 160). It shows us that, in physical appearance, Presley fashioned himself in a decidedly black image, and the inscription—"Jackie, you got yourself a friend. . . ."—indicates his reverence for Wilson, the African American rhythm and blues idol. A further reading of this snapshot reveals how much a composite of African American culture Presley was and offers an interesting case study on the dynamics of race and class in these United States. Like Wilson, Presley is dressed in a tight-fitting, three-button suit. Neither man wears a tie. Wilson sports a white shirt, buttoned at the neck. Presley takes the look a step further and wears a turtleneck pullover. Wilson wears the high pompadour hairstyle popular among African American male entertainers of the period. Presley has added his particular touch, again. His "do" is not an exact replica of Wilson's but a modified version—not as high on the top, with the front wave (or "pomp," as that crown was called in Harlem when I was a child) tilted a little off to one side. Presley, a poor, lower-class, Southern white, was excluded by birth from the socially sanctioned, WASP-dominated, middle-class world of college, crew cuts, and coming out parties. Like the nineteenth-century white minstrel (who was frequently of Irish or Jewish immigrant heritage), he was a white Other to middle-class, urban white America. Yet, solely on the basis of race, any member of the white underclass could exert power over any black Other. Presley could take what he wanted from the African American world and enter that world at will, symbolically or literally. By imitating the African

American vocal style, body movements, "Concolean" hairdo, and sharp suit, Presley put himself outside the ken of the 1950s scrubbed, close-cropped, "goodwhiteboy" image and became a "bad white dude."[6] Only bad—"baaaad"—whites imitated blacks. His song style was carefully cultivated to replicate the black sound. And his movement style was a watered-down, slightly spastic version of the Snakehips, a sophisticated, sinuous dance, notorious for its torso articulation, that reached superb levels of irony, complexity, and sophistication when performed by African American males such as Earl "Snakehips" Tucker (See Chapter 2). Presley aligned himself with generations of European Americans— males, in particular—who, since the era of blackface minstrelsy, imitated and identified with the Other, be they African American or Native American, in a rite of passage to adulthood. Another irony in this photograph is that African American males of the 1940s and 1950s "conked" their hair in imitation of European American movie idols of a previous generation such as John Barrymore and Robert Taylor. Thus Presley is imitating blacks imitating whites.

This merry-go-round of appropriation is not uncommon in our Creolized society. In the nineteenth century, a dance called the "Cakewalk," created by enslaved blacks who stole and mockingly imitated the high-falutin' mannerisms of whites at plantation balls, was the traditional minstrel show finale. Later it became a popular white social dance, another example of whites copying blacks copying whites. The equation also travels in the other direction. For example, in minstrelsy the white entertainers imitated blacks and made up their faces with burnt cork in order to complete the picture. This theatrical form became the first legitimate stage for African American performers. What happened when they entered the genre? They, too, blackened their faces: blacks copying whites copying blacks. Mimicry by both groups has been a way to exercise social control. Irony is inevitably implied on both sides: the playing-with-power irony of miming-to-master the master, or the love-hate irony of imitating-to-demystify the Other. Legend has it that Thomas "Daddy" Rice, an Irish American known as the father of minstrelsy, copied the "Jump Jim Crow" song and dance routine of an African American menial laborer down to the specifics of body posture, movements, and vocal accompaniment. His final touch was to blacken his face. Thus began the formal tradition of blackface minstrelsy, and Rice's routine was one of the first documented "cover" acts for African American invention (see Chapter 6).

An interesting example of Creolization from the black end of the spectrum is in the Africanist transformation of European set dances, discussed by Szwed and Marks (1988, 32):

It was Lafcadio Hearn who in 1876 observed the black roustabouts on the river-front of Cincinnati dancing a quadrille to the "Devil's Dream," . . . gradually transforming it into a Virginia Reel, and then changing it again, this time to a "juba dance" done to a shout-like call-and-response song. Again there is the sense that these European dance forms were flexible and open to transformation and improvisation, at least within the performances of Afro-Americans.

Mixing and borrowing have been the stuff of American culture since whites and blacks set foot on this continent. Cultural exchanges were well established by the late eighteenth century. Edward Brathwaite cites diary entries from the Jamaican colonial era that show the pervasive Africanist influence (1971, 302). Young white females, influenced by their African female servants, picked up the "drawling, dissonant gibberish. . . aukward [sic] carriage and vulgar manners. . . . & by insensible degrees almost acquire the same habit of thinking & speaking."

How powerful was the influence that could undermine the mores of the dominant culture, in spite of the fact that African peoples were subjugated and silenced. The observer was correct. Whether we like it or not, verbal appropriation brings motional and cognitive assimilation. As is the case with Elvis, and in other examples of young whites taking on the look and sound of blacks, their flirtation runs more than skin deep and transforms the whole person. Perhaps this is a primary fear, that self will become Other. However, the greatest fear is in perpetuating this condition of Other-as-self through sexual intercourse, intermarriage, and procreation. Yet, through the centuries, these boundaries have been broken almost as a matter of course. In particular, all classes of white males have engaged in sexual intercourse with women of color. It is a known fact that the wide spectrum of skin tones among African Americans attests to this practice. However, common sense, not even science, tells us that intersexual contact and intermarriage are two-way streets that affect both cultures, black and white. European Americans seem to ignore the fact that interethnic mixing may account for variations in skin tone, facial features, and hair texture for white Americans, too. There may well be a drop of the Other in all of us.

The Presley example also confirms the presence and power of the subculture. According to ethnomusicologist and folklorist John Szwed, "the fact that, say, a Mick Jagger can today perform in the same tradition [minstrelization, or imitation of African American styles] without black-face simply marks the detachment of culture from race and the almost full absorption of a black tradition into white culture" (1975, 263). The tradition is assimilated, yet its creators are systematically excluded. What is remarkable is who is allowed to borrow, on whose stage, and how. Given the politics of racism, it is predictable that the powers-that-be attempt, against all odds, to stricture this exchange into a one-way

street. The "high" is sanctioned to borrow from the "low," whites from
blacks, ballet from folk dance, and so forth. When the exchange goes in
the reverse direction, a condescending, patriarchal tone of ownership
prevails. For example, since the minstrel era phenomenon of African
American concert artists singing European music—from Elizabeth
Greenfield in the 1850s (known as the "Black Swan"), the Fisk Jubilee
Singers of the 1870s, and Sissieretta Jones of the 1880s (known as "Black
Patti") through the African American conductors, composers, and ballet
artists in the twentieth century—the road for the black artist borrowing
from high-culture white forms has been posted with "no trespassing"
signs. In the following passages Szwed elaborates on this theme of the
high group's appropriations from the low group as it plays out in the
white male rite of passage:

There was a stage, when we were about thirteen, in which we 'went Negro.' We
tried to broaden our accents to sound like Negroes, as if there were not enough
similarity already. We consciously walked like young Negroes, mocking their
swinging gait, moving our arms the way they did, cracking our knuckles and
whistling between our teeth. We tried to use some of the same expressions, as
closely as possible to the way they said them, like: 'Hey, m-a-a-a-n, what you
doin' theah!,' the sounds rolled out and clipped sharply at the end for the hell of
it. (quoted in Szwed 1975, 263)[7]

In our very lives, we have to come to repeat this pattern, individual biography
recapitulating cultural history. Born theoretically white, we are permitted to
pass our childhood as imaginary Indians, our adolescence as imaginary Negroes, and only then are expected to settle down to being what we really are:
white once more. (quoted in Szwed 1975, 264)[8]

"White once more" is put in question by the tenor of the quotes.
Who is whom and what is white become moot points for, surely, all past
experiences are brought to bear on the present moment. All texts are
intertexts. Johnny Otis, a rhythm-and-blues singer who happens to be
white but has lived his life symbolically passing for black, honors the
African American legacy as a pivotal choice for his survival:

I don't think it's so unique in America for white kids to grow up with black
youngsters and come up together as brothers and sisters. What might be unique
is not to veer away. I could not veer away, because that's where I wanted to be,
those were my friends, that's what I love. It wasn't the music that brought me to
the black community. It was the way of life. I felt I was black. . . . You know,
different cultures have different characteristics. And the characteristics of the
African American community became my own. And I just wasn't willing to give
that up to go become part of the mainstream community where people felt superior to black people and they oppressed black people and they preached democ-

racy and practiced racism. I didn't want to be part of that. I wanted to stay in that sweet, beautiful black place in the black community. (Otis 1989)

Otis may have wished to stay in that "sweet place," but he was constantly reminded by the powers-that-be of forces to the contrary:

I remember once in 1939 [Otis was born in 1921], we went to Treasure Island where the World's Fair was holding forth. . . . to the dance where Count Basie was playing and two big peckerwood cops stopped me, "Where you going boy?" So I said I was going to the dance and one of them says, "You can't go in there, that's for coloreds only!" Well, Rudy, my buddy [African American] had presence of mind, and said, "Well he's colored, he's my cousin." Then this one big cop says, "Let me see your fingernails," And he looked at my nails and looked back at his partner and says, "Yeah, Bill, he's a boogie all right." We laughed about that one, and cried about it. . . . So ridiculous you had to laugh, but so bitter and so hurting you had to cry. (quoted in Carter 1995, 54)

Otis could enter the black mini-world of a blacks-only dance in an otherwise white World's Fair only after having his black pedigree validated by a white male authority figure. He is so much a part of the Africanist ethos that he both laughs and cries at the irony of the condition. These are occurrences that he knows are part and parcel of the American double standard. His friend, Rudy, answers quickly and smartly, a measure of how intimately he lives with these ironies. As sympathetic as he is, Otis is still white. Rudy's retort confers on Otis the temporary privilege, as well as the pain, of being black. Unlike his black counterparts who might try to find a place in a white community, Otis was embraced by the black community. He had a choice. African Americans do not.

Otis and Presley are an interesting study in contrasts. As the extracts demonstrate, not only does Otis acknowledge his debt to the black community, but he also heralds it and takes pride in it. He acquired his black heritage directly from the inside, as it were, having grown up black, for all intents and purposes. He was not a bohemian or a voyeur; he was raised and bred in "the 'hood." Presley grew up in poor, white, segregated, racially polarized America. African American culture was implied in every part of his aesthetic education, even though African American peoples were held at bay. His "blackenizing" was received from the Africanist intertext of American society, which we all inherit as Americans, black or white, despite segregation and discrimination. This presence was directly manipulated and exploited by his producers and managers who created and marketed him as a highly profitable product. There is extreme irony in the fact that it was Johnny Otis who produced for Big Mama Thornton the original version of "Hound Dog" (Carter 1995, 52). Otis has spent his life producing and supporting black artists.

In his forthright exposition on the importance and, as he describes it, the blessing of the Africanist influence on his development, Otis cites as a strong conditioning factor the neighborhood sanctified churches that he attended during the Depression. The teenager was attracted by the free milk and cookies they dispensed, real treats in a lean era. He also mentions the girls. Then he mentions the music and, in the same breath, the preaching. This is a significant point because in the African American church tradition, the liturgy of music and the liturgy of the word exist as a continuum. Both are forms of music and, conversely, both exemplify *Nommo*, the power of the word. He also mentions a neighbor who was a Pullman porter who would return from his Chicago runs bringing new blues records. In many ways Otis had a direct line on Africanist invention, but these same influences infused the culture, even in white forms. They were essential in defining American musics.

Well, you know blues and gospel are the foundation for every form of music we have. Of course, there's Scottish, Irish, Celtic music and the Western scale. And yes, this music didn't develop on African instruments. *But the forms, the psychology, the poetry, the songs, the humor, the wit, the pathos, the way voices are used, that's all American black people.* (quoted in Carter 1995, 56; emphasis added)

Otis recognizes the catalyzing effect that black forms have had on shaping white America. The connections are thick, deep, and dense. A European American male student of mine at Temple University put it this way:

What does it mean to be white? How do we as whites construct our cultural identities, and how do blacks figure in this construction? What are the cultural costs and prohibitions that obtain in subscribing to "whiteness?" How do these costs and prohibitions contribute to the perpetuation of racism?[9]

Now, let us take a brief look at some ways in which the Africanist presence is implied in a small but representative sampling of "white" performance genres.

PERFORMANCE

On the concert stage, modern and postmodern trends have redefined European concert music. It may be polyphonic, syncopated, chromatic, dissonant, atonal, jazzy, or more. It may be composed of silence, improvised sounds, or random noise made on found instruments. African American musicians have been making *musique concrète* for centuries, without the cachet accorded by a French term. Playing on found instruments, making instruments from found objects, or doctoring traditional instruments (especially keyboards) to give them the twang and chromatic characteristics of African scales are all part of the Southern black American music tradition. Such practices may be elevated to the status of art when, in the John Cage tradition, members of the dominant culture finesse these influences to a concert standard.[10] This is not to say that experimental forms of European concert music are not original, creative, and innovative in their own right, for they are, and highly so. These observations only point out that, again, the Africanist quotient was one of the presences in the waters that spawned them.

Theater played a large part in the "whitenizing" of the Africanist aesthetic. To overcome the stranglehold of mainstream theatrical conventions, experimental groups during the 1960s and thereafter looked not only to Asian sources (which are well documented as inspiration for avant-garde arts) but also to Africanist stimuli. In that era I was a performing member of the Open Theater, one of the pioneering groups that, along with the Living Theater and the Performance Group, was a leader in New York's experimental theater movement. We borrowed materials ranging from the "Cakewalk" to Candomblè (an African Brazilian religion) in our theatrical explorations. A signature Open Theater study was called "vocal jamming." We were instructed to be like jazz musicians with our voices and to "jam" (improvise sounds) in conjunction with the other actors in the exercise. The value put on improvisation by American experimental theater groups is an Africanist presence from African American cultural intertexts such as jazz music and social dancing.[11] Questions arose as to what makes a performance; when it begins and ends; where it happens; and what constitutes the audience's role in the process. Answers were sought in cultures indigenous to every place but Europe. The recent work of theater innovator Jerzy Grotowski (whose Polish Laboratory Theater blazed a trail of innovation in the 1960s and 1970s) with a group of collaborators based in Pontedera, Italy, provides a useful 1990s example:

There are few discernible words, but these rhythmic, highly structured vocal works—some derived from African and Caribbean initiation rites—have an uncanny resonance and vibration. . . . Their carefully controlled movements, based on ancient forms of concentration, include a special way of holding the spine and protruding the backside, much like the warrior's position in primordial tribes. The stance, silent and attentive, is supposed to energize and enliven the body and awaken a certain innate physical power and mindfulness. (Croyden 1992, 42)

The vestiges of that stance, still discernible in the posture of contemporary peoples of African lineage, have been maligned in the ballet world and used as evidence to prove the inappropriateness of the black dancing body for ballet. Now it is being celebrated in Grotowski's theater.

Broadway theater of the 1960s was rejuvenated and revitalized as, by third hand (that is, in the wake of off-Broadway and off-off Broadway), it assimilated and distilled some of the theatrical innovations pioneered by the avant-garde. Musicals such as "Hair," "A Chorus Line," and "Jesus Christ, Superstar," are just a few benefactors of this Other-inspired legacy. Noteworthy, too, is the earlier, 1920s, rejuvenation of the Broadway that had belonged to Florenz Ziegfeld and the Shubert brothers. Historical black Broadway shows inexorably redefined the character of American musical theater, bringing with them innovations and a style, speed, and rhythm that spread a wash of color and a pulse of change over white Broadway. From the 1900s through the teens, black musical directors and choreographers working in segregated black communities, especially Harlem, evolved a musical comedy style that drew white choreographers and impresarios uptown and invariably resulted in appropriations. One of the legendary examples is the story of Florenz Ziegfeld and the African American production (by J. Leubrie Hill and his Darktown Follies repertory company) of a show called "My Friend in Kentucky":

Night after night Florenz Ziegfeld sat admiringly in a box at this show, drinking in the details of the admirable stage direction, the spontaneity of the performers, their characteristic lax ease, and the delightfully abandoned tunes. Several of these he bought, together with their accompanying action, and transplanted them into his "Follies of 1914." (Van Vechten 1974, 38)

Moreover, the precision chorus line (of "girls" dancing in unison with rhythm and a sense of swing) was a black innovation that replaced the English music hall-Broadway-showgirl tradition of elaborately costumed chorus ladies who performed marches and drills.[12]

From a 1990s vantage point it may seem obvious that a host of definitive ingredients in American social, musical comedy, and cabaret dance forms are of Africanist origin. Earlier, this legacy was denied. Here is a 1930s quote from an article on the Lindy Hop by Carl Van Vechten, a swing-era photographer, critic, and novelist who was a loving commentator on and devotee of Africanist arts—if you will, an "Afrodisiac":

Nearly all the dancing now to be seen in our musical shows is of Negro origin. But both critics and public are so ignorant of this fact that the production of a new Negro revue is an excuse for the revival of the hoary old lament that it is pity the Negro can't create anything for himself, that he is obliged to imitate the white man's revues. This in brief, has been the history of the Cakewalk, the Bunny Hug, the Turkey Trot, the Charleston, and the Black Bottom. It will probably be the history of the Lindy Hop. (1974, 39)

The European American collective memory has been thorough in invisibilizing African American *lieux de mémoire*. The late Honi Coles cited an example that echoes Van Vechten's contention and indicts a major American choreographer:

They [Coles and his partner, Cholly Atkins] joined the cast of "Gentlemen Prefer Blondes" in 1949 and . . . . were featured in the second act, singing and dancing to "Mamie is Mimi."

They ran into a snag at the start. "During rehearsals Agnes de Mille didn't know what to do with us, " says Coles, "so finally Julie Styne, who hired us, took us aside and said, 'Look, why don't you fellows work up something, and I'll get her to look at it.'" They located arranger Benny Payne. . . and the three of them worked out a routine. "One afternoon, Miss de Mille took time off to look at it," says Atkins. "She liked it and told us to keep it in."

On went the show with the Coles-Atkins-Payne routine a hit, and Agnes de Mille listed as choreographer in the program. "Later on we had to get her permission to use our [own] routine on Jack Haley's "Ford Hour," says Coles. "She was very nice about it." In her autobiography Miss de Mille writes that the "Mamie Is Mimi" number, along with several others, was devised "in a single short rehearsal," presumably by Miss de Mille. (Stearns and Stearns 1979, 309)

For the African American performer, insult is added to injury. Perhaps the most baneful layer is the final one: Not only are they not credited for their choreography during the run of the show, but they remain invisibilized in De Mille's autobiography. Who is doing the documenting? By whose criteria? And what is being recorded?

After examples such as these there is some small solace in reading current popular literature, which makes an attempt to bring Africanist sources to light. For instance, the following sentence appeared in a *Dance Magazine* obituary for Hollywood choreographer Hermes Pan, who made dances for many musicals, including all the Astaire-Rogers films for RKO: "His fascination with dance evolved from watching the impromptu dancing of black youngsters in Nashville, and through informal instruction from his family's black chauffeur" (Roman 1991, 30). By borrowing the artistic forms created by a caste of people who were designated as servants and confined to dancing on street corners, Pan rose to a fame and fortune that was inaccessible to his earliest mentors.

Similarly, according to a dance article on the Nicholas Brothers tap team in *The New Yorker* (1991, 6):

For that program [a Nicholas Brothers film tribute at a Manhattan alternative film house] Mr. Goldstein will also be screening an entire 1942 feature, called *Orchestra Wives*, starring the Glenn Miller orchestra and featuring the Nicholas Brothers in a number called "I've Got a Gal in Kalamazoo." There Harold

[Nicholas] performs a double air turn into a split, Fayard [his brother] tags a wall with his foot and comes down into a split, and Harold runs clear up the wall, rocketing off it into a back flip to land in a still more stretched-out split. Ten years later movie audiences would discover Donald O'Connor's madcap version of the same stunt in the "Make 'Em Laugh" number of *Singin' In The Rain*. But Harold was there first, and with elegance.

Brief and random credits in specialized publications are appreciated, but they do not compensate for the ongoing trivialization of the Africanist presence in our society. To a lesser extent it was an ingredient in European culture, as African American performers brought their art to stages far and wide, from the Soviet Union to England, France, and Germany. This influence has a remarkable way of popping up in unpredictable, unexpected venues. Take, for example, the case of a renowned ballet choreographer. In a few lines in her autobiography, Bronislava Nijinska (the sister of Vaslav Nijinsky) explains that her first dance lessons (at age four) were in tap dance and were given to her by Jackson and Johnson, an African American vaudeville team that was well known on the European music-hall circuit. While they were on tour in Russia, they "brought a small plank to our home one day, spread sand on it, and taught me how to tap dance on the plank" (quoted in Gutman 1983, 2).

Indeed, Africanisms are at play on both sides of the Atlantic and on both sides of the footlights. Many of the contemporary American audience's verbal responses are appropriated from the vocally forthright, participating-observer spirit of Africanist sacred and secular traditions. Verbal signifying or encouragement of performers ("cook," "burn," "work it," "go, girl"); physical response to performers (by audience members in the aisles, sometimes actually jumping onstage); applauding as the spirit moves them; hooting (as in the ubiquitous "Whooooh," a common post-1960s feature in European American concert performances and a direct steal from the gospel church tradition); and, in a broad spectrum, the appreciation of hot-and-cool are signature Africanist spectator stances that have been assimilated by European American audiences. Once a practice like the hooting catches on in the European American community, African American grassroots culture reaches into its bag of surprises and comes out with something new. Thus, the cutting edge kudos at some early 1990s black performances was a "hunh-hunh-hunh-hunh," a guttural, simian-like, rhythmic sound of approval. Will this, too, become public domain?

Let us examine a few more threads in this interlocked fabric. Some have their roots in Europe.

EUROPEAN CORRELATIVES

Africanisms are part of the European American landscape primarily through American culture, and tangentially through European exports. (This exchange implies that European cultures are also Africanized, but that is a topic for another essay.) One such export merits some attention here, because it influences how African peoples are perceived and/or allowed to perform, both on stage and in everyday life. It is a set of metaphoric ideas and images — namely, the primitive trope — which has seduced and played havoc with Europe since the Age of Enlightenment. European Americans may reach out to the Africanist aesthetic in their quest for the illicit, the dangerous, the hip, the Other. The primitive trope allows complex cultures to be seen as either lowly and inferior or as idealized, early forms of superior European endeavor — either hated or loved, but in either case objectified as Other. By the nineteenth century, the institutionalization of academic disciplines developed by a bourgeois European scholarly community put the final stamp of approval on the doctrine of European superiority, a theory that was implied by the work of Linnaeus in establishing the taxonomic discipline in the previous century.[13] The newly evolved and revised Victorian-era categories of science, history, sociology, psychology, anthropology, and medicine helped enforce the primitive trope. This way of thinking posits that "primitives" are childlike and may be irrational, violent, dangerous; yet, they may be noble savages. They are free in some sense, and they are sexually promiscuous. They are lowest on the evolutionary ladder, while Europeans are highest. Their culture is insignificant; European culture is civilization. The Charles Darwins, Sigmund Freuds, and Karl Mullers — nineteenth-century European scientists, psychologists, and historians — contributed to this grand delusion, by accident and/or by design.[14] Borrowing and reshaping these nineteenth-century theories for their own twentieth-century illusions, the Nazis termed as *entartete* (that is, degenerate or, literally, without a species or kind) all artists and works they considered "tainted" by primitive, non-Aryan influences. As psycho-historian Sander Gilman explains, the term "degenerate" was picked up by the Nazis from scientific jargon of the previous century and was widely understood as "a general term of opprobrium or deviance from the norm" (1993). The Third Reich masterminds were very clever, in fact. They recognized the power of these non-Europeanist inspirations and tried to control them by banning them and their creators. Their list of degenerates was long. It included musicians like Stravinsky and Hindemith, whose work showed jazz-Africanist aesthetic principles of syncopation, dissonance, and use of chromatic scales; German-born expressionist artists who, like African sculptors, did not depict the natural world but rendered that which lies beneath, around, and above the real—the spirit and the psyche; and performers such as Josephine Baker. All of these "types" were conflated as Jews, blacks, and degenerates. The Nazi example is an extreme variation on a theme that nevertheless underlies the Enlightenment-modernist construct of a European identity. Utilizing the primitive trope as its base line, Europe conceptualized the Other and projected its forbidden fantasies on her. She is called "Third World," a disenabling phrase that means neither you nor I, neither first nor second person—three strikes, and you're out. As Roland Barthes (1979, 37) so aptly put it, "Ultimately the Black [*sic*] has no complete and autonomous life [in the white gaze]: he is a bizarre object, reduced to a parasitical function, that of diverting the white [*sic*] man by his vaguely threatening *baroque*: Africa is a more or less dangerous *guignol*".

On the early end of this primitive spectrum was the so-called Hottentot Venus, whose buttocks and vulva held a pathological fascination for the "scientists" of early nineteenth-century Europe. This person (a South African woman who was also known by the name Sarah Bartmann) died in Paris in 1815, at age 25, after five years of having been exhibited semi-nude throughout Europe. According to Gilman,

The audience which had paid to see her buttocks and had fantasized about the uniqueness of her genitalia when she was alive could, after her death and dissection, examine both, for [Georges] Cuvier [who wrote *Extraits d'observations faites sur le cadavre d'une femme connue à Paris et à Londres sous le nom de Vénus Hottentote*, in 1817] presented to "the Academy the genital organs of this woman prepared in a way so as to allow one to see the nature of the labia." (1985, 232, 235)

More Hottentot Venuses followed Sarah Bartmann and became the object of "scientific" attention by European medicine men. We can only imagine what happened when these males played "doctor" with no legal strictures on their actions, for, of course, African women were regarded as subhuman and were outside the realm of the law. Once these women were characterized as having animalistic sexual appetites and likened to apes, the European male pundits had free rein over them, in every sense. As fascinated as they (and all of "enlightened" Europe) were about her vulva, the Europeans also marveled—with typical repulsion cum longing—at Sarah Bartmann's buttocks. What is ironic is that the bustle became the mode of dress of Victorian Europe, and we all know what part of the anatomy is emphasized by that accoutrement. This butt-bustle relationship is almost predictable. The love-hate, attraction-repulsion model is the leitmotif that informs the primitive trope and accounts for the repression and distortion implied in it. European culture ends up doing the very thing it detests and characterizes as Other. It becomes blackenized, even though the process may involve a transformation and finessing from the nude, raw African model into one covered in silk and lace. Ironically, European culture and bodies become a repository for internalizing and preserving the Other. In fact, *they are the Other*.

Performance is my topic, and performance is implied in the primitive trope. Performance, after all, was one of the few professions open to Africans in Europe (as was the case for other Others, such as Gypsies), whether their stages were lecture halls, museum exhibitions, medicine shows, circuses, street corners, or brothels. Beginning with the Hottentot Venus example, the Enlightenment-Victorian-modernist discourse on bodies and phenotypes bears a direct relationship to performance and the way performers are conceived, perceived, and received. Without this historical legacy, a phenomenon like blackface minstrelsy could not have developed. Thus, the primitive trope combined with nineteenth-century anthropology to bring other Africans on parade across Europe. By the end of the century, groups of Africans were "educationally" displayed in the European counterpart of the American medicine show. It became fashionable for Viennese women to take on African lovers (thus, the phrase, "Ashanti Fever"; see Gilman 1986, 36–42). Michel Leiris is seduced, in part, into becoming an anthropologist by the influence of jazz, Montmartre, "Negroes," and the primitive trope as played out in 1920s Paris (Torgovnick 1990, 111). By the advent of the twentieth century, Europeans were captivated by African Americans. Stars like Florence Mills, Josephine Baker, and many others unwittingly carried on the primitive legacy, their real contributions misinterpreted and their greatest potential untapped. Fantasies and fables about African sexuality came with this conquered territory, and the black dancing body was the battleground.

Josephine Baker was a trope in and of herself, and her career illustrates this battle. The animal correspondence and the Hottentot Venus connection is evident. Baker, too, was exhibited seminude, her buttocks on display as much as her breasts.[15] Not only were African fauna part of her elaborate cabaret acts; she also kept them at home, at various periods in her career. She would appear on a Paris street accompanied by the cheetah from the Revue de Paris, or with a monkey on her shoulder. Correspondingly, her talents were considered inborn, rather than learned. A journalist who saw "La Bakaire's" first appearance in Paris at the Folies Bergère described her as "the Black Venus, the animalistic black woman; a gold-colored body, her breasts revealed, dedicated, lost, ecstatic: spasms of passion and lust. Long legs that dash arbitrarily, quivering sides, fingers that alternated between stroking and clawing" (quoted in Muller 1985, 20). This male journalist could well have been the same French male protagonist who starred opposite her in "Princess Tam Tam," one of two extant films in which Baker had a leading role. In that film Baker is depicted in a state of lustful longing for the white male.

The following description by Baker points to the fact that she perceived herself quite differently: "Not a dancer, not an actress, not even black: Josephine Baker, that's who I am. I can go on my heels and I can run on all fours, when I want to, and then I shake off all piercing looks. . . . Because I'm not a pincushion either" (quoted in Muller, 1985, 22). This quote is particularly interesting. Here is a woman who does not want to be pigeonholed by stereotyping. No categories fit her, so she rejects all of those that we might have thought applicable—dancer, actress, black. And why not, since all were perceived as pejoratives? She tells the reader she can choose to stand tall or "get down." The significant point is that she tells us that she can do so at her own choosing, when she wants to. Perhaps most revealing is her conclusion. It is a sexualized statement. In effect, she tells us that she is more than a screen for sexual "projections" ("piercing looks"), and that she refuses to be pinned down—impaled, pierced, punctured—by labels and categories. A description of one of her early routines shows how difficult it was for the European male to brand her:

And now a strange creature takes the stage. It dashes around with bent knees, at a tremendous pace. A pair of ragged pants is its only attire. An incredible mixture of chewing gum, a boxing kangaroo, and a bicycle racer. Josephine Baker. Is it a man? Is it a woman? Lips painted black. Banana-coloured skin. The short hair cropped close to the head—a wig made of caviar. The voice is piercing, trembling with incessant movement. The body squirms like a snake. . . . Making faces and grimaces, she leers, puffs up her cheeks, twists and turns, does splits, and finally runs away on all fours, with stiff legs, her behind higher than her head like a young giraffe. . . . It's not a woman, it's not a dancer, it's as incomprehensible and as extraordinary as music itself. (quoted in Muller, 1985, 20)

Of course, Baker was imprisoned by the white male gaze, defined and confined within the parameters of the primitive trope. The fact that she thought that she was free is only a measure of the relativity of the concept of freedom.

The modern art movement is another significant link in this discussion. My brief comments on it are included because of its effect (subliminal and conscious, direct and tangential) on performance. It subtly reinforced the primitive trope and, in its rejection of academic European high art, offered a model for the modern dance movement to reject European concert dance (ballet) and expropriate aspects of the Africanist aesthetic. Art historians have done the work for us in addressing the African presence in European modern art. How ironic, that the high art of modernist Europe, a "wholly artificial cultural construct created by and for white males," should contain important principles derived from Africanist sources.[16] And what a paradox, that European sources needed infusions—or transfusions—from African cultures for revitalization. This appropriation could have been an enlightening fact of history, a wonderful occurrence, were it not for discrimination against African peoples and cultures. Excited by exposure to African and Oceanic art of an unimagined power and beauty, a group of artists was significantly influenced by these works, which were brought to their doorstep as spoils from colonialist exploits. (One of them went to live with the Other and created a specific, large body stereotype to represent the Tahitian female, ascribing to her, as did Cuvier with the Hottentot Venus, a sensuality and overt sexuality that were off-limits for proper European females.)

Around 1905, an exhibit by this group of artists inspired their critics to christen them "Fauves," or wild beasts. The connection with "primitives" is clear in this received nomenclature. The wildness was in their color choices and unexpected juxtapositions of compositional elements. Radical juxtaposition is an Africanist trait in music, movement, verbal forms, fabric art, and sculpture. Painters such as Picasso and Braque used other principles and intimations derived from African sources to stretch even further the boundaries of European high art. Picasso and Braque were early collectors of African masks. Braque stated that they "opened up a new horizon: they put me in contact with instinctive things, with direct manifestations running counter to the false tradition that was so hateful to me" (quoted in Leymarie 1972, 217). Selected works of many others, including Modigliani, Klee, Leger, and Lipschitz, show a clear relationship to these masks (Palmer et al. 1990, 3–7). Matisse, Klee, and Klimt owned Kuba (Zaire) textiles. "The Knife Thrower," one of the pieces in Matisse's "Jazz" collection, is directly attributable to Kuba influence. Besides the Africanist-primitivist subtext implied in the Fauvist period, the works of Matisse's later cut-out period show the bold use of color and superimpositions that European artists adopted from Africanist standards in the visual arts.

A recent art history example is the case of European American Jackson Pollock. His was both a Native American and an Africanist attitude in the conception and execution of his work. Placing canvases on the floor requires full body engagement in the act of painting and is the working style for "folk" artists throughout Africa, the Americas, and much of Asia. This process deletes the linear relationship of painter to canvas (affixed to a wall or easel) and inserts, instead, the circularity and dimensionality of a potentially 360-degree approach. Pollock, who grew up in the Southwest, attributes this influence to Native American sources:

I hardly ever stretch my canvas before painting. I prefer to tack the unstretched canvas to the hard wall or the floor. . . . On the floor I am more at ease. I feel nearer, more a part of the painting, since this way I can walk around it, work from the four sides and literally be *in* the painting. This is akin to the method of the Indian sand painters of the West. (quoted in O'Connor 1967, 40)

Earlier (32) Pollock stated that "some people find references to American Indian art and calligraphy in parts of my pictures. *That wasn't intentional; probably was the result of early memories and enthusiasms* (32; emphasis added). Later he states that "the Orientals painted on the floor" (80). African processes are not mentioned.

Although Pollock does not credit any Africanist resonances in the creation of his work, he was also an avid jazz enthusiast who was known to listen to the music while he worked and to utilize it occasionally as an aid in helping him overcome painter's block.[17] According to his wife, painter Lee Krasner, "He would get into grooves of listening to his jazz records — not just for days — day and night, day and night for three days running, until you thought you would climb the roof! Jazz? He thought it was the only other really creative thing happening in this country" (Kagan 1979, 96). It is notable that Pollock was a great admirer of Picasso: "The example of Picasso provided reassurance that such references [to black art forms, for example] could be acceptable in high art" (Kagan 1979, 98). As a young artist he combined cubist and surrealist techniques. They were abandoned as he adopted and adapted the jazz trope — specifically, improvisation — as a modus operandi in the evolution of his legendary drip technique. Breaking from the principles of grid composition — which had dominated the Europeanist canvas since the High Renaissance, even in the works of modernists like Picasso — Pollock's work made the canvas passé and showed that "high" art could be successfully produced by pure improvisation. It is strange that this important, pervasive jazz-Africanist resonance in Pollock's work has slipped through the cracks.   Yet, we know how frequently that is the case. It is a problem characterized in other contexts by Harold Bloom (1973) as the "anxiety of influence" and by Warren Robbins, former curator of the Smithsonian Institute's National Museum of African Art, as a "dilemma of derivation" (Palmer 1990, 3).

A key player in this discussion is Picasso's "Les Demoiselles D'Avignon" (1906–7), which has two figures on the right directly influenced by African masks. This work dissected the pictorial plane into angles and wedges. Critics, historians, and scholars classify and order the work of creative artists, and they are the ones who ultimately are responsible for acknowledging sources. Critics called the new style initiated by this painting "cubism," a term that highlights the gridlike angularity but hides the Africanist presence in this breakthrough work. Now, what if it had been called "Africanism?" What an exhilarating, stimulating effect that title could have had on the art world of colonialist, post-Victorian Europe. Had that been the case, one can only fantasize on the relationship that might have developed between modern art and its Africanist sources. But there is a disturbing trope encoded in this painting. Picasso has fallen prey to the primitivist trap of associating promiscuous sexuality with the image and symbols of Africa, thus placing this signature work on a symbolic continuum with the early nineteenth-century investigations of the Hottentot Venus. These "demoiselles" are prostitutes depicted in a brothel.[18]

Many examples from the modern art canon show that, in the case of Europe's borrowings from Africanist aesthetics, intertextuality is not, as the theory implies, a matter of anonymous formulas of unidentifiable origin. These works are directly indebted to African art and were not produced until the European artists had been exposed to African art. They probably qualify as unconscious quotations minus the quotation marks. They are certainly not exact replicas of their African models, yet the African presence in them is more than coincidence.[19] Some examples show direct influences, and some show subtextual presences. Rather than blame the artist for this invisibilization, we need to examine ourselves and our culture. We take from Other cultures, from traditions where the artist remains unnamed, and we credit our individualist tradition for innovations that have come from Others. We call "their" art "folk art"; when a European adopts it, it becomes "high art." There seems to be a general assumption on the part of Europeanist cultures that African visual arts, music, and dance are raw materials that are improved upon and elevated when they are appropriated and finessed by European artists. Like diamonds and gold, they are natural resources for colonialist domination and exploitation. But these things are products of cultures and individuals who are as complex and highly developed as Europeans. If we shuffle the cards to a revisionist perspective, it is equally natural for an African to look upon European "art" as folk work. This brings us back to Joann Kealiinohomoku's point (1983) that ballet—and, by extension, any other European cultural artifact—is no more or less than a European ethnic product.

Despite Rudyard Kipling's claim that "East is East, and West is West, and never the twain shall meet," Africanist influences have laced through European culture for centuries. In thirteenth-century Spain, at a time when that nation was an ascendant European power, illuminated manuscripts showed African and European musicians playing side by side. Spanish culture was a rich landscape of Jewish, African, and Latin strains. Songs by the thirteenth-century Spanish King Alfonso (such as the "Cantitas De Maria") were accompanied by Africanist rhythms played on the dumbek, an African drum from Islamic culture.[20] The Moorish (read African) presence was an integral component in shaping Spanish culture and may well have been one of the elements responsible for the sensual hip, arm, and torso movements of many Spanish dances, as well as the percussive and improvisatory nature of flamenco music and dance.[21] Blacks and/or blackface characters (Moors) appear in mummers' plays, courtly masques, and military and court bands. Their music and performance aesthetic put a permanent stamp on European styles. By the eighteenth century, the expressive, ecstatic person of medieval Europe was superseded by the "rational man" of the Enlightenment. Concomitantly, the rise of repression (the Inquisition), colonialism ("improved forms" of slavery and the "discovery" of America and the rest of the world), and Protestantism (new and more efficient enforcers of the mind-body split, with the body progressively devalued in the equation) marked a shift in European consciousness. This change was completed by the end of the nineteenth century with the rise of the Darwin-based sciences and social Darwinism, which led to phenomena such as the Hottentot Venus, cranial measurement to ascertain intelligence, and the emergent theory of white superiority. All are part of a taxonomy that placed European males at the top of the evolutionary ladder.[22] The Age of Enlightenment belied its name. Instead of offering an expanded worldview, that era launched a European perspective that became increasingly intolerant of variety and insistent upon the hierarchy and uniformity of class, caste, and race. Add to this "scientific" sociology the late-Victorian discovery of the psychological subconscious, layer them both on top of the dogmatic church traditions that determined European ethics and values, and the distortions of racism reach the epic, institutionalized proportions that we have learned to accept as normal in our twentieth-century lives.

It is my hope that this bullet-brief telescoping of several centuries of European art and cultural history seems neither arrogant nor presumptuous. Although the bleak focus was purposeful, it should in no way be construed as a denial or rejection of the beauties and achievements of European culture. However, we all know very well the good side. That was and still remains the bulk of our formal and circumstantial education as Americans — black, white, or brown. My task is not to repeat what countless scholars have done before me, but to fill in the missing pieces. I do not consider European culture as Other; I own it as mine, as I equally own my Africanist heritage. Both must be claimed, reclaimed, and embraced, with their conflicts and contradictions acknowledged, if we hope to understand how we arrived at this juncture and how we might conceive of making changes for the future. I tried to include here the essential historical flashpoints, the informational scaffolding, for understanding the broad contexts undergirding the African-European-American cultural edifice. Now, let us move on to examine the Africanist aesthetic in concert dance.

NOTES

1. Cheryl Willis, in conversation with the author, March 1989.
2. Allan Jabbour, keynote panel discussion, "Congress on Research in Dance" conference, Williamsburg, Virginia, October 1989.
3. Lawrence Sullivan, in conversation with the author, October 1989.
4. Originally the term "cover record" denoted a recording made by a white performer that was a copy (frequently, an exact imitation) of a piece originally created, styled, or performed by a black performer. Generally, little or no financial reward or documentary credit was accorded the original artist. The rationale for the cover record phenomenon was that the mainstream white public would not purchase recordings featuring black artists. This line of thinking enforced separate recording industries, radio stations, theaters, nightclubs, and ballrooms — one set for whites, and another for blacks — with both industries utilizing black-inspired forms as their basic commodity.
5. Milhaud visited Harlem in 1922, was overwhelmed by hearing jazz, and described it as

absolutely different from anything I had ever heard before, and [it] was a revelation to me. Against the beat of the drums the melodic lines crisscrossed in a breathless pattern of broken and twisted rhythms. . . . Its effect on me was so overwhelming that I could not tear myself away. More than ever I was resolved to use jazz for a chamber work. (quoted in Machlis 1961, 222)

6. "Concolean" is the commercial brand name of a chemical hair-straightening and waving process used by African American men. "Conk" is the abbreviated form.
7. Quoting Willie Morris, *North Toward Home*, Boston: Houghton Mifflin, 1967, 81.
8. Quoting Leslie A. Fiedler, *Waiting for the End*, New York: Stein and Day, 1964, 134.
9. William Yalowitz, final project proposal for Black Performance course, Temple University, February 1992.
10. According to Robert Farris Thompson,

John Cage's infamous 'prepared piano,' Judith Wilson relates, emerged when 'the legendary African-American dancer/choreographer Syvilla Fort's request for music for one of her dances led Cage to attempt to compose an African-sounding score. . . [by attaching] screws or bolts' to the piano strings. (1991, 92)

As Thompson points out, doctoring their instruments was a traditional practice with African American blues and jazz musicians. John Szwed made the same point about Cage's indebtedness to Africanist invention in a lecture, "Afro-Modernism and Afro-Postmodernism," given at Temple University in October 1992.

11. The concept of improvisation is not present in classical modes of Chinese performance, and the I Ching principle of chance, as used by Europeanist composers and choreographers, involves the random ordering of set phrases. It is a principle that values process, but it is not concerned with improvisation, per se. In the fusion of forms that characterizes American culture, Asian, African, and European principles are merged to define modern and postmodern styles.

12. See Stearns and Stearns (1979) for a detailed account of this era. On the black musical stage, the late minstrelsy, early vaudeville innovation of females dancing unison versions of the "Cakewalk" may have been the forerunner of the precision chorus line.

13. Carolus Linnaeus (1707–78) was a Swedish botanist and taxonomist who originated the system of scientific classification of plants and animals that is the basis for modern taxonomy.

14. I do not mean to imply that these and other scholars represent a monolithic perspective. They do not. Their work differs widely in degree and scope of ethnocentricity. Darwin was a progressive for his time but, for example, he regarded the people of Tierra del Fuego

to be . . . late-surviving remnants of ancestral, primitive humans. Like many others of his day and class, he simply did not believe that these savages ('absolutely naked and bedaubed with paint, . . . their mouths, frothed with excitement, . . . their expression. . . wild, startled and distrustful, . . . like wild animals') were human in the same sense that he himself was. He was more horrified by their lives than he was impressed with their similarity to those among whom he had grown up. (Shipman, quoted in Wright 1994, 7)

Social Darwinism, or the belief that social abilities are conditioned by biological variations rather than cultural adaptation, is the most deleterious extension of Darwin's work. Although he may not have intended that his canon be used as "grist for racist mills," the question remains: Where does the responsibility rest for "predictable misuses" of nineteenth-century science, history, and scholarship?

Karl Muller was an early nineteenth-century German historian. His work helped advance the Aryan Model of Greek history, to use Martin Bernal's terminology. This model purged ancient Greece of Egyptian and Semitic influences, which were discounted by Muller and characterized as delusionary, romantic "Egyptomania" on the part of the Greeks (see Toni Morrison in the *Michigan Quarterly Review*, 1989: 7). Martin Bernal is the author of *Black Athena: The Afroasiatic Roots of Classical Civilization, Vol. I. The Fabrication of Ancient Greece, 1785–1985*.

15. Baker's biography by one of her adopted children, Jean-Claude Baker, opens with this paragraph: "What an ass! Excuse the expression, but that is the cry that greeted Josephine as she exploded onstage in "La Danse de Sauvage.""

(Sixty years later, her friend and sometime lover, Maurice Bataille, would say to me, 'Ah! ce cul, . . . it gave all of Paris a hard-on')" (Baker and Chase 1993, 3).

In all fairness, Baker's nudity and exoticism must be considered in light of the general exploitation and commodification of the female body in twentieth-century entertainments. White "girls" were simply the object of a different set of white male fantasies.

16. The phrase quoted was made by a white, female colleague of mine who read an early version of this chapter and commented that my examination of the modernists was too harsh. She suggested that I discuss modern art in terms of the "wonderful paradox" of Europe needing Africa. She mentioned the profound effect that Picasso's "Demoiselles" had had on her early aesthetic development. Her implicit message, though not delivered in these words, was: "I don't really care what you say about Elvis, but don't take my Picasso away from me." I sensed that I was treading on sacred ground.

17. See Powell (1989, 31 and 33). For a thumbnail discussion of the Pollock-Picasso-Africanist intertextual schema, see Andrew Kagan (1979).

18. This, like the "cubism" title, was not Picasso's idea, but the popular name that stuck (see Leymarie 1972, 216). Picasso's preference was simply "The Brothel of Avignon," a title that still retained the subliminal association between the face of Africa and the prostituted woman.

According to Torgovnick (1990, 104): "Respectable medical theory ventured the opinion, around this time, that syphilis originated in Africa and that black skin was 'caused' by syphilitic sores. The adjectives *horrible* and *death-like* were often used in the early part of this century to describe primitive statues." In a recent book devoted totally to this painting, the Africanesque masks are explained in a Freudian sense, "in which emotions too painful to confront directly (here the artist's conflicted feelings triggered by the inherent savagery of sex and fear of death) are dealt with by substituting 'cover' images" (Rubin, Seckel, and Cousins, quoted in Frey 1995, 18). This explanation of the masks reinforces Torgovnick's and my contentions: Picasso is here associating sexuality, fear, and death with mother Africa.

19. An excellent example of the recursive nature of these cultural borrowings was related to me in a conversation with medical anthropologist Sydney White (April 1995), who did field work in Yunnan Province in Southwest China. According to White, in the 1980s, when things were opening up on the Chinese cultural landscape, artists left social realism behind and turned to modern styles. Cubism was even more popular than Impressionism, and "Picasso was really big." The Yunnan School was a movement by a group of mostly male artists who turned their attention to (Chinese) minorities, especially minority women, in a way that is correspondent with the primitive trope of the noble savage. They concentrated on cubist depictions of nude female bodies in a way that White characterized as "internal Orientalism." She added that there are fifty-six recognized minorities in China, twenty-five of which reside in Yunnan Province. Perhaps needless to say, I relate this anecdote to point out the irony that these Chinese should find Picasso the correspondent and contemporary vehicle for expression of their own preexistent primitive trope, a phenomenon that definitely has its own peculiar history.

20. Interview and program with the Ensemble for Early Music. "St. Paul's Sunday Morning," National Public Radio, May 6, 1990.

21. Following the lead of contemporary Africanist continental scholars such as Mazrui (1986), I do not make a racialized separation between North Africa and sub-Saharan Africa. Due to centuries of transcontinental migration, so-called "black" Africans inhabited North Africa, North Africans inhabited "black" Africa, and both groups inhabited and influenced European cultures and each other. In addition, both North and sub-Saharan Africans were included in the Muslim population. Culture and skin color vary on a wide scale on both sides of the Sahara. The separation of the African continent into North and South according to skin color, religion, or culture is regarded as an arbitrary, "Eurocentric" conceit based on the old and biased taxonomies of "racial" characteristics. When we use the term "European," we signify a vast array of cultures stretching from Finland to Spain, Italy, and Greece; from Poland, Roumania, Bulgaria, Hungary, parts of Russia, and even Turkey, to England and Ireland. What a range, yet no issue arises in identifying them all as European. The same holds true for Africa, and Egypt is included in this panoply—not only by its Nubian, Kemetic history, but also its present.

In their research on flamenco roots and culture, Meira Weinzweig-Goldberg and Carolynn Hine Johnson, flamenco dancers and scholars, have discovered in the literature and the practice historical connections and working correspondences between flamenco and Africanist forms of music and dance. Johnson quotes Spanish American dancer Matteo who, in his book, *The Language of Spanish Dance* (Norman, Okla.: University of Oklahoma Press 1990, 31), hypothesizes that the origin of castanets is traceable to the similar use of sea shells in ancient Egypt.

22. European females of all classes but especially of the lower class were regarded as inferior to males in ways that reached far deeper than the denial of suffrage. They were regarded, in some cases, as a sub-species of the European male. See Gilman (1985).

4

Barefoot and Hot, Sneakered and Cool: Africanist Subtexts in Modern and Postmodern Dance

We have two primitive sources, dangerous and hard to handle in the arts, but of intense psychic significance—the Indian and the Negro. That these influence us is certain.

Martha Graham (1930), quoted in de Laban 1945, 55

This statement, made by the grande dame of modern dance, acknowledges influences that have been essential in the birth and evolution of that art form. Yet there exists no dance book or monograph to document these presences, and attention to them remains the exception rather than the rule in academic classrooms and scholarly conferences. These forces may be part of the air we breathe, but acknowledgment of them has fallen through a crack in our historical memory.

Two premises drive the discussion in this chapter. The guiding principle is that of intertextuality, the fact that cultures influence each other, and their products, processes, and people cross paths and exchange information in ways that we see and in ways that are invisible yet felt. Deborah Jowitt's statement about looks in the air that influence us is a simple but effective reduction of this concept. Second, there is the theory of "home truths." Sara Maitland, a contemporary British writer, gave this title to one of her novels. (Unfortunately, the designation for the American edition was changed to *Ancestral Truths*, a title that misses the mark.) A home truth is described as "'an indisputable fact or basic truth, especially one whose accuracy may cause discomfort or embarrassment.' It hits you, so to speak, where you live" (Kenner 1994, 12). Africanisms are home truths in European American culture. They are the bastard child, the muffled scream that still can be heard in spite of efforts to hush it. They are the asymmetrical threads breaking the desired and mythical uniformity of the American fabric. Respectively, these two premises fall into two categories already discussed, namely, influences and invisibilizations. Keep them in mind, along with the Africanist aesthetic premises discussed in Chapter 2, as you read on.

Louis Horst, Martha Graham's companion and one of the pundits of modern dance, gave a proscribed credence to Africanist influences in his book, *Modern Dance Forms* (1987). His acknowledgment is framed by the convention that regards these resonances as "primitive" and, therefore, open territory for appropriation. At first, we don't know that this will be his perspective. He states that "primitive art is evident as a strong quality in every contemporary style" (53). Then he compares Africanist-inflected modern dance poses by Graham and other modern dancers with modern art paintings that were similarly influenced. He connects for us the borrowings in modern art and modern dance with specific pieces of African sculpture. He contends that most modern dance is "primitive to a degree," and that some works have totally adopted the primitive mold (65). It looks and sounds as though he is giving credit where it is due. However, we begin to understand the nature of his acknowledgment when we read, "The primitive did not create works of art, but magic weapons" (57). Like his peers and colleagues, and in keeping with the tenor of his times, Horst believes that these appropriations are not really appropriations (and, of course, he never uses this terminology in his discussion) but, instead, an elevation of the status of primitive raw materials to a higher, cultured, European aesthetic standard of excellence. In a chapter devoted to what Horst terms "jazz dance," he attributes the roots of that genre to enslaved Africans and states that jazz does not "imitate the typical ethnic African, but it retains many of the attributes brought from Africa," which he specifies as "jerky, percussive movements and accents," "syncopation," and "melancholy and lassitude" (111). He mentions the pervasive intertextuality of jazz in America:

Although jazz is by now cosmopolitan and international, and has proved its affinity to the whole modern world by its popularity with all races and cultures, still it is most typically American. It is natural to all Americans, as deeply and subconsciously understood as any other folk dance is understood by the people from whom it grew. It is specifically the expression of present-day urban America. It is an intimate part of our daily life and shows in the urban walk, the posture, the rhythm of speech, the gesture, the costumes, of the city. It belongs to a certain way we have of standing—a slouch, one hip thrown out—of sitting in an informal sprawl, of speaking in slangy abruptness. Jazz is the trade mark of the city. (Horst 1987, 111–12)

Perhaps it is my "paranoia of origin" that causes me to interpret this passage as a classic example of "anxiety of influence," but I am made uncomfortable by Horst's diffused stamp of Americanness on the jazz attitude. He seems to responsibly acknowledge the African roots of the jazz aesthetic, yet there is an air of patronization, if not condescension, in stating that jazz does not reflect the "typical ethnic African." To state his case in this way, using that choice of words, is a giveaway as to where he ranks "the ethnic African" in his hierarchy. Moreover, he simply ignores the African American quotient. His conclusion is not so different than mine—that the pervasive Africanist influence defines American culture. But his process colors and shapes the idea to a different focus and end. He seems to give credit with the one hand and take it away with the other. He deftly loosens and extrapolates jazz from its Africanist moorings and accords it a Europeanist pedigree by defining it as "natural to all Americans, . . . as any other folk dance is understood by the people from whom it grew." It is too easy for the African American part of the equation to become invisible when jazz dance is described as an American folk dance. The jazz characteristics described by Horst are indeed Africanisms that infuse every aspect of American endeavor and can be summed up by the phrase, "the aesthetic of the cool." In addition, these forces have also influenced the mood and attitude that underlie American postmodern dance.

It is important to remember that, beyond the "primitive" and jazz influences that Horst acknowledges, there are specifics that he does not discuss: the torso articulation so essential to modern dance; the legendary pelvic contraction coined as the signature statement in Graham's movement vocabulary; the barefoot dancers reifying contact with the earth, touching it, rolling or lying on it, giving in to it. These particular components of the New Dance had no coordinates in European concert or folk dance traditions. Those traits live in African and African American dance forms, and modern and postmodern dance received this wisdom from Africanist-inspired American vernacular and pop culture. Robert Farris Thompson mentions the influence of Sea Island women on some of Graham's "basic ideas for costuming, and stance, and gravity-indulgence" (1991, 92). In another essay he suggested that African "apart dancing" (his phrase for improvisational solo dancing) may have been an influence on the improvisatory impetus in modern dance (1980, 106). The value placed on improvisation in modern and postmodern dance stems from the pervasive presence of Africanist improvisatory forms in American popular music and social, ballroom, cabaret, and revue dance genres.

Let us turn to the postmodern moment. As is the case with acknowledging the Africanist presence in modernism, nothing is taken away by arguing that Africanisms are added to the picture. The European, historical, avant-garde roots of modern and postmodern art and dance forms have been well documented by established mainstream scholars. Recapitulating that research is not my aim. My task is to fill in and strip away and, thus, to reveal what has been hidden. Unlike the case of pop cover records, and despite Horst's presumption that European modern dancers make a conscious acquisition of the primitive, appropriation in many postmodern dance instances is not a matter of direct stealing. Indeed, here we are deep in Barthes country, dealing with texts as intertexts, because the Africanist presence in postmodernism is a subliminal but driving force. To compute this factor into the postmodern equation does not reduce the whole to any one source but enriches and broadens the movement and corrects the historical miscalculation that omitted it. I am not suggesting that the postmodern aesthetic does not have other, more direct and deliberate historical roots in Dadaism and other movements from the modernist period (although it should be clear from modern art history, and clear even from Horst's and Thompson's sparse though pointed ruminations on modern dance, that Africanisms are an intertext inherent in nearly all modernist genres). I am also aware that a generic, popularly espoused approach to multicultural, recursive, and Creolization theories endorses a pluralist perspective that examines in tandem the broad range of diverse cultural contributions to American society. But that is not my task. Due to the historical, systematic denial and invisibilization of the Africanist presence in American culture, I have taken the particularist (namely, Africanist-centered) approach that seems justified, in this case.

So much of what we see as avant-garde in the postmodern era is informed by recycled Africanist principles and parallels traditional, characteristic Africanisms that we all grew up with as Americans, black, white, and brown. In her characterization of early postmodern dance, dance historian Sally Banes states that "the key postmodern choreographic technique is radical juxtaposition" (1987, xxiii). Similarly, in describing Africanist visual arts, dance, and music, Robert Farris Thompson and others have pointed out the centrality of high-affect juxtaposition:

A gifted Egbado Yoruba dancer maintains the whole time she dances a "bound motion" in her head, thus balancing a delicate terra-cotta sculpture on her head without danger, while simultaneously subjecting her torso and arms to the most confounding expressions of raw energy and force. It is not difficult to find similar instances of control in other African dancers. Thundergod devotees, for instance, sometimes dance with a burning fire in a container coolly balanced on the top of their heads. (Thompson 1980, 109)

The coolness, relaxation, looseness, and laid-back energy; the radical juxtaposition of ostensibly contrary elements; the irony and double entendre of verbal and physical gesture; the dialogic relationship between performer and audience — all are integral elements in Africanist arts and lifestyle that are woven into the fabric of our society. Postmodern dance, like other postmodern trends, has as a keynote the quoting of styles from past eras. When dancer Douglas Dunn "quotes" ballet without straight legs or heroic energy, or Yvonne Rainer creates a solo, titles it a trio ("Trio A," 1966), and bases it on movement clusters and an indirect approach to the audience, they redefine their idiom.[1] They may not be aware that the Africanist aesthetic is nonlinear and values dance steps that come in overlapping, self-referential clusters. (This approach to dance making, from a European perspective, has been regarded as "cluttered" or naive choreography.) But they probably do know that, in hip talk, "that's bad" means "that's good," and "that's down" means "that's up." Irony, paradox, and double entendre, rather than the classical European, linear logic of cause, effect, and resolution, are basic to the Africanist aesthetic and offer a model for postmodernism subconsciously and, at times, deliberately. It is probable that Dunn, Rainer, and others were not aware that in traditional Yoruban performance modes, the categories of play, ritual, and spectacle are fluid, multidimensional, multicentered concepts that put to shame the Europeanist idea that Africanist ritual is rigid or static. Margaret Thompson Drewal's work with this culture reveals such a vitally alive, multiplex, and improvisatory picture that she concludes that "unfixed and unstable, Yoruba ritual is more modern than modernism itself" (1992, 20). Due to continuities and retentions throughout the African diaspora, these values have come to the Americas, along with African peoples. Maya Deren's descriptions of Haitian Vodun performance in her book and film, *Divine Horsemen* (1991), point to similar factors about the vitality and improvisational nature of this highly creative and original Africanist tradition. My point is that it is naive to assume it is coincidence that postmodernism and Africanist traditional performance share parallel processes. The fact that postmodern culture exists inside of, around, and on top of Africanist cultures is a fact of intertextuality, not merely parallel development. The problem is that the chroniclers of postmodern performance have credited sources from the European historical avant-garde. They have also credited Asian sources in Zen and other Buddhist philosophies, yoga and other Hindu practices, and in the martial arts. They have not given credence to the Africanist aesthetic as a pervasive subtext in postmodern performance.

In her exposition on postmodern dance, Banes (1987, xxii) states that "the bodies of their dancers were relaxed but ready, without the pulled-up, stretched muscle tone of the ballet or classical modern dancer. . . . The discovery and understanding of their forms and processes, . . . the down-to-earth style, the casual or cool attitude, the sense that "it is what it is". . . constituted a crucial aspect of the dance's import.

The same specifics could be used to describe the operative principles of tap dance or jazz music, two Africanist forms predating postmodern dance that are part of the black or white, urban or rural, twentieth-century American experience. Banes unconsciously uses a bit of African American urban street orature in borrowing the phrase, "it is what it is." Although to some ears, that phrase may have the ring of a Zen koan (and, certainly, African Americans have taken on alternative religious practices such as Buddhism), it emanates from the existential street jargon of the 1960s black drug subculture. Pieces of that "talk" have quietly been embraced by the mainstream, particularly the liberal fringe. In the film, "About Tap," the superb tap artist Chuck Green says, "You have to know how much dancing to do. You can't just do all you want to do; you've got to give what's needed" (1985). Thus, he expresses a sentiment of balance and cool that is pervasive in Africanist forms such as jazz music and tap dance and reverberates in postmodern dance. This quote may also have the ring of Asian philosophy, but it comes from the nitty-gritty experience of black popular performance.

Rhythm tap dance offers strong attitudinal modeling for postmodern dance. Its cool, laid-back energy is mirrored in the "no skill, few accents, unhurried control" principles espoused as an aesthetic by postmodern dancer Yvonne Rainer in the film "Beyond The Mainstream" (1980) and in her "'Trio A." A noteworthy aside is relevant here. White American females of the 1960s through the present era have made a major contribution to the continuity of African American tap dance. They studied, apprenticed, and performed with an older generation of black male tap masters and brought the form to the attention of white concert dance audiences at a time when the African American middle class most frequently sent their children to study ballet and modern dance. This black tap presence in white concert dance venues influenced postmodern dance and, in turn, was influenced by it. Conversely, tap always remained a popular staple in African American grassroots culture. But the costs for such cross-pollination are always at some group's expense, in this world of commodified art objects. The losers, in this case, were the excellent African American female tap artists who were excluded, by both racism and sexism, from white concert venues.

Jazz dance offers another model for the postmodern dancer. Performer and teacher Billy Siegenfeld echoes the Africanist principles of embracing the conflict and the aesthetic of the cool in the quote below (and the writer quoting him repeats the common conflation of the cool aesthetic with Zen practice):

'To dance jazz, you have to relax about not getting it right the first time; you have to be able to embrace the error and go on.' [Siegenfeld] As in Zen archery, you start to hit the target when you stop thinking about hitting it. You can't really swing unless you forget the cultural imperative to be square. [staff writer] (quoted in Mazo 1991, 54)

The postmodern dance aesthetic also mirrors the attitude of the 1940s-1950s bebop jazz musicians who broke away from the established jazz tradition, literally turned their backs on the audience, took their own, sweet time, and redefined jazz improvisation. Charlie Parker, whose nickname was "Yardbird," wrote songs that were inversions of ballads and, in a wonderful play with words and names, gave them titles like "Ornithology." Yvonne Rainer's solo-trio, based on poses and gestures that never bring the performer in frontal contact with the audience, is an offshoot of Parker and the jazz-Africanist ethos. Both artists used Africanist aesthetic principles that came to them on the wings of American life and culture. Rainer and others said "no" to the seduction of the spectator and, like the bop musician, did not play to or even face the audience, but reversed the traditional spectator-performer roles and required the audience to stretch, flex, and reach out to the performer. Just as some spectators greeted this new form of jazz by saying that it wasn't music, so a criticism of postmodern dance was that it was not really dance. And, from the European American mainstream dance critics, a criticism of African and African American dance has been that it is not "real choreography" (which seems to mean choreography based on European concert dance principles) but simply steps strung together. It is interesting to note what happens, however, when the "steps strung together" approach is given a Europeanist pedigree. Then it is quite likely to garner critical praise as a plotless, avant-garde experiment in "pure movement." In fact, "Trio A" is a case in point. But, as choreographer David Gordon explains in *Beyond The Mainstream* (1980), his work does not represent "a second rate, underrehearsed modern dance company, but another way of doing something from a different perspective." Rainer's and Gordon's work, like that of the modern jazz musician, involves the medium and the task, with the performer's focus at a cool, meditative state of concentration.

Returning to the film "About Tap," dancer Jimmy Slyde, in describing his smooth style (indicated by his surname) suggests that his movement is so seamless that it travels faster than the conscious mind:

I like to move a lot. Sometimes they call it a blur, because you move so fast you get out of focus. So you have to catch up with yourself. That's where the slides come in. You can't just meter out slides and. . . . there's not a certainty you'll end up where you want to.

A postmodern correspondence to Slyde's explanation is stated by Trisha Brown in "Beyond The Mainstream" (1980), where she describes her style as "very kinesthetic, very articulate and silky—so much so that sometimes while I'm working I think I will slip off of the air if I don't insert another kind of movement." Choreographer Laura Dean talks about both dance and music stemming from the same sources, rhythm and energy. These sources are predominant characteristics in the Africanist aesthetic. In addition, postmodern dancers do things that are basic to Africanist aesthetics but new to the European perspective. They dare to be repetitious, awkward, or ungraceful, not only in the formalist-primitivist style of Martha Graham in the 1930s, but also in the street-wise, deadpan, laid-back attitude of black-inflected contemporary popular culture. They may risk being off-center which, from a revisionist perspective, is not "off," but represents a shift of the center from the vertical spine to some other part of the body. A tap dancer's center may be in his feet, not his spine. In fact, for many styles of tap and postmodern dance, the concept of center may be a categorical error, a misleading, misapplied term that fabricates a reality that is untrue to the genre. Like Snake Hips Tucker, the postmodern dancer redefines performance as playing oneself, rather than a role, and redefines what a dance is—not a psychological reenactment of emotional expression but, as in African dance, a constellation of steps and/or tasks with feeling as a kinesthetic concept intimately connected to the movement itself. In both, expression comes from feeling for, with, and through the movement, rather than the movement serving as a vehicle for expressing emotion.

One way to approach tap dance is as though it is a simple act, like walking. Postmodern dance took the next step and put actual pedestrian movement, like walking, on stage, whether that stage was a loft, a gym, or a sidewalk. In both cases and, unlike ballet and some other forms of European concert dance, the intended message is inclusive, to show that dancing is as easy as walking, to impress us by giving the illusion that we could just get up and do it ourselves (rather than intimidating us by showing how difficult it is). The following description of Savion Glover, a young tap artist, illustrates this point:

A tall drink of water bounded up from the front row and made his way to the stage. It was Mr. Glover, wearing slacks, a Bart Simpson T-shirt, and a necklace of golden links. He began to slouch and saunter around, casually pigeon-toed, just ambling. The only difference between him and any other ambling teen was that he somehow managed to produce so many tap rhythms so nonchalantly that even eyewitnesses couldn't quite believe it. Within a couple of minutes, he had shaken out a boatload of tarantulas. (1990, 6)

The final point in this comparison of postmodern dance and tap dance aesthetics through the films, "About Tap" and "Beyond the Mainstream," is that both genres privilege a cool, mellow state that can be termed "flow." Jimmy Slyde calls it "swinging," a state in which the dancer performs with ease and finds common denominators with the music, the musicians, and the audience. Steve Paxton, the father of contact improvisation, talks about the mind of the contact improviser in the comparable place and state as it is when one plays basketball: open, receptive, "apolitical," to use his word. One description mirrors the other.

Contact improvisation is the postmodern dance form that put an absolute premium on improvisation.[2] A powerful subliminal flashpoint for that dance genre is the black Civil Rights movement of the 1950s and 1960s. As the site of a nationwide revolutionary spirit culminating in a move toward reorganization of political and social structures, this grassroots, originally black movement had a phenomenally pervasive effect on the lifestyles of Americans from many different walks of life. For example, feminist poet and essayist Adrienne Rich describes its effect on her development in an essay, "Split at the Root: An Essay on Jewish Identity":

The emergence of the Civil Rights Movement in the sixties I remember as lifting me out of a sense of personal frustration and hopelessness. Reading James Baldwin's early essays in the fifties had stirred me with a sense that apparently "given" situations like racism could be analyzed and described and that this could lead to action, to change. (1983, 183)

The movement became the prototype for the subsequent women's, anti-war, and environmental protest movements, offering an immediate model for liberation. It showed that an alternative form of social organization — a subculture — could exist and even thrive within an alien superculture. It lifted Americans beyond the impotence and stagnation of the McCarthy 1950s era and indicated that, through action, change was possible on many fronts. Similarly, contact improvisation seems to have unconsciously drawn from the movement the inspiration and model for its own freedom movement in dance — not in content, of course, but in attitude. The contact community began as a subculture that thrived in spite of establishment modern dance. In an example of perhaps inadvertent borrowing, even the contact improviser's "jam" takes its name from the jazz musician's "jam session," a designation for group improvisation. (Indeed, the word "jam" has crept into the American vocabulary as a descriptor for many non-jazz situations.) These jams see contactors from far and wide converge to hold a marathon, paralleling the traditional form of African American revival meetings. And in contact improvisation, as in its jazz paradigm, the participants improvise, allowing their improvisations to be inflected and modified by what the others are doing. Like their Lindyhopping predecessors, contacters and other postmodern dancers may revel in the sheer acrobatic, kinesthetic pleasure of movement. They share with Lindyhoppers a gender-democratic concept of partnering in which it is just as likely that a female will lift a male as the other way around. Contacters and postmodern dancers took this "Lindy" innovation a step further and gave credence and visibility to same-sex lifts.

Postmodern performers such as Deborah Hay, Meredith Monk, Simone Forti, and Carolee Schneeman, along with other European Americans of their generation, were influenced by the Africanist presence in American popular culture. While I was living the life of a Manhattan–New York State "hippie" (and the Africanist origin of that word suddenly jumps off the page at me) during the 1960s, my path crossed that of the women named above and others of their — no, *our* — ilk at parties or clubs in the Big Apple (coincidentally, this name for Manhattan was originally the name of an African American social dance of the swing era) or in rural New England and New York State communes. At these venues, dancers and non-dancers alike danced as part of the "we are all artists" democratic spirit of the era. All-night social dancing influenced the "art" dancing created for the lofts, churches, and open fields where these dancers performed in the 1960s. Creating choreographies that had no clear beginning or end and ascribing to a fluid concept of audience-performer interaction paralleled dancing all night at parties or discos to pop music in open-ended, participatory social situations. And, whether we were aware of it or not, the ethos and ambiance of our communal, chemical explorations (pot, hashish, LSD, cocaine) symbolically and somatically fed our romanticized, illicit, or politicized fantasies of a non-bourgeois Other. We staged our own Africanist-inspired, Native American inspired rituals on stage and in life. In both arenas the choice role to play was oneself. A style that emulated the communal, collective standard of African and Native American cultures and the high-affect aesthetic and specific movement vocabulary of the Africanist inevitably affected "artistic" output and influenced the creation of theatrical dances that were termed postmodern. Similarly, the risk-taking that occurs in early postmodern dance parallels the experimentation basic to jazz music and tap dance. Each genre flirts with the danger involved in playing the edges of one's instrument, so to speak.

European American concert dancers have utilized the Africanist aesthetic, and so have African American artists. Moreover, African American postmodernists such as Blondell Cummings, Jawole Willa Jo Zollar, Bill T. Jones, Bebe Miller, Donald Byrd, and David Rousseve have deconstructed, refashioned, and preserved European American concert dance aesthetics in their own image. They are latter-day followers in the African American tradition of wearing many hats and inverting-subverting codes, descendants of folks who did so long before there were words like deconstruction or postmodernism. To know the mainstream culture and play its game, but also to remember and keep one's own — that is and has always been the task. The flip side of this coin is the fact that Cummings, Zollar, and others preserve Africanisms in their particular postmodern styles.[3] The inverse of this equation is demonstrated in the way that Molissa Fenley, a white dancer exposed to Africanist influences by growing up both in Africa and the United States, draws upon this aesthetic in her choreography — not in steps, but in attitude and attack. What I mean is, for example, the driving ephebism of her solo to Stravinsky's "Rite of Spring," plus her choice to dance it barebreasted. Other postmodernists have more directly appropriated movement vocabularies. According to the late Burt Supree (1991, 98), dance editor of the *Village Voice*, choreographer Doug Elkins has "built a dizzy, cheeky style on steals from flamenco as well as break dancing, martial arts, and traditional dance vocabularies."

In his book, *The End of Humanism*, Richard Schechner (1982) addresses the difference between modernism and postmodernism and characterizes the latter as a nonnarrative, nonlinear, ritualistic means of organization. Those Africanist characteristics are basic to the African American culture that is the legacy of all Americans. Jazz and tap dance are nonnarrative portraits in rhythm that demonstrate the postmodern concept of "dance for dance's sake." Traditional African dances are constellations of polyrhythmic, polycentric steps, movements, and gestures that may refer to a theme, but the real story told is about the dancing itself — the steps, rhythms, movements, and the dancing body that generates them. Like postmodern dance, these Africanist dance forms are self-referential and nonlinear. Africanist forms focus on process rather than product and exhibit flow rather than cause-and-effect organization, all of which are basic principles integral to the definition of postmodern performance. Africanisms pervade American culture and are inherited by blacks and whites, modernists and postmodernists alike. The conclusion is inevitable: The Africanist presence is a deep-structure conditioning force in the definition and practice of modern and postmodern performance.

NOTES

1.   The full title of this dance is "The Mind Is a Muscle, Trio A." It was choreographed to be performed by three soloists simultaneously, which is why it could justifiably be called a trio. However, the three perform the same movements independent of one another. They "relate" neither to each other nor to the audience. A 1979 film version of the "Trio" is performed solo by Rainer herself.

2.   According to researcher Cynthia Novack,

Contact improvisation is most frequently performed as a duet, in silence, with dancers supporting each others' weight while in motion. Unlike wrestlers, who exert their strength to control a partner, contact improvisers use momentum to move in concert with a partner's weight, rolling, suspending, lurching together. They often yield rather than resist, using their arms to assist and support but seldom to manipulate. Interest lies in the ongoing flow of energy rather than on producing still pictures, as in ballet; consequently, dancers doing contact improvisation would just as soon fall as balance. Although many contact improvisers demonstrate gymnastic ability, their movement, unlike that of most gymnastic routines, does not emphasize the body's line or shape. Even more important, they improvise their movement, inventing or choosing it at the moment of performance. (1990, 8)

3.   Choreographers such as Garth Fagan, Alvin Ailey, Rod Rodgers, Blondell Cummings, Bebe Miller, Ralph Lemon, and Donald Byrd, to name a few, are African American by ethnicity. However, they are not choreographers of African dance. They are forgers of an American concert dance tradition. I point out this distinction to correct the categorical error that assumes that all dancers who are black make "black dance." The creations of these artists, like the work of their white counterparts, are influenced by both Africanist and European aesthetics. For an expanded discussion of the issue of "black dance" and "dancers who are black," see Dixon (1990, 117–23).

5

STRIPPING THE EMPEROR:
GEORGE BALANCHINE AND THE
AMERICANIZATION OF BALLET

Note on Commercial Theatre

You've taken my blues and gone —

Langston Hughes 1974, 190

Some people imagine that ballet is about as far away from the Africanist aesthetic as black supposedly is from white, but things just aren't as defined or clear-cut as that, not even black and white. In spite of our denials, opposites intermingle more often than we admit. Cultures borrow from each other, and fusions abound.

George Balanchine had a profound influence on the Americanization of ballet. That is ironic, since he emigrated to the United States as an adult, professional choreographer schooled in the Russian ballet tradition. Sometimes it takes an outsider to see what the real flavor of a culture is all about. The Africanist presence plays a subtle but substantial role in defining American ballet. This component has been glossed over in the past, if touched upon at all; certainly, no consistent inquiry has been accorded it. As early as 1934, the same year Balanchine arrived in the United States, Arnold Haskell in his book, *Balletomania Then and Now*, noted: "During the past twenty years or more, Harlem influence upon all branches of art and life has been as great as the Diaghilev influence and has been felt even in the ballet, stronghold of tradition itself" (1977, 205).

While the African presence in modern art has received fluctuating attention over the course of the century, from the start the Africanist influence in American ballet has been tucked away in an interstice of history where it has been overlooked.[1] It is frustrating to read the literature on Balanchine's Broadway musical comedy career. Writers lavish praise upon him for bringing dance-as-art to the musical comedy stage, but they have nothing to say about what he learned and gleaned from that genre, a venue that manifests a harmonious marriage of Africanist and Europeanist aesthetic principles. In a typical dilemma of derivation, they state the case so that it seems that culture is a one-way street, with the traffic moving from "high" to "low," when it should be clear that borrowing and exchange are interactive processes. Not only a donor, Balanchine was also the fortunate recipient of a rich, partly Africanist-inspired legacy during his musical comedy years. Furthermore, the term "jazz dance" functions as a smokescreen in a case like this. Like the Horst example in the previous chapter, it serves to conceal the Africanist presence.

Although the Africanist influence has been invisibilized, it shadows ballet and almost every American cultural pursuit. How could it be otherwise? When different cultures share the same geography, it is inevitable that they will also share the same biography, regardless of who is in power. Once we acknowledge this fact, we may begin to discover the presence of Africanist sources in Europeanist high art forms. I acknowledge and celebrate the stock influences on American ballet—Russian, French, Italian—that Balanchine brought with him from Europe. Those are understood and are well documented in the annals of ballet history. They are the subject of innumerable scholarly conferences, symposia, and academic discourses on both sides of the Atlantic. My purpose here is to retrieve the hidden legacy, the black text in Balanchine's Americanization of ballet. It's not the case that Balanchine was a choreographer of black dance. On the contrary, it is clear that he was a ballet choreographer who worked in the ballet medium and subscribed to a ballet aesthetic. I hope to make equally clear that throughout his career, he introduced to the ballet canon Africanist aesthetic principles as well as Africanist-based steps from the social, modern, and so-called jazz dance vocabularies. He brought these innovations to ballet while maintaining his grounding in the ballet aesthetic. The result was still ballet, but with a new accent. I hasten to add that, from its European beginnings, ballet has always borrowed from folk culture and popular motifs for replenishment. The appropriation of European folk forms was particularly rampant in ballet and other high art genres during the mid-nineteenth-century Romantic period. Choreographers like Jules Perrot and Jean Coralli made ballets like "Giselle" (1841); August Bournonville created a canon of folk-inspired works for his Danish troupe; and specific vernacular dances like "La Cachucha," an adaptation of a Spanish dance akin to the "Bolero," were adapted for and performed by the preeminent ballerinas of the era. This transition from vernacular to elite supplies essential lifeblood for the continuity of the ballet tradition.

There would be every reason to expect that the same process would occur in the Americas except that here, the popular cultural icons happen to be infused with Africanisms, patently and subliminally.

SECOND PREMISES

My guiding principles, listed and explained here, are grounded in contemporary revisionist scholarship:

1. Ballet is a form of ethnic dance (an observation made by dance anthropologist Joann Kealiinohomoku) and, like all (ethnic) dance, is subject to the influences and presences that are valued in its cultural context.
2. Influences from past and present cultures are woven into, intermeshed with, and redistributed in any given cultural form (such as ballet, for example) at any given moment in time.
3. The Americanization of ballet by a Russian immigrant, George Balanchine, shows both African American and European American influences.
4. An Africanist perspective can be used to reveal the Africanist presence in American ballet.

Ballet's Ethnicity

To state that ballet is a form of ethnic dance lends a democratic perspective to this cultural form. Along with European orchestral music, it has been lionized as "classic" — that is, beyond classification, in a class by itself — so that it is isolated from and raised upon a pedestal above other world art forms. To separate ballet in this way, to deem it "high" art while other forms are considered something less, sets up an unreasonable, ethnocentric hegemony. By revising our perspective and redrafting the rules of the game, we may see ballet for what it is — one form of world dance, amongst scads of others, representing the aesthetic choices of one group of people at a particular period in history. To regard ballet as another form of ethnic dance returns it to its place in the world community of dance. It is embraced, not debased, by its ethnicity, and it (and the world view that produced it) is recognized not as the supreme answer but as one possible solution to the question: "What is dance?"

When we examine the dictionary for the word "ethnic," we may begin to understand why people react with shock at the suggestion that ballet is ethnic. We also realize that the term, Greco-Roman in origin, was used by Europe to define Other in opposition, inferiority, and subordination to self. The following definitions come from the *American Heritage Dictionary* (1980, 450):

ethnic — adj. — 1. Of or pertaining to a social group within a cultural and social system that claims or is accorded special status on the basis of complex, often variable traits including religious, linguistic, ancestral, or physical characteristics. 2. Broadly, characteristic of a religious, racial, national, or cultural group. 3. Pertaining to a people not Christian or Jewish; heathen; pagan. [Late Latin *ethnicus*, heathen, foreign, from Greek *ethnikos*, of a national group, foreign, from *ethnos*, people, nation.]

The Latin-Greek origins show the degree of bias that was present in the original casting and usage of the term. According to the first definition, supposedly the accepted contemporary definition, ballet would be considered ethnic, just as European peoples, be they Irish, French, or German, are specific ethnic groups. Although it is an outmoded connotation given in an out-of-date publication, the third definition is the one that prevails and holds sway in general American usage.

Influences

This principle is summed up by the concept of intertextuality, discussed in Chapter 1.

Ballet's Americanizer

"There are other ways of holding the interest [of the audience], by vivid contrast, for instance. Imagine the effect that would be produced by six Negresses dancing on their pointes and six white girls doing a frenzied jazz!" (quoted in Haskell 1977, 98). So suggested Balanchine to Arnold Haskell, his interviewer, in New York in 1934. Balanchine had recently arrived in the United States, invited by Lincoln Kirstein, who can best be described as the dream-come-true impresario. What Balanchine proposed was quite interesting, and I am sorry that he didn't try that black-white ensemble back in 1934. Although he was playing on the shock value of putting "primitives" on *pointe* and having the civilized "get down," such a cast might have helped change the racial tenor of American dance relations at a time when there were no mixed casts and no blacks were on *pointe* in white ballet companies. In fact, the idea is very non-European. He proposes a high-contrast, high-affect trick that is far beyond the parameters of good taste, in the European sense. Balanchine did not have to hit American soil for the Africanist aesthetic to wash over him. He had sharpened his performance teeth during his apprenticeship in Europe during the Jazz Age of the 1920s. (Substitute "Africanist" for the word "jazz," and the focus of that era becomes clearer.) He had choreographed "Apollo" (1928) for the Diaghilev Ballets Russes. After Diaghilev died, Balanchine worked in major European cities as a ballet master and choreographed revues for the popular stage. He also created musical routines for "Dark Red Roses" (1929), the first feature-length English talking film. Europe's play with Africanist influences in music, dance, and the visual arts grew proportionately with colonialist expansion starting in the mid-Victorian era and came to full, ribald blossom as "the continent" reveled in these influences during the 1920s.

Perspectives

A revised picture from a particular vantage point, be it Africanist (discussed in Chapters 1 and 2), feminist, or other, yields and reveals information that otherwise remains concealed. Freudian and Marxist theories may be seen as the forerunners of twentieth-century revisionist thinking. Each methodology presents a new lens for refocusing our perspectives.

AESTHETIC VALUES AND CONDITIONING INFLUENCES

Why did Balanchine become the conduit for the (African) Americanizing of ballet? Katherine Dunham gives us a clue. "Balanchine liked the rhythm and percussion of our dances," she said, referring to her own African American dance company and to their work with Balanchine on the musical, "Cabin in the Sky" (1940). "I think most Georgians have a good sense of rhythm from what I've seen" (quoted in Mason 1991, 193). Balanchine was the perfect catalyst for defining and shaping American ballet. The groundedness and rhythmic sense that he inherited from the Georgian (Russian) folk dance tradition was the open door that allowed him to embrace the Africanist rhythmic landscape of his adopted homeland. With talent and initiative he was able to merge those elements from the two cultures, just as he fused ballet's cool aloofness with the Africanist aesthetic of the cool. Mixings such as these can occur only if compatible components and favorable conditions exist on both sides. According to Deborah Jowitt, "Certainly, Balanchine's take on Americans and America affected his style as profoundly as his background" (Jowitt 1988, 255). It is implicit and evident that things African American are part of his "take" on America.

A word about coolness: the cool of a Balanchine ballet like "The Four Temperaments" (1946) is of a different ilk than the cool of a classic like "Swan Lake." Balanchinian cool, like its mother, the Africanist cool (let us say that the cool aloofness of European ballet is its father) is tongue-in-cheek, sassy, somewhat ironic. It leads to open-endedness and double entendre, not to the resolution of traditional European ballet. It is not the aristocratic, haughty coolness of that tradition but the cool arrogance of people with an *attitude*—Americans, black, brown and white. Some people think Balanchine ballets are brash; some people think African

American youth are brash. The Balanchine dancer and the African American social or street dancer share a remarkable quality — the juxtaposition and balance of hot and cool. Thus, for both, the intensity of a body involved in a speedy, complex combination may be balanced by the radical opposition of a cool, masklike face.

Vital to Balanchine's Americanization of ballet was his love of classicism, combined with an active interest in contemporary life and culture. As recounted in Francis Mason's *I Remember Balanchine* (1991, 161), he once told one of his young dancers, who asked him how she could become a choreographer, "Your eyes is camera and your brain is a file cabinet." He was an avid observer of the culture, not only its dance and dancers, but people, places, and things in general. African Americans held a particular fascination for him. According to one of his close friends, this curiosity manifested itself at least once in his choice of a sexual partner: "He was interested in trying a female of the species [*sic*] he had never had before, including one of our black entertainers who was famous in Paris. He did that purely to see, 'I wonder how a Negro woman is?'"[2] (Mason, 133).

His idea of having black ballerinas dance on *pointe* while whites perform "a frenzied jazz" indicates Balanchine's desire to use black skin as a color value in his modernist stage picture. The same intent figured again in his casting of "Agon" (1957), as described by ballerina Melissa Hayden: "The first time you saw Diana Adams and Arthur Mitchell doing the pas de deux it was really awesome to see a black hand touch a white skin. That's where we were coming from in the fifties. It was marvelous what Balanchine did" (Mason, 359). In the racially segregated world of pre-1970s United States, this pairing — specifically, the arch taboo of black male and white female — was a near-revolutionary move, especially in the all-white, elite world of the ballet stage. According to Arthur Mitchell, the only black member of Balanchine's New York City Ballet Company for many years: "There was a definite use of the skin tones in terms of Diana being so pale and me being so dark, so that even the placing of the hands or the arms provided a color structure integrated into the choreographic one" (Mason, 395).

The visual value of skin color also played a part in other ballets, like "Midsummer Night's Dream" (1962) and "Figure in the Carpet" (1960). However, Balanchine's stage fascination with blacks was not limited to skin tones. He was also seeking to use (or, from the Europeanist perspective, to improve upon) qualities that he saw as native to the black dancing body. In the early 1930s he wanted to establish an integrated dance school. Black dancers would be sought for their superb "combination of suppleness and sense of time" (quoted in Mason, 116). It is ironic and unfortunate that, first, the integrated school was never

established; second, Balanchine therefore sought out these same movement qualities in white dancers; and third, he perpetuated the ethnic
status quo by maintaining a basically segregated ensemble (with less
than a handful of exceptions over a period of four decades). Balanchine's
preference for this type has been a significant force in changing the preferred body shape of the present-day ballerina. No longer the long-
waisted, short-legged body type of the classical Russian ballerinas from
Pavlova to Plisetskaya, she is the reverse: a long-legged new woman with
a proportionately short torso. According to Mitchell,

There was a fallacy that blacks couldn't do classical ballet—that the bodies were
incorrect. But then you talked to Balanchine, who was the greatest master of
them all and changed the look of ballet in the world today. He described his
ideal ballerina as having a short torso, long arms, long legs, and a small head. If
that's ideal, then we [peoples of African lineage] are perfect. (1987, 36)

Dancer Francisco Moncion had this to say about one Balanchine
choice: "This dancer [ballerina Marie-Jeanne], Balanchine's favorite at
that time, had an extraordinary body. Her legs seemed to start up in her
chest. She had long feet, too" (quoted in Mason, 200). According to ballerina Moira Shearer: "Balanchine liked a certain type of shape in a
dancer—*long legs* and not too much flesh. . . . He liked *strength* very
much—*actual physical strength and stamina.* . . . I think he liked *speed* and a
good jump as well" (quoted in Mason, 337, emphasis added).

The italicized qualities are attributes that, by racial stereotyping,
have been commonly attributed to dancers of African lineage and used
to point out the difference between the black and white dancing body.
They were frequently the characteristics that pre-Balanchine white choreographers avoided in their choice of female dancers, not knowing how
to use them and, perhaps, thinking that they were traits that made the
black ballerina seem "masculine." Along with the overall tenor of racism
in America, this evasion also meant that white ballet choreographers
were not obliged to consider using black dancers. They could excuse
themselves by declaring that they were not racists, but that black bodies
were inherently unfit for ballet. Then enter Balanchine, who secures
white bodies with these characteristics, recasts them culturally and cho-
reographically, and, in so doing, redefines the feminine ideal in ballet.

The issue of black body attributes as ideal, but black dancing body as
taboo on the ballet stage, is a convoluted matter of fear, power politics,
and the love-hate relationship between self and Other, black and white.
The possibility that the shape of the white dancing body—or any body
used for specific cultural purposes—changes over time due to the prefer-
ences of people in power says a mouthful about cultural conditioning
and imprinting and points to environmental and societal factors as po-

tent forces in determining how we look and, in every sense, how we "perform." If we open any high fashion magazine or go to the movies, we see the post-1950s ideal woman. Like the stereotyped African body (not the Hottentot Venus stereotype, but its binary opposite, as epitomized in Josephine Baker), although finessed and edited down to a white standard, her boyish frame is long, lean, and leggy. The relatively short torso is sensually accentuated by the arched spine, which puts a revisionary, modified emphasis on the buttocks. Women diet, exercise, and train, from early adolescence onward, to mold their frames into this ideal form.

Much of the vilification of Africanist culture and peoples of African lineage is focused on the image of the black body, the dancing body, the grounded, freely articulated body—sexualized and therefore dangerous—and the fear of it. It is a site that is charged with tension. Given this condition, and its special virulence regarding the black male, it should come as no surprise that John Martin, the reigning New York dance critic of the era and a leading advocate of Martha Graham, criticized in 1940 the young Talley Beatty (then a member of the Katherine Dunham dance group) for what Martin paternalistically described as Beatty's "serious dallying in ballet technique" (quoted in Emery 1988, 255). For Martin, Beatty's appropriation of ballet was inappropriate for "the Negro," and out of character with "the essence of Negro dance itself," which he characterized as "not designed to delve into philosophy or psychology but to externalize the impulses of a high-spirited, rhythmic and gracious race" (quoted in Emery, 255). There is more than a little of the primitive trope at play in that statement.

When I was in high school, I remember reading one of Martin's *New York Times* reviews in which he complained about the casting of black Arthur Mitchell as the male soloist to partner a white ballerina in New York City Ballet performances of Jerome Robbins' "Afternoon of a Faun" (1953). It was the early Civil Rights era and Martin carped that, because the nation was in the throes of that movement, an integrated pas de deux was unrealistic and unacceptable (although the ballet has nothing to do with civil rights or any other social issue). Could he have accepted that partnership before the Civil Rights movement? Was there any reason to believe he would ever deem it appropriate for a black—specifically, a black male—to be featured in a ballet *pas de deux* with a white female simply as a dancer, and not in a color-coded role?

Let us return to the claim that the black dancing body is unsuitable for ballet. To quote dance writer David Vaughan, "Ballet technique has always accommodated itself to human bodies in all their variety" (1988, 27). Or, as ballet master Richard Thomas put it, "Anybody can *do* ballet. It's not a matter of how you're built but of whether you have a brain"

(1991, 8). Balanchine, whose preferred body type (albeit on white dancers) ran contrary to classical European standards, helped change the picture. In 1969, former New York City Ballet soloist Arthur Mitchell took Balanchine's vanguard move a step further. By creating the Dance Theater of Harlem, a ballet company composed principally of dancers of African lineage, he made a formal institution of the ultimate taboo in ballet—the black dancing body. (Prior to Mitchell's initiative there had been a handful of all-black ballet companies in the 1940s and 1950s. Mitchell's was the first to survive and gain ongoing attention in the powerful white ballet establishment.) Mitchell's ensemble has earned an international reputation for excellence and is, moreover, one of the American ballet troupes lauded for its execution of the Balanchine repertory.

Balanchine's Africanist apprenticeship really began before he came to the United States and even before he went to Western Europe. Early on, he was introduced to the Africanist aesthetic through the work of other artists whom he admired. Among this group was the Russian constructivist Kazian Goleizovsky, "whose cool, erotic-gymnastic etudes and interest in American jazz stimulated the Russian art world of the twenties" (Jowitt 1988, 255). Balanchine's work is marked by speed and density, with more dancing packed into his phrases than had ever been seen before in ballet. Heightened speed and densely laden phrases are common characteristics in most forms of African-based dance and music. They are underlying Africanist correspondences in Balanchine's work. In the Africanist aesthetic, the opposite of beauty is not ugliness, but incompleteness, or unfulfillment. Similarly, Balanchine stated the following in the 1934 Haskell interview: "It is a deep down love that is important [in ballet, as opposed to the requisites for careers such as museum study or academic knowledge]; there must be a strong reaction to things seen. Even if they are ugly things, it doesn't matter. Apathy is the only enemy" (Haskell, 96).

Elements appeared in Balanchine ballets—angular arms, turned-in legs, bent knees—that certainly were considered ugly by the ballet establishment. These same elements are basic syllables in Africanist dance language. According to some early members of the New York City Ballet, this Africanist aesthetic has been slowly leaching out of the choreography since Balanchine's death in 1983. States Barbara Walczak, who danced with the company in the 1950s:

The difference between the original and today's "Barocco" ["Concerto Barocco," 1940] is a timing difference, an energy difference. It was never meant to be lyrical. One difference was that many of the steps were very off-center. We were supposed to fall off. It was like waves on an ocean. The energy behind the steps was different. They were attacked more than they are now. They were not meant to be done with a soft attack. (quoted in Mason, 259)

The specific qualities of energy, attack, speed, timing, and off-centeredness that Balanchine brought to ballet were partially informed and influenced by his exposure to Africanisms in the culture, and his particular sensitivity in using them to serve the ballet aesthetic.

Maria Tallchief, New York City Ballet ballerina and one of Balanchine's former wives, tells a similar story:

Phrasing and timing were the most important aspects of the technique as I learned it. In a demonstration with Walter Terry [dance critic] and Balanchine, I did an eight-count *developpé* [leg extension], straight up and out with the *port de bras* [arm positioning] in the manner in which we most often see it done. Then George turned to me and demanded, "Now out in *one* count and hold the rest." That is an example of the simplicity of his style. The speed was not hard for me, because I always had more of a propensity for allegro dancing than anything else. Standing still was the tricky part. (quoted in Mason, 239)

What is interesting about this quote is not only the reference to speed and timing, but also the last point about standing still. Balanchine asked Tallchief to simultaneously move fast and attack hard, and immediately follow by being still — in other words, to demonstrate the aesthetic of the cool by a hot-cool, high-affect juxtaposition. The nontraditional timing Balanchine introduced into the ballet canon, like his introduction of torso articulation and off-center movement, stretched the parameters of ballet and served to revitalize and Americanize the genre. In these excerpts Walczak and Tallchief inadvertently pointed out his use of the Africanist aesthetic.

Choreographed when Balanchine was only twenty-four, the ballet "Apollo" contains many of the elements that shaped his subsequent career, including Africanist presences. It was first presented by the Diaghilev Ballets Russes in Paris in 1928. It advanced his credibility as an experimentalist and innovator in rank with those in literature, music, and visual arts who also reached out to African, Asian, or Oceanic vocabularies to expand their creative options. This ballet also marked the first of Balanchine's collaborations with Igor Stravinsky, whose radically rhythmic, chromatic scores were influenced by Africanist, Asian, and vernacular European principles outside the European classical music tradition. ("Agon" [1957], "Jewels" [1967], and other landmark Balanchine ballets were also choreographed to Stravinsky scores that were marked by jazz-Africanist inflected elements.) Balanchine described "Apollo" as a turning point in his career, and so it was. Through it he appropriated Africanist conventions that were present in European popular performance, adapted them for use on the ballet stage, and imported (or exported) them to the United States where, with considerable additional input, he changed the face and shape of ballet.

Balanchine's early American career included a substantial apprenticeship on Broadway. Between 1936 and 1948 he choreographed or co-choreographed a number of musicals, including "The Ziegfeld Follies" (1936), "On Your Toes" (1936), "Babes in Arms" (1937), "I Married an Angel" (1938), "The Boys from Syracuse" (1938), and, with Katherine Dunham, "Cabin in the Sky" (1940). His sense for contrasts and the erotic-exotic play between blacks and whites onstage was illustrated in the 1936 "Follies," in which he had Josephine Baker surrounded by a chorus of white males in Zouave uniforms. (Apparently, blacks were insulted and whites were horrified; see Kisselgoff 1987, 38.) African American choreographer Herbie Harper worked with him on the choreography for Ray Bolger in the "Slaughter on Tenth Avenue" ballet in "On Your Toes" (Long 1989, 38). Balanchine worked with the Nicholas Brothers, two extraordinary tapdancing kids, in "Follies" and "Babes," and with Josephine Baker in "Follies." In 1949 he staged the New York City Opera production of "Troubled Island," using Jean Léon Destiné's African American dance company. He withdrew as choreographer from the African American musical "House of Flowers" (1954) before the New York premiere (Long, 83). Thus, he had direct contact with African American dancers and choreographers and with genres that were highly influenced by the Africanist aesthetic.

We are told in his biography that, in making dances for the opera "Aida," Balanchine created routines for white dancers that were based on black dance movements (McDonagh 1983, 89). Inversely, he worked with an all-black cast for "Cabin in the Sky." In this instance, he stated,

What is the use of inventing a series of movements which are a white man's idea of a Negro's walk or stance or slouch? I only needed to indicate a disposition of dancers on the stage. The rest almost improvised itself. I was careful to give the dancers steps which they could do better than anyone else. (McDonagh, 89)

But Balanchine was not the sole choreographer of the musical; Katherine Dunham collaborated with him. The reason that he did not need to invent movements (apart from the creativity of the dancers themselves) was that he had a seasoned, talented African American colleague to work with. To state that "the rest almost improvised itself" is to fall into the trap of assuming that African peoples do not work, train, or practice in order to perform successfully, that dancing, for them, is an inborn trait. Did Balanchine give them the steps to do or did the dancers suggest and show him steps from which he then chose? Why does he resort to the passive voice in the only section of the quote that deals, not with him, but with the black dancers? Thus, it is not even stated that the black dancers improvised the routines, but that the routines improvised themselves, as though the black dancers had no agency in the process. There is a subtle difference, but the documented description makes the African American dancers seem like Balanchine's puppets, while the modifications suggested by these questions would indicate some initiative and creativity on the part of the African Americans, which is the more likely scenario.

Balanchine's statement parallels what choreographer Agnes de Mille said about the Honi Coles and Cholly Atkins number in "Gentlemen Prefer Blondes" (1949), as related in Stearns and Stearns' *Jazz Dance* (1979, 309), that the dance was created in one brief rehearsal. (Without flatly stating it, De Mille implies that she did the choreography when, in fact, Coles, Atkins, and arranger Benny Payne had worked out the routine in separate rehearsals prior to the one in which they showed their work to her for her approval.) In both cases the work created by African Americans is attributed to intuition, not technical acumen and creativity. The European choreographer is given the formal credit and made to seem superior in ability, if not intelligence. But the evidence belies this picture. Without acknowledging its significance, Don McDonagh (1983, 79–95), in his book on Balanchine, tells us that the choreographer directly used Africanist material in "Aida," "Cabin," and "Follies." Although he does not discuss Balanchine's contact with the Nicholas Brothers in "Follies," he mentions the fact that Balanchine "designed" the two Josephine Baker numbers, which she danced "in her own style no matter what the choreographer did for her." And the author describes the jazz-inspired "Slaughter on Tenth Avenue" (whose co-choreographer was Herbie Harper, a name not mentioned by McDonagh) as the saving grace for "On Your Toes." With these points in mind about bodies and choreographies, let us now take a detailed look at some of the Africanist influences, presences, and correspondences in Balanchine's ballets.

THE AFRICANIST MIRROR

There are many ways in which the Africanist legacy comes bursting through Balanchine's choreographies. The most noticeable is the new approach to movement vocabulary, which he introduced to the ballet stage. The displacement and articulation of hips, chest, pelvis, and shoulders, instead of vertical alignment of the torso; leg kicks, attacking the beat, instead of carefully placed extensions; angular arms and flexed wrists, rather than the traditional, rounded *port de bras,* all of these touches usher the viewer into the discovery of the Africanist aesthetic in Balanchine. Moreover, this presence goes beyond surface characteristics such as movement vocabulary and is a significant subtext in Balanchine's work. One such example is in the play between energy and form in the Balanchine canon. In European academic ballet, energy is subordinated to form; energy is measured and contained by form. In Africanist-inflected dance, form is subordinated to energy, and energy situates and determines form—for example, where the leg will end in an extension, or how the arm will be raised in a gesture. It is energy that predicates and mandates the form. Balanchine finesses and plays with the edges of this difference, and gives ballet a new life blood in the process. Surface and deep structure Africanist components appear in works throughout his career and are highlighted in ballets such as "Apollo" (1928), "The Four Temperaments" (1946), "Agon" (1957), "Stars and Stripes" (1958), "Jewels" (1967), and "Symphony in Three Movements" (1972), among others. If and when they appeared in European ballet, these elements were reserved for lesser, "ignoble" characters and represented comic, rustic, vernacular or exotic components. Balanchine crafted them in a decidedly nontraditional fashion and assigned them to soloists and principals in serious ballets, thus assuring them integral significance in his work.

In the first movement of "Symphony," the corps dancers lunge from side to side, with the straight leg turned in and one arm angularly jutting downward in a style unknown in traditional ballet. Later, a male sextet makes a prancing entrance that can only be described as an updated, balletic version of the "Cakewalk," with the upper torso leaning deeply backward. The second movement opens with torso isolations as a central element in the first duet (the same isolations used more baroquely in the orientalist "Bugaku" [1963], which, without irony, utilizes Africanist movement vocabulary to depict a Japanese wedding ritual). "Cakewalk"-inspired variations are also a leitmotif in the "Rubies" section of "Jewels," as are Africanist-inflected ballroom dance partnering conventions in this ballet's pas de deux work. Balanchine struts and parades his Broadway heritage to the hilt in this red-hot gem of a suite and blatantly uses his ballerinas as showgirls. The "Rubies" choreography is "in your face" (meaning brash, challenging, and up-front), to borrow a phrase from African American pop culture. In these two and in a variety of other ballets, the Africanist influence allows Balanchine to expand the ballet idiom by introducing the articulated torso to its vertical standard.

Two of the three thematic duets that form the opening suite of "The Four Temperaments"—the allegro second duet and the adagio third—share some of the same Africanist-inflected vocabulary. In both, ballroom dance references are as evident as the traditional pas de deux conventions into which they have been inserted. Additionally, both duets contain particular passages that make them look like a deconstructed Lindyhop. Let me explain.

In each duet the male twirl-turns the female in place, as social dancers do, except that she is "sitting" on the air in *plié* (that is, with knees bent) while on *pointe*. In the allegro she maintains this position, with right arm akimbo and the left overhead. She is supported by her partner, who stands behind her and clasps the wrist of her lifted, left arm. With his free hand, he twirls his partner by touching her elbow and giving her a little push to propel her around. It is ballroom dance sleight-of-hand. At this point, the couple performs a very interesting lift, which reappears a few beats later in this duet, then again in a variant form in the third duet and, later on, in the finale. The male, again positioned behind the female (she has her back to him), supports her with his hands at her waist. He lifts her while she swiftly and simultaneously spreads her legs in the air in a neat, clipped, second-position scissor. She is in this pose for a split second, while he lowers her to allow her to momentarily alight, touching her buttocks upon his "lap" (which, in this case, is an open seat: he has his legs apart and knees bent, in a parallel *plié* position, to support her in her descent). This way of allowing a female dancer simultaneously to be lifted and "sit" on her partner was a popular "Lindy" sequence during the 1930s and 1940s. It occurs in any number of film clips and photographs of Lindyhoppers in action. To be sure, a ballroom aesthetic is not a ballet aesthetic, even though my point is to note the commonalities and interrelationships. Thus, in the "Lindy" version of this lift, the female is helped into the air by the male dancer who bumps her buttocks with his knee (the leg of the gesturing knee may be bent or straight). Balanchine finessed this lift to an acceptable ballet standard and omitted this direct contact between male knee and female butt. The "Lindy" version is faster, more explicit, and more dynamic, but the lift is the same, in principle.

Let us continue to analyze the allegro duet. Still positioned behind his partner, the male supports the female by steadying her against his torso, gripping her waist with one arm and using the other to grip the thigh of her right leg, which is lifted in arabesque. All the while she has her back facing him, so that his role is to clutch and exhibit her. In this position he pumps her hips forward and back as he clunkily propels her through a turn in place, the *pointe* of her standing foot dragging the floor. He could pull her off her feet, speed it up, and take her out on the ballroom dance floor in an airborne "Lindy" variation. This movement is capped off with jazzy little side lunges, straight, outstretched arms, and flexed wrists, as the two dancers face each other. Once more they perform the scissor-leg lift, and the female lightly perches on her partner's open lap. They exit, making "Egyptian" arms (Euro-American dancer's lingo for arms raised to shoulder height and bent perpendicularly from the elbow).

The third duet, the adagio, manifests some of the same movement characteristics of the second, but in slower tempo. While remaining on *pointe* the female sinks into a *demi-plié* on the right leg, with the left leg lifted in a modified *passé*, the foot of her lifted, bent leg resting above the knee of the standing leg. As in the allegro, the male supports his partner by holding the hand of her left arm, which is lifted overhead, and propels her into sustained twirl-turns in place by pumping the elbow of her right arm, which is extended in front of her. The male leads his partner into deep, parallel-legged crouches (it would be misleading to call them pliés), which she performs while still on pointe. Then, standing, he offers his back to her. Facing his back, she wraps her arms around his neck, drapes the full length of her body against his, and leans on him. He moves forward for several steps, dragging her along. This looks like a cleaned-up, slowed-down variation of a typical "Lindy" exit. (And only in the "Lindy" have I seen as much female crotch as in these two duets.) As they conclude, the male supports the female, again from behind, by allowing her to rest the armpits of her outstretched arms in the bend of his elbows. In this potentially awkward position he drives her across the floor as she *rond-de-jambes* (or circles) one leg and the other leg alternately, each time ending in the scissored position of the lift described in the allegro. The difference is that, in this adagio, the ballerina is not lifted to achieve this pose. Her toes touch the floor, with her crotch momentarily resting on her partner's thigh, before she is propelled by him into repeating this pose with the other leg.

What is so interesting about these duets is how they deconstruct and defy the traditional European ballet canon of verticality and male support of female centeredness, essentials in the classic pas de deux. Rather than maintaining her alignment and acting as the buffer to bring her back to center (as is the classic European ballet role model for its *danseurs;* see, for example, the adagio pas de deux of the Prince and Odette in "Swan Lake"), the males in these duets push, thrust, or manipulate their partners off center. They seem to play with letting the female fall. It is a ballroom dance risk-taking that Balanchine has crafted to meet the needs of the ballet aesthetic and the concert stage. The themes from these three duets are then played out in the four variations that follow.

In the first variation, the "Melancholic," a trio composed of male soloist and two females echoes some of the themes established in the duets. Then four women enter. Their arms are in second position, not in a traditional *port de bras*, but straight, with flexed wrists. They perform high kicks, which are resolved by pushing the pelvis forward on the second count of a 1–2, kick-thrust beat, and their legs are parallel as they *bourrée* (or take evenly-paced, small, quick steps on *pointe*) around the male soloist. Throughout this variation, the turned-in, "primitivist" position of early modern dance (as inspired by the African and Oceanic statuary that influenced modern art) is deployed as an equal partner with the turned-out legs of traditional ballet. The choreography for the male is heavy, grounded, intense, and most probably comes by its Africanist resonances via the modern dance vocabulary of the 1940s Graham/Humphrey/Weidman tradition. It is marked by low lunges, deep, acrobatic back-bends, and dramatic backward falls, with the male catching his weight on his arms just before reaching the floor. Taking his lead from the music, he "gets down," as if this were a melancholy blues. He leans on Paul Hindemith's score, which intimates the chords and intervals associated with blues and jazz. His fluid ephebism is balanced by the quartet's cool. He exits in a deep, acrobatic, nonacademic backbend, his outstretched arms leading him offstage, the center of gravity in his head and arms, not his spine.

There are many instances in the "Sanguinic" variation, especially in the choreography for the female soloist, in which the movement is initiated in the forward thrust of the hips. This and the exit described in the "Melancholic" section are examples of the simplest version of polycentrism. Several centers are not occurring simultaneously, but the center has shifted from the vertically aligned spine to other parts of the body. The "Phlegmatic" solo opens and closes as a study in torso isolations and asymmetry.

The finale is a recapitulation of important themes. The Egyptian arms exit of the second duet; the forward thrusting hips and high kicks of the female quartet in the "Melancholic" variation; and those second and third duet scissor-legged lifts, ending with the females momentarily straddling their partners—all are featured as the ensemble brings this extraordinary work to its finish.

Although the Africanist aesthetic influenced continental European culture (and affected Balanchine before his emigration), it comes to full flower in the European American landscape because of a larger and deeper Africanist presence here. For that reason, if no other, European Americans pick up the Africanist aesthetic in the very air they breathe. It is second nature for them, but not necessarily for Europeans. For example, according to an anecdotal report, on their first rehearsal shot at it, the La Scala ballet ensemble missed the point and erased the American-flavored nuances in "The Four Temperaments." Instead of imitating the American rehearsal director in performing the jazzy hip displacements and angular arms, they inadvertently adjusted and "corrected" the movements so that they were centered and aligned in accordance with traditional ballet standards.[3]

In contrast, Balanchine's "Apollo," although choreographed in Paris before his emigration to America, is bathed in the Africanist aesthetic.

As the three muses enter together, they perform the same high kicks with pelvis thrusting forward that reappeared in "The Four Temperaments" nearly twenty years later. There is a delightful moment when they move by waddling on their heels, their legs straight. On another stage and in another mood, that would be a tap dance transition step. And their asymmetrical poses diverge from traditional ballet but are akin to Africanist dance, via the moving poses struck in Africanist-inflected stage and social dance styles of the 1920s. The title character's first solo is a twisting, lunging affair. He simultaneously jumps, bends his lower legs so that his heels touch his hips, and torques his hips so that they angle against his upper torso. His landings dig into the floor as one leg releases and kicks downward on the beat. Indeed, these jumps explore the downbeat—the earth, not the air—and the soloist, like a jazz musician, hits the beat on the "one" count, not taking the preparatory "and" count that is traditional in ballet. This dance passage may be a clear example of the fusion between Africanist influences and vernacular dance influences from Balanchine's Russian past.

In his third solo,[4] Apollo performs several moves in which he pulls his weight off center as he lunges and stops short in an asymmetrical *plié* on the forced arch. His turns and lunges are grounded and abrupt. He stops suddenly, as if on a dime. Unlike traditional ballet practice, the turns are not resolved; they simply stop. Both solos manifest ephebism in their speed, attack, and force. Apollo's solos and the "Melancholic" solo from "The Four Temperaments" are dances about weight and groundedness, not defying gravity but meeting and embracing it. The jumps are performed not to highlight the going up, but to punctuate and emphasize the coming down—to highlight rhythm and percussion, rather than melody and ethereality. Ballet's traditional airborne quality is not present here. Instead, we find the connection to the earth characteristic of Africanist dance and American modern dance. This solo is followed by an amusing vaudeville chorus that seems to come out of nowhere. The muses join him. With no preparation and on an abrupt change in the mood of the score, they all *plié* in an asymmetrical position, settle back into one hip with buttocks jutting out, and bounce in unison to the rhythm. They are setting time for a change in rhythm, and this is the "break." It is a radical juxtaposition, set against the previous mood and movements. It is also a quotation from popular dance styles. The work ends as the three muses lean their bodies against Apollo's back, their legs in gradated *arabesques*, while he poses in a lunge, legs parallel, arms raised, hands flexed.

Accounts by Balanchine dancers unconsciously attest to the Africanist presence in his work. In working on "Concerto Barocco," described by former New York City Ballet dancer Suki Schorer as a ballet with "a very jazzy feeling" (quoted in Mason 1991, 459), Balanchine aimed for clarity in syncopation, timing, and attack. Schorer states that Balanchine characterized a particular step as "like the Charleston," which may have meant the timing, rhythm, speed, movements, or all of these. Patricia McBride, who danced for Balanchine from 1959 until his death in 1983, says, "Dancing Balanchine is harder—the patterns, the way they change in Balanchine ballets. The ballets are so fast, and they travel much more than a lot of the more classical companies" (Mason, 444). Abrupt and unpredictable changes in speed, timing, and attitude are key elements in Balanchine and are key to the Africanist aesthetic. They are not signature components of the ballet world from which he emerged.

It seems ironic that when Schorer compares the Russian ballet companies with Balanchinian ballet, she states that the Russians don't understand "phrasing, counting, the timing within a step. They've never seen anything. They only know what they know" (Mason, 462). What they don't know, and what Balanchine was exposed to, is the phrasing, counting, and timing that comes from the Africanist influence in American culture, so native to us that we take it for granted. By embracing these elements that he encountered in the United States, Balanchine expanded the definition of ballet. There is no doubt that his redefinition included both Africanist and European elements, fused into a spicy, pungent brew.

Balanchine's legacy, like the Africanist aesthetic, is a living one, much of which cannot be codified or contained by "the steps." In the words of another former Balanchine dancer, Paul Mejia, "You don't learn Balanchine, you live it" (quoted in Mason, 480). Arthur Mitchell worked well with Balanchine, and Mitchell's cultural background and training helped. His description of "Metastaseis & Pithoprakta" (1968) shows the Africanist aesthetic in Balanchine's process-oriented way of working through rhythm, rather than steps, and in requiring the dancing body to be laid-back, cool, and free to receive his messages:

Suzanne Farrell and I danced a pas de deux that was one of those eerie things that didn't use steps per se. He'd say, "I want something like this," and he would start moving. You would just have to be free enough to let your body go and do it. I think one of the things that helped me so much with him was that, *being a tap dancer, I was used to rhythm and speed* [emphasis added]. Many times when he was choreographing he would work rhythmically and then put the step in. If you were looking for a step, it wouldn't be there. But if you got *dah, da-dah-dah-dah*, it would come out [emphasis in the original]. The rhythm was always the most important. The choreography was set in time and then space. (quoted in Mason, 395)

According to Mitchell, Balanchine sometimes referred to Katherine Dunham in his teaching and sent his dancers to study with her. He also regularly called on Mitchell to "come in and show these kids, because they don't know old-fashioned jazz" (Mason, 396). It seems that he was asking Mitchell to demonstrate an energy field and an attitude toward the movement as much as he was requesting the mere steps. More of the hidden story is intimated in Balanchine's original intentions for his new American ballet school, as recounted by Lincoln Kirstein:

For the first he would take 4 white girls and 4 white boys, about sixteen yrs. old and 8 of the same, negros [sic]. . . . He thinks the negro part of it would be amazingly supple, the combination of suppleness and sense of time superb. Imagine them masked, for example. They have so much abandon—and disciplined they would be *nonpareil*. (quoted in Mason 116–17)

Thus, even before his arrival in the United States, Balanchine was calculating how he could draw upon the energy and rhythm of the black dancing body. Of course, the primitive trope is at work here, with the concomitant allure of the exotic. Even so, if his dream had been realized, what a different history might have ensued for American ballet and its relationship to peoples of African lineage. That plan was not carried forth, however. Balanchine and Kirstein did engage Talley Beatty, then a promising young talent, to work with Ballet Society, the post–World War II forerunner of the New York City Ballet. For whatever reasons, Beatty appeared in only one work under their auspices, and, irony of ironies, that work was Lew Christensen's ballet, "Blackface" (1947) (Dale Harris 1995, 28). One can only imagine that, innocent and ignorant of American racism, Balanchine understood, once here, that his dream school was infeasible.

The Africanist presence in Balanchine's works is a story of particular and specific movement motifs, of which numerous examples could be cited from ballets that span the course of his career. They are not decorative touches that marked one or two ballets; they were essential building blocks in his canon. The story continues. More significant are the underlying speed, vitality, energy, coolness, and intensity that are fundamental to his Americanization of ballet. The tale proceeds with the radical dynamics, off-center weight shifts, and unexpected mood and attitude changes in Balanchine's work that create a high-affect juxtaposition of elements uncommon in traditional ballet but basic to Africanist dance. His legacy lives on in an American—and increasingly, a European—ballet tradition that will never be the same as it was before. It is due to his influence and, to a considerable degree, his crafting and shaping of the Africanist aesthetic, that a new, energized, and expansive standard has become commonplace in contemporary ballet practice.

Less innovative artists might have held onto the old, but Balanchine didn't settle for that. He was enticed by what he saw as American qualities, and they rest as much on the African presence as the European. It simply will not suffice to say that jazz dance influenced his work. That term serves to misname the Africanist legacy that, buried under layers of deceit, has been invisibilized. Surely Balanchine himself would not have willingly disavowed this presence.

BLUE NOTE

We cannot quantify attitudes or impulses, but we can record appearances. And we can expand the lens through which we view our world and try for a wide-angle shot. Through the Eurocentric lens, Balanchine used "jazz" and Broadway influences as an occasional, decorative touch. This perspective sees Europe and Europeans as the alpha and the omega of American culture, with everything-everyone else as marginal. However, from an Africanist study of Balanchine, heretofore concealed information may be revealed. From this enhanced perspective, the Balanchinian flexed foot, angled arm, retracted hip, or thrust pelvis are essential parts of a larger, polycentric whole, not merely interesting twists on an otherwise Europeanist turn. American culture is both heated and cooled by the Africanist presence, and this particular intertext of borrowings, receivings, and exchanges influences us all, not only in outside form but also in underlying attitudes that can be felt, even if they cannot be quantified. When we are able to see the African reflection as the image of our culture, then finally we will behold ourselves fully — as Americans — in the mirror. At that point it will be silly to talk about Africanist presences as "the Africanist contribution." That is the outdated language of disenfranchisement, the mindset that implies that the European is something bigger or better into which the African — the Other — is subsumed. But there is no Other, *we are it*.

The body — the Africanist body as mover, shaper, and shaker of the American body — is the origin and the outcome of my thesis. I call this chapter "Stripping the Emperor," but we all know that this is impossible, for the emperor is what he is — a naked body. What needs stripping is our way of perceiving. Once we dare see the naked truth, as the child in Andersen's tale, we shall see a body, the American dancing body. It is a black-and-white portrait, an affirmation of opposites, in which the negative contains the positive.

NOTES

1.   The 1984 New York Museum of Modern Art mega-exhibit, "'Primitivism' in the Twentieth Century: Affinity of the Tribal and the Modern," revitalized this discourse in modern art.

2.   Evidence revealed by Jean Claude Baker, one of her adopted children, indicates that this person was Josephine Baker (Baker 1993, xxiii).

3.   Conversation with Clyde Nantais, former dancer-choreographer with the Boston Ballet and doctoral candidate, Temple University Dance Department, May 1990.

4.   This description is based upon the Dance in America (WNET-TV, NY) production, *Baryshnikov Dances Ballet* (broadcast 5 February, 1988) in which Mikhail Baryshnikov dances the title role in *Apollo*. In 1978 Baryshnikov left the American Ballet Theatre to work with George Balanchine as a member of the New York City Ballet, where he remained for one year. Bringing his own jazzy, eclectic touches to his performance of this classic, Baryshnikov's interpretation of Apollo is a unique triangulation of Balanchine, Baryshnikov, and the jazz-inflected Africanist presence.

Earl "Snake Hips" Tucker. This swing-era cabaret dancer based his act on the traditional Africanist dance variation that became his appellative. Africanist principles are clearly evident in his routine. Photo courtesy of the Frank Driggs Collection.

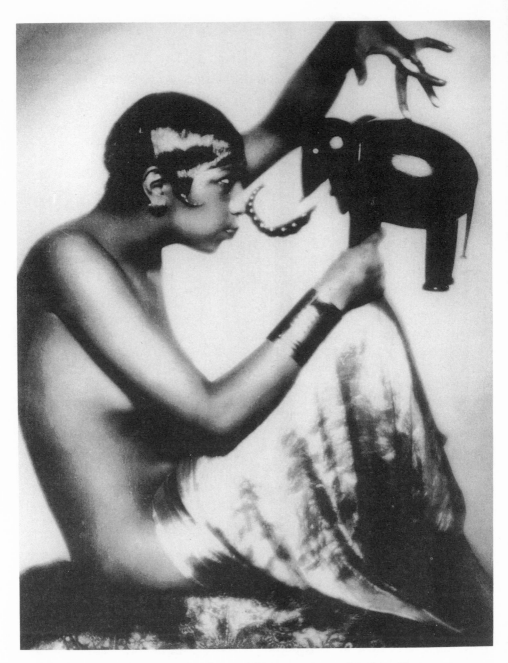

Josephine Baker poking fun at her "image." Photo courtesy of Archive Photos.

George Balanchine horsing around with Katherine Dunham (co-choreographer on this production) and cast members of "Cabin in the Sky," the Broadway musical. Photo courtesy of Black Star.

George Balanchine with danseur Arthur Mitchell. Note the subtle difference in hip position between the choreographer and the dancer. It is Mitchell's off-center pose that adds the Africanist touch and extends Balanchine's aligned pose beyond the traditional ballet aesthetic. Photo courtesy of Martha Swope, © Time, Inc.

George Balanchine with ballerina Violette Verdy. Note the relationship between dancer and choreographer, which is the inverse of that in the preceding photograph. Here Balanchine gives a more Africanist turn to the movement than his European-born dancer. Photo courtesy of Martha Swope, © Time, Inc.

George Balanchine's "The Four Temperaments": a shot of the ensemble in the finale. The females have descended from a Lindy-like, scissor-leg lift and momentarily "sit" on their partners' laps. Photo courtesy of Martha Swope, © Time, Inc.

Whitey's Lindy Hoppers rehearsing a sequence for the 1941 film, "Hellzapoppin'" (Left to right: Mickey Sales/William Downs; Norma Miller/Billy Ricker; Al Minns/Willa Mae Ricker; Frank Manning/Ann Johnson). The sense of improvisation that bursts through this variation is evident in the individuality of each couple's lift. Photo courtesy of the Ernie Smith Collection.

Ole Virginy Breakdown. Like other generic terms (such as "jig" and "buck dancing"), "breakdown" was a catch-all that included a constellation of Africanist characteristics. The breakdown depicted here includes several jig steps that were common on the minstrel stage, particularly in the white minstrel era. Photo courtesy of the Schomburg Center for Research in Black Culture.

DARK ARTILLERY; OR, HOW TO "MAKE THE CONTRABANDS USEFUL.

Dark Artillery. Here the sinister side of the minstrel trope is interpolated in a political context. "Contraband" human beings are conflated with the minstrel stereotype: in the original, color rendering of this newspaper sketch, the African Americans were depicted with burnt-cork faces and red lips. Photo courtesy of the Schomburg Center for Research in Black Culture.

Contraband Ball at Vicksburg, Mississippi. The minstrel stereotype, more modest than in the preceding illustration, still obtains, particularly in the facial features and expressions of the males. Photo courtesy of the Schomburg Center for Research in Black Culture.

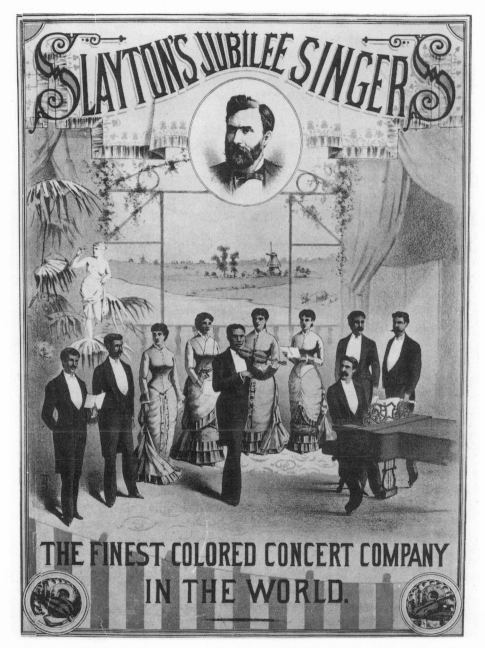

Slayton's Jubilee Singers. This type of choral ensemble was common fare on the African American minstrel show lineup and introduced a concert dimension to the genre. Photo courtesy of the Schomburg Center for Research in Black Culture.

Black Patti Troubadours. Sissieretta Jones, "Black Patti," was an opera singer whose only professional outlet was the minstrel stage. She headed her own performing group, the Troubadours, formed in 1895. The first portion of their performance closed with a buck dancing contest. Photo courtesy of the Schomburg Center for Research in Black Culture.

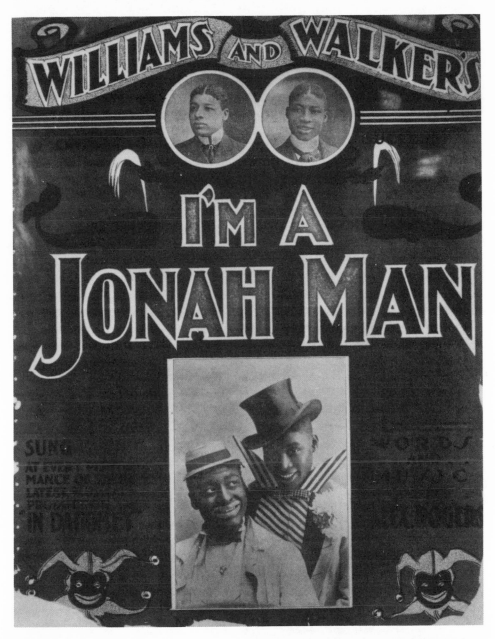

Sheet music cover for Bert Williams' and George Walker's song, "I'm a Jonah Man," from their hit musical "In Dahomey." The renowned African American team adopted the practice of white minstrels by showing themselves in character (and, for Williams, in blackface) as well as in everyday appearance. Photo courtesy of the Schomburg Center for Research in Black Culture.

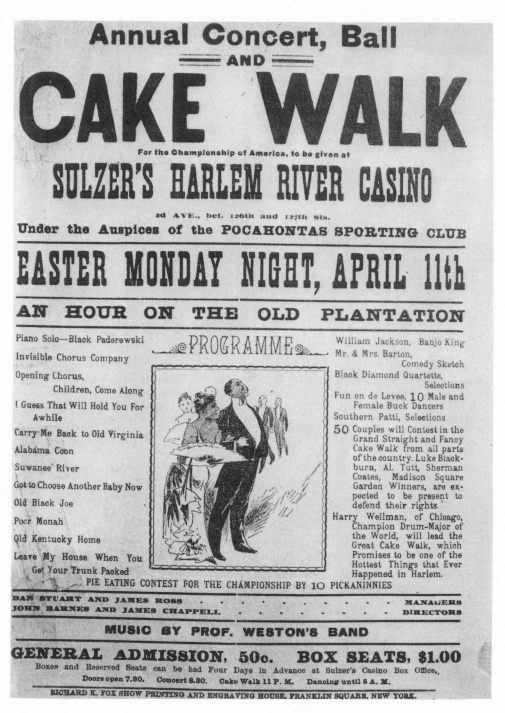

Annual Concert, Ball, and Cakewalk. Photo courtesy of the Schomburg Center for Research in Black Culture.

The Greatest Colored Aggregation in the World Today. Photo courtesy of the Schomburg Center for Research in Black Culture.

Revue Nègre. The minstrel stereotype was alive and well in Josephine Baker's Paris of the Jazz Age. Photo courtesy of the Schomburg Center for Research in Black Culture.

"Entartete Musik" was one section of the Entartete Kunst (Degenerate Art) exhibit assembled by the Third Reich. It was the most largely attended art exhibit in history. For this program cover the Nazis have conflated African and Jewish peoples, using the minstrel stereotype and jazz music as the hook. Photo courtesy of the Los Angeles County Museum of Art.

Rennie Harris, dancer, choreographer, and artistic director of Pure Movement, his dance company: bringing hip hop to the concert stage. Photo courtesy of Bob Emmott.

6

PAST IMPERFECT: PERFORMANCE, POWER, AND POLITICS ON THE MINSTREL STAGE

The theatrical stage itself, more than any other cultural phenomenon, opens a perspective into the pathology of American race relations. It exposes the white-black dependency which has defined race relations in the United States and which persists despite all reform.

Nathan Irvin Huggins 1971, 245

If they hate me I'm still whipping them, because I'm making them laugh.

Billy Kersands, quoted in Stearns and Stearns 1979, 51

THE MINSTREL TROPE

The previous chapter focused on George Balanchine and the highbrow world of ballet. This one does an about-face and looks at a "peculiar institution"—not slavery, but one of its "kissing cousins"—blackface minstrelsy.[1] In a sense, this book would be incomplete without a chapter devoted to the topic. This is where the precedent was set. The European American appropriation of Africanist forms and principles was systematized, validated, and institutionalized in the minstrel construct. It is because of this form—and its colossally convoluted relationship to Africanist invention—that the Africanist presence in American performance continues to be invisibilized and exploited. Almost everything that occurs in African-American performance, on stage and in life, is somehow predicated upon and circumscribed by the minstrel trope—the love/hate contestation of the white-black exchange; the self/other dichotomy implicit in the white male gaze on the black object; and the cunning ways in which the black object obfuscates and intercepts that gaze so as to become its own subject and, as Ralph Ellison puts it, "change the joke and slip the yoke" (1964, 45).

It was an appalling experience to research this material and encounter the brute force of nineteenth-century antiblack sentiment. At the same time, it was problematic to sort out the myth from "the genuine article." Beneath its layers of mockery and distortion, what, in minstrelsy, was really Africanist? Dating from this era, African American invention and style have been obliged to reinterpret and counter the dominant stereotype, yet the stereotype persists. The paradoxical masking and mirroring of a black self (or, really, a counterfeit black self) has informed both black and white modes of popular performance by the likes of Amos and Andy,[2] Stepin Fetchit, Elvis Presley, Sophie Tucker, Al Jolson, and Madonna, to name a few. These representatives of various degrees of minstrelization are some of the more blatant examples.

The full story of the minstrel trope, like the vaudeville comedian's explanation of the abbreviation Ph.D., is "piled high and deep" and has yet to be told. It is layered with conflicting narratives. With the exception of Rourke (1931), most mainstream authors (Nathan 1962; Wittke 1930; Paskman, et. al. 1928) examined the topic from the white minstrel perspective. Works by Winter (1948), Ellison (1958), Stearns and Stearns (1979), Huggins (1971), and Toll (1974) give credence to the minstrel experience from an African American perspective. The topic has recently been reworked by Eric Lott (1993), who focuses on the white, male, working-class milieu of antebellum minstrelsy.

What are my intentions in exploring this subject? Building on the solid ground and unsurpassed work of Robert Toll, I survey the Africanist presence in both pre– and post–Civil War minstrelsy. The works of Lott and Toll are used as markers of alternate perspectives. Second, the white appropriation of Africanist cultural forms is discussed in relation to the stereotypical minstrel image that serves to contain and control black performance. This discussion leads into issues of power, which may help in understanding the why and how of minstrelsy. Finally, I review the black minstrel period, the innovations brought to the genre by African Americans, and the function of black minstrelsy as a transition medium into early African American vaudeville.

Whites in minstrelsy set out to master and mock African American expressive styles of performance. These two aims worked in tandem to keep them in control. They could appropriate Africanist forms, to the degree that it was possible, by entering black enclaves and observing black performance on Southern plantations and Northern streets. Partly because their lack of understanding of what they saw allowed them only to skim the surface, whites created from their appropriations a product that grotesqued and demeaned the people represented by those forms.

That is, whites in minstrelsy used the minstrel construct as a way to have their cake and eat it, too—to have the power to be both outsider and insider in relation to Africanist life and culture. Because other performance outlets were closed to them, African Americans, on entering minstrelsy, had no choice but to step into a white-constructed mirror that distorted their reflection. Required to claim themselves as the original upon which the stereotype was modeled, they imitated the imitation. Yet they introduced genuine black presence, invention, and creativity into the genre. They faced the formidable task of amending the stereotype (in any way possible, while still appearing to go along with it) and redefining what a black role in minstrelsy could be; refashioning, through black design, the white-inflected form that was assumed to faithfully represent them. In other words, blacks had to do a job of reappropriation. It was a minefield of paradoxes through which the African American had to tread with caution and skill. Minstrelsy reflected the basic contradiction of being black in white America, living in two worlds and being both seen and unseen.

Those who read and write about it today need to regard minstrelsy as, on the one hand, a white conceit having little to do with African American anything and, on the other hand, a genre that expropriated and imitated bona fide Africanist expressive forms. The fantasy parts included the claims of "real" plantation life as played by "real darkies," and, of course, the grotesque characterizations of blacks as primitive, childish, ignorant, oversexed, and so on. The genuine article included the widespread dissemination and use of the banjo, an instrument of African origin; Africanist musical invention centering around rhythm and syncopation; and the presence of plantation-derived dances such as the walkaround, the "Virginia Essence" and, in late black minstrelsy, the "Cakewalk"—all stylized and refashioned as stage forms but nevertheless, rooted in Africanist origins. But, as in the Balanchine case, beyond any laundry list of patent traits, the Africanist subtext was, above all, what the white minstrel hoped to capture. This underlying attitude stood in stark contrast to Europeanist frames of reference (and had engendered white fascination, desire, and disgust since the first Afro-Euro contacts in the Americas). In their eyes, it was a complex, confusing stance—careless, "shiftless," dangerous, defiant, sometimes preposterously and (self-) mockingly humorous—a bold combination of comic and tragic subtexts that could be interpreted as anti-authoritarian, anarchistic, or even revolutionary. Numerous Colonial and antebellum diary entries by whites in the United States and the Caribbean bemoaned this expressive, Africanist influence on the young masters and mistresses who exuberantly imitated their personal servants and often participated in African American plantation festivities. Above all, and underneath it all, the (male) African body was the seat and center of difference, the site of contestation, and the focus of white minstrelsy.

Although minstrelsy for African Americans represented oppression in the dreaded minstrel format and its stereotypes, it was the first (and for a long time the only) professional performance outlet for African Americans on the legitimate stage in the United States. The work of some artists was outside the minstrel pale, but racism dictated that there was no other place for them to go. The operatic vocalist known as "Black Patti" (the stage name of Sissieretta Jones, given to her as an honorific after the international opera star of the era, Adelina Patti) and the choral groups who followed the Fisk Jubilee Singers (pioneers in rendering African American spirituals in a Europeanist concert song style) appropriated European genres and made them their own. These artists were successful as long as they "stayed in their place." Thus, Jones was never allowed to sing opera on the concert stage. Although she and the Fisk Singers performed for the president of the United States at the White House, they couldn't find lodging or be served at restaurants in Washington, D.C. There is political as well as symbolic significance in their plight. Blacks could amuse and entertain whites, even in the White House, but were not their equals. The minstrel (or, later, vaudeville) stage was where they belonged, regardless of the fact that they were concert artists.

The intertexts of imitation-masking-disguising-displaying self as Other and Other as self are dense readings. When they first entered minstrelsy, many African Americans blacked up, and some did not. White minstrels made sure that the audience knew that they were white, and programs or handbills frequently showed them in two depictions, normal appearance and blackface character.[3] Some African Americans engaged in this practice, at least occasionally. For example, the sheet music cover for "I'm a Jonah Man," a song from "In Dahomey" (one of the late-minstrel, early-vaudeville musicals by George Walker and Bert Williams which premiered in New York in 1902 and played in London for seven months in 1903) follows this convention in showing Bert Williams in both aspects. Williams was one of the many African Americans who continued to perform in blackface after leaving minstrelsy and entering vaudeville. Blacking up meant taking on the mask that afforded him the freedom to be ridiculous. Apparently, it allowed him to assume a stage persona that announced, as much as for any white minstrel, "This is a character — not *me*. I am playing a role here." In this sense, blacking up can be seen as similar to applying whiteface and taking on the attendant persona of the clown. Blackface presented a paradoxical freedom for the white performer and an even more contradictory liberation for blacks. While wearing the abhorred mask created by whites in blackface, African

Americans filled it with *self*, the shape and sound of real black bodies. Yet, it was still a mask, an assumed persona.

Now, African peoples are well-versed in the art of role playing and role reversal, concealing and revealing, double entendre and innuendo. These are positive characteristics and basic integers in the Africanist aesthetic. They long predate the oppressive conditions of slavery and minstrelsy. Traditional Africanist cultures embody and impart the lesson of embracing the conflict and balancing discord. This culturally transmitted performative skill can be activated as needed, in good or bad circumstances, and it plays a role in black minstrelsy. By necessity, Africans in America have had to mask themselves and use disguises to survive in hostile, often life-threatening environments. In fact, performance is a common requisite enlisted to support the double identity maintained by diasporan Africans; it is a way of life, not just a stage convention. Donning a mask, literally or symbolically, is a survival mechanism for mediating the conflicting waters of mother culture and dominant society. For the African American minstrel performing for African American audiences, blacking up could be perceived as an ironic underscoring of what he/they were expected to be and how he/they were treated in everyday life, at some level or other. Thus, the minstrel mask was the external, visible, tangible sign for a conflicted narrative in African American daily life. As Toll rightly points out,

To survive, blacks had developed masks and facades that allowed whites to indulge their racial fantasies, while blacks created their own hidden culture within. Thus, the same words and actions could have very different meanings for whites, for the black bourgeoisie, and for members of the black subculture. In this, as in many other ways, black minstrelsy was a microcosm of black history. (Toll 1974, 262)

Or, as African American minstrel Billy Kersands put it, "If they hate me, I'm still whipping them, because I'm making them laugh." Kersands and his cohorts were masters in the fine African American art of "shucking 'the man'. . . while winking at an observing brother or sister" (Gay and Baber 1987, 10). The average white spectators did not understand that the minstrel persona was a mask, an assumed character, and they ultimately believed that these depictions, whether played by white or black minstrels, were true-to-life delineations of African American "types." Thus, the insidious stage stereotype permeated the everyday lives of African Americans.

Though they may have been regarded by whites as buffoons, onstage and off, African American minstrel stars were respected by the grassroots black community. Many of them, like Kersands and James Bland, were national and international stars who had performed for royalty in

England and were household names in the United States. In the difficult times of the post-Reconstruction era, with the reality of Jim Crow segregation and the threat of lynching, African American life was particularly perilous for the black male. Minstrelsy was a decent, legal means of employment in a world of few options. Like the railroad porters who later were organized (and led, for many years, by A. Philip Randolph) as the Brotherhood of Sleeping Car Porters, the black male regularly employed in minstrelsy could gain the respect of the black community and even become a part of its middle class. (There still exists a vast difference in the parameters that define the black and white American middle class. Since their community possesses less capital, fewer economic resources, and a smaller range of opportunity than its white counterpart, the black middle class is a more flexible concept, by necessity. It is significant that in both communities, money is the true marker of class status.)

When, how, and why did blackface representation begin? Earlier researchers have sought the answers to these questions. These characters appeared in late eighteenth-century Europeanist plays such as "The Padlock" and "Oronooko." By the early nineteenth century, song-and-dance interludes performed in blackface were inserted between the acts of a play or performed in popular arenas such as dance halls or the circus.[4] Some topical reference to Africans might be part of the lyrics and, thus, the excuse for blacking up, but the dancing consisted of jigs (Irish) or clogs (English).

Mura Dehn, a Russian immigrant who spent her life in New York documenting African American dance, reflected on the European origins of blackface characters. (I take this opportunity to put her work in the spotlight. Because it is unpublished, it suffers from the same invisibilization as her topic, black dance.[5]) She reads them, collectively, as Africans in exile who afford Europeans a means of using the Other to define self (Dehn n.d., n.p.). In addressing this history and its importance in medieval and Renaissance Europe, she cites

the imprint which the African humor, motion and imagery left on the tradition of the popular theatre. According to it the African in exile served as a prototype which gave to the Western folk theatre its outstanding characters: the Greek satyr, the Roman comic slave, medieval devils in pageantry and puppets inherited many of the satyr traits, and in the Renaissance he reappeared in the guise of Harlequin. [6]

She mentions Aesop, "the African slave of Greek antiquity so seldom referred to as 'African.' Aesop's fables became a basic part of European folklore enduring to present times." Dehn uses the Aesop example to make a case for the "universal quality of African creativity in exile" and reemphasizes the fact that Europe's African roots are invisibilized.[7] She even suggests a conspiratorial subtext in the silencing of the Africanist presence. By bringing into the discussion the commedia dell'arte characters of Harlequin and Brighella (often depicted with black face and white hands and neck), Dehn posits the American white minstrel in a long lineage of theatrical convention—the blackface character on the white stage, who is

infiltrated into this family of nations. He is closely woven into the folklore and more so into the folk entertainment. He appears on the podium of fairs and carnivals and in the puppet shows. He is a member of all European countries, even of faraway Russia: a Blackamoor, a devil, a harlequin, a minstrel man, a Tambo and Bones. He never identifies himself with any nationality, but he thoroughly knows the ways of each people. . . [H]e is at home but he is not one of them. For a people to choose and to retain as part of their national folklore a stranger, especially if he is also of a different color, is of great significance. This character must represent something meaningful and vital to the people. He always adds spice to the situation. Throughout different countries and different centuries he remains recognizably the same, although he always appears in a different guise. He is black. He has African features. He is extremely nimble and adroit physically. He may be bawdy or insolent. . . . He represents something desirable and forbidden. . . . He is the embodiment of an appetite for life. The caucasian actors finally claimed him. With time his color fades, his origin is forgotten, he becomes white.

However, there are important distinctions to be made between the classical, European depiction of blackface characters and their appearance in minstrelsy. Americans evolved an entirely new theatrical genre to contain the curious intruders. The African stage stereotype was systematized and institutionalized to a degree and in a manner that was unique to and dependent upon the United States' special brand of black-white power relations, shaped and tempered by slavery. The "American Way" never allowed the color line to be forgotten. Origins of dance steps and musical forms were not duly credited, and their African American creators were never allowed to "cross over." Unlike its European antecedents, the American stereotype's color does not fade, and the persistence of the stereotype(s) remains a perpetual marker of white supremacy. White American delineators claimed and owned these stock characters and loudly proclaimed them as "genuinely Negro," while declaring themselves "genuinely white." The American system went further than any European prototype in claiming Other as self while preserving the distance between the two. The political implications of American minstrelsy, with its ramifications for the resident African American population, gave it a thrust and a sinister power that far outstripped any European cognate.

Yet, Dehn was on the right track in focusing on American minstrelsy as a paradox. The blackfaced Other, in Europe or America, allowed for a radical level of social commentary. The mask of blackness permitted whites to say things in another voice, to move with a surrogate body, to be released from normal restraints by means of a socially sanctioned form of ritualized abuse. In reviewing the reigning social and cultural constructs of the era—Victorianism and its attendant Protestant ethic, combined with the white ambivalence (guilt-anger-hate-love) toward blacks, which is epitomized in the institution of slavery—it is no wonder that a ritualized form of American theater would involve masking and mockery as the means, with African Americans as the target:

The mask was the thing (the "thing" in more ways than one) and its function was to veil the humanity of Negroes thus reduced to a sign, and to repress the white audience's awareness of its moral identification with its own acts and with the human ambiguities pushed behind the mask. (Ellison 1972, 49)

Well before the construction of the black mask in white minstrelsy, American whites were aware that Africanist culture was different from theirs. Visitors from the North and Europe were regularly taken to the African American quarters of Southern plantations to witness the singing and dancing, with no distinction acknowledged by these guests between secular and sacred performances. Conversely, they were frequently treated to performances by enslaved Africans that were staged in the white quarters. In the North and West, free and enslaved African American laborers, boatmen, and artisans were observed, copied, hired, imitated, and exploited by whites for their performative abilities. The dancing body of minstrelsy is informed by deep-structure Africanisms that were already a recognized but sublimated part of the American landscape. And the strange, elusive, contradictory meanings of minstrelsy are embedded in its central paradox: *It is and it isn't black.* As twentieth-century writers try to get to the inside of this conundrum, we are confronted with new measures of ambiguity and complexity. I may be "quoting" from the past by positioning myself in a similar relationship to Eric Lott's work as did Ralph Ellison with regard to the work of Stanley Edgar Hyman. In both cases, although three decades separate us, it is a matter of an African American scholar challenging the argument of a European American scholar on the interpretation of this institution and its relationship to black "folk" culture.[8] And, in both cases, the person of color is saying, "Hey, there's something you've missed." As Ellison pointed out Hyman's good intentions, so I point out the same in Lott's brilliant exposition.[9]

My main concern with Lott's work is that it may function as a mirror for the postmodern, reflexive turn, shedding light on white intent, while

decentering the Africanist presence in the process. For the sake of pluralist cultural theory, it may serve to underplay the tragic effect of white
American racism on African American life and arts. It is an issue that I
take up in opposition to cultural recursive theory, inasmuch as the Africanist presence is concerned. It is too easy for the theory to serve as a
new invisibilization of the already "invisible man." As I took issue with
and extended the (post)structuralist theory of intertextuality in previous
chapters, so I apply the same argument here. Africanist and Europeanist
threads, though interwoven, are also frequently distinct, and it is their
independence that afforded white minstrels the opportunity to construct
the alien, black minstrel stereotype. I would hasten to remind the contemporary scholar that it is the Africanist presence, absence, and distortion that are central to the minstrel trope. Lott addresses minstrelsy's
purposes, aims, and intentions as instruments of power deployed by its
white subjects. Ellison, as well as Huggins and Toll, addressed the function and the effect of the minstrel mask on the black object (with function, here, implying action). Actually, it is not a matter of the one
argument being right and the other wrong but, simply, that the two
complement each other. Lott's perspective is incomplete without those
contributed by his scholarly predecessors. His work is best understood
not as a replacement for those forerunners, but as an addition.
(Incidentally, this would be an excellent time for the publishers of the
Toll work—who are the same publishers of Lott—to reissue Toll's *Blacking Up*; the two works need to be read in tandem.)

Lott's focus is Eurocentric. In spite of his revisionism, he places
white perspectives and motives at the center of the discourse as he examines minstrelsy's effect on the white male subject. (To state the obvious, a Eurocentric or Afrocentric perspective has little to do with the
researcher's ethnicity; it is a matter of focus.) The forerunners that he
evaluates—Toll, Huggins, Frederick Douglas, Ellison—examine minstrelsy from the perspective of the African American object. Once African Americans enter minstrelsy in the post-Civil War era, the issues of
exploitation and borrowing take on added convolutions that are not considered by Lott due to his central focus and cut-off date.

One of Lott's most important points, which is never diluted in his argument, is that minstrelsy was driven by the white male obsession with
the black male body. This body becomes a battlefield for acting out the
binary, love/hate, oppositional discourse of the black–white interaction.
Veering from those scholars who preceded him, Lott delves into a psy-
chocultural interpretation of this syndrome and attempts to replace earlier premises of racial domination with psychohistorical revisionism. He
deploys the concept of racial desire (and, particularly, sublimated psychological urges) as a central drive in the minstrel trope, and he does so

at the expense of the sociopolitical argument of his precursors. Of course, as he correctly contends, the category of race works in tandem with other pertinent categories and divisions. But that does not mean that the notion of race is not the central presumption of minstrelsy. A poststructuralist discourse may be concerned, as he contends, with "a dismantling of binary racial categories in favor of multiply determined and positioned subjects" (Lott 1993, 8), but it is shortsighted to allow one's contemporary lens to blur the racially weighted focus of the minstrel era and the minstrel trope.

I concur with Lott's assertion that, although he is totally unaware of it, the white American male has so grossly and unconsciously internalized black male style that it has become a second-nature, basic component in his "equipment for living" (53). He claims that the kind of white men who entered minstrelsy did so in order "to indulge their felt sense of difference" (51). As differences, he cites, among other things, temperament, alcoholism, and sexual orientation. The same elements could be significant markers in the personal profile of one who makes a career as an actor, businessman, politician, fireman, or any other profession, for that matter. There is no way to authenticate such a claim. From a sociopolitical perspective, the significant fact is that those who were marginalized in Protestant American culture on the basis of race — Jews and the Irish — were most likely to be drawn to minstrelsy. Like the blacks they represented, they, too, were outsiders, and minstrelsy was one of the few outlets that was open to them. Their "felt sense of difference" was due to mainstream American racism against newly arrived immigrants. This was the same reason that blacks entered minstrelsy around the time of the Civil War.[10]

The psychosexual claims go further. Lott cites adolescent minstrel memories in which the subjects think and dream of the minstrel life before they enter the profession. A reminiscence about an imagined tambourine in hand and burnt cork on face is enough to have Lott compare that circular musical instrument to a symbolic penis and, alternately, a hymen (54). He claims that "in a real sense, the minstrel man *was* the penis, that organ returning in a variety of contexts" (25). It is not that the psychosocial interpretation of history is invalid. But in this case, these musings privilege the psyche of the white male subject over and above the soma — the actual, mortal body — of the black male object. They separate white motives from their black outcomes and examine one side of the coin but not the other. Lott states:

[E]ven the ugly vein of hostile wish fulfillment in dime minstrel songbooks reads as a sort of racial panic rather than confident racial power (though, to be sure, the result was hegemonic enough). We are still in the world of the child, the fantasies of omnipotence barely concealing the vulnerability they mask. One notes in particular the relentless tranformation of black people into things, as though to clinch the property relations these songs fear are too fluid. The sheer overkill of songs in which black men are roasted, fished for, smoked like tobacco, peeled like potatoes, planted in the soil, or dried and hung up as advertisements is surely suspicious; these murderous fantasies are refined down to perfect examples of protesting far too much. (150)

In spite of the primitive quality of these fantasies, Lott acknowledged in his parenthetical aside that "the result was hegemonic enough." Now, that is a very important phrase. We can only guess at impulses and motives, but we can see (and, for African Americans, experience) products of the white social, political, economic, and cultural perception and reception of African Americans. Lott may choose to read this ugliness as impotence but, for the black object of the white male gaze, what matters is the result: racial power politics, oppression of blacks, and white supremacy. Psychological occurrences need to be interpreted in a context that embraces the full picture, if we hope to get a handle on our racialized identities and to reach beyond them. The white minstrel icons of "overkill" are the seeds that, with the right racist climate, blossomed into the lynchings, castrations, and physical abominations that African Americans were and sometimes still are subjected to. And there lies the rub in Lott's theory. The staged joke is lethal and all too real for blacks. This fact cannot be minimized. Although I appreciate the attempt to examine the white side of minstrelsy, I am alarmed by this neglect of the black side. No treatment, psychological or otherwise, of a black perspective, real or imagined, is presented. Lott's layered psychological insights need (or lack) the undergirding of comprehensive social and political analysis. He stops short of the promise and potential offered by contemporary cultural studies to lead us beyond our exclusive hegemonies toward an inclusive picture.

To reiterate, I do not take issue with Lott for what he does — analyzing white working-class motives in the minstrel trope. This side of minstrelsy is important and must be examined to complete the full picture. I take issue with how he goes about it and who is left out.

Lott states: "I take as normative a long, conflicted history of racial exchange that significantly 'blackened' American culture as it creolized African cultural imports, a history that in a sense makes it difficult to talk about expropriation at all" (39). He continues, "Moreover, practices taken as black were occasionally interracial creations whose commodification on white stages attested only to whites' greater access to public distribution (and profit)" (39). I quote these statements because they illustrate exactly what I fear: the disempowering of the Africanist component in American culture and a new, deconstructionist way of disowning this presence. There is no doubt that interchange and Creolization are the name of the game in America. That is why American culture, black, white, and brown, is a fusion of cultures, black, white, and brown. That is how African Americans absorbed Europeanist influences; incorporated them into the Africanist; on the one hand, became the primary musicians for white fancy balls; and on the other hand, changed the shape and sound of New World Christianity. Still, the Africanist and Europeanist strands of the fabric can be deciphered and identified, to a surprisingly large degree. If, as he contends, interracial creations were commodified by whites and drew profits for whites, this, too, is an example of expropriation, and the fact that whites, not blacks, were the profiteers is an important point. Lott further states:

The creolized character of black forms themselves, of course, not to mention their casual and undocumentable influence on white ones, muddies this whole question considerably and makes all cultural labeling a provisional matter. Indeed, the heated debate about black secular music's "origins" (as with minstrelsy) turns up highly speculative, straining, even bizarre arguments as to its definitive (white or black) "source." (94)

It is unfortunate that Lott's sometimes brilliant treatise is "muddied" by offhand statements such as the above. His own argument about the influence of black (male) style and presence on the white minstrel refutes the idea of this exchange as casual. And it is not that the influence is "undocumentable" but, rather, that documentation has been sparse and frequently skewed. All American forms, black and white, are Creolized. Yet there are clear markers indicating basic differences in Africanist and Europeanist aesthetic concepts that have been discussed and detailed by a number of researchers in the past three decades, of whose research Lott must be aware. (A cadre of these authors was mentioned in Chapters 1 and 2; there are others, as well.) I am unaware of the "speculative, straining, bizarre arguments" about the origins of black secular music. I do know of solid, intelligent sources that document, record, and analyze the black side of this black–white equation.[11] Given the fact of American racialized history, for Lott to either trivialize or be unaware of the rationale and validity for documentation of the black threads in our Creolized culture is beyond my understanding. He knows, from his exposition on the white male acquisition of black male body language, that the minstrel dancing body of America, both black and white, is the repressed and misrepresented *black* dancing body.

This is a good juncture at which to introduce some of Toll's findings, lest we forget the racist intent of the form (which is possible in Lott's recursive convolutions). Toll, from his vantage point, highlights the other side and tells us that even some elements that were assumed to be white were probably black: "Since cultural interaction between blacks and whites was common in Southern frontier areas, minstrels probably unwittingly included elements of black culture in some of what they thought was white frontier lore" (Toll 1974, 42). He further points out that minstrel dances were clearly a blend of African and European forms. He adds: "The normal direction of the adaptation, however, was from blacks to blackface, and the 'borrowers' were white men who consciously learned from blacks" (43). To be sure, the kinds of fusions that were practiced by white minstrels were directly geared to profits and were, as Toll points out, conscious acquisitions—made possible by the already present, subliminal force of the Africanist in their American lives. Fusions are significant, and they are a given in our culture. But what is not given—and is often stolen, trivialized, or misnamed—is the significance of the back side, the black side, of the fusion coin: "Minstrelsy was the first example of the way American popular culture would exploit and manipulate Afro-Americans and their culture to please and benefit white Americans" (Toll, 51).

In spite of Creolization and interracial levels of exchange, American society was, then as now, highly polarized. In discussing the advent of the Virginia Minstrels and other popular white minstrel troupes of the antebellum era, Tolls states:

Although most Northerners did not know what slaves were like, they believed or wanted to believe that black slaves differed greatly from free white Americans. Thus, minstrels emphasized Negro "peculiarities," described themselves exotically as "Ethiopian Delineators" and/or "Congo Melodists," and called some of their acts "Virginia Jungle Dance," "Nubian Jungle Dance," "African Fling," and "African Sailor's Hornpipe." (34)

White, working-class racism—an equal partner with white, working-class fantasies—was a strong operative in minstrelsy and should not be underestimated. We must remember that, North and South, then and now, it is frequently poor, working-class whites who exhibit the most physical, blatant, and heinous racism against African Americans, because they are the ones who feel most immediately threatened by African American advancement and are most likely to be in direct contact and market competition with African Americans. But it is noteworthy that, when push comes to shove, both poor and well-off whites have been known to bond and find common ground by using racism as a way of distancing the black Other in order to measure and define the white self. It seems superfluous, on Lott's part, to talk about white working-class "ambivalences" as reason to "disallow simplistic ascriptions of racism to the [white] working class" (130). One need not propose a monolithic, racist intent on the part of the white working class, then or now, in order to validate the contention that the effect of white (working-class) practices, in the workplace and in leisure life, has been to perpetuate anti-black racism. Minstrelsy was a white-engineered construct that allowed white entry onto a simulated black turf and simultaneously sanctioned white suppression of and agency over the black male body.

"Ambivalence" means a two- (or many-) sided perspective. Toll looks at another side of it. He points out minstrelsy's "fundamental ambivalence" about slavery (84). Thus, although some minstrel material sympathized with slaves, never was a fugitive portrayed as successful and, increasingly, the image of the "happy darky" longing for the simple joys of plantation life prevailed. Taken in tandem with minstrelsy's grotesquing and lampooning of blacks, a strong case may be made for a basically antiblack, proslavery bias in white minstrelsy (most virulent in the late 1850s) and, by extension, in its white minstrel creators. Furthermore, the white minstrel made it clear that his pro-Union sentiments should not be misinterpreted as antislavery:

"To go in for de Union," one of Hooley's minstrels succinctly observed during the war, "ain't nigger abolition." Leaving no doubt about where they stood, minstrels sought to discredit abolitionists by charging that blacks had been content in their places until these agitators put "de debbel in de nigger's head." (Toll, 113)

WHAT'S YOURS IS MINE

Let us now turn to some of the ways in which the Africanist presence was commodified and appropriated in minstrelsy. What we see in this regard is a mass of mixed messages and a grand example of the dilemma of derivation. Here are the words of J. Kennard, from an 1845 issue of *Knickerbocker Magazine*, as quoted by musicologist Eileen Southern (1971, 103) and Lott (99), although each author endows it with a different reading:

Who are our true rulers? The Negro poets, to be sure. Do they not set the fashion, and give laws to the public taste? Let one of them, in the swamps of Carolina, compose a new song, and it no sooner reaches the ear of a white amateur, than it is written down, amended (that is, almost spoilt), printed, and then put upon a course of rapid dissemination, to cease only with the utmost bounds of Anglo-Saxondom, perhaps with the world. *Meanwhile, the poor author digs away with his hoe, utterly ignorant of his greatness.* (emphasis added)

Southern uses the quote at face value to point out that white America was and is dependent upon the Africanist aesthetic in forming an American aesthetic. Lott examines Kennard's motives and deconstructs the 1845 American moment (when Americans felt culturally superior to African Americans and inferior to Europeans) to say that Kennard meant this statement as a sardonic comment on the blackening of America. Although that might have been the motive, the outcome is the same. The quote remains a telling statement about the power of the Africanist aesthetic in American traditions. Either way, an anxiety of influence is indicated. Lott omits the final sentence of the quote, which I have emphasized. Both he and Southern do point out that minstrel music was a fusion of Africanist, Scottish, and Irish influences. Southern emphasizes that "the black man was behind it all" (103). That phrase must be (re)constructed and (re)membered for each generation of Americans — white and, sadly, even black — because, generation after generation, the fact is covered up and forgotten. During the white minstrel era, the "delineators" wanted to have it both ways, to say they were performing authentic black material while claiming that they were inventing original creations. And the writers of their era, including those who wrote for publications like the *New York Clipper*, were of the same bent. Then, during the early twentieth century, the likes of T. Allston Brown (1912), Arthur Gillespie (1909), LeRoy Rice (1911), and others writing theater history highlighted white male invention in minstrelsy and ignored its black counterparts. Brown went so far as to disclaim the banjo as an African instrument. (His argument was based on evidence that the instrument is Egyptian. Like most other white writers, he ignored the fact that Egypt is an African nation whose history is rooted in and predicated upon Africanist precepts.)[12] The same historical erasure is met in mainstream writers of the 1930s and 1940s. The writers of the late 1950s through the 1970s, obviously fueled by the black Civil Rights movement, were the first generation since the lone voices of African American intellectuals W. E. B. Du Bois (1903) and James Weldon Johnson (1930) and white Constance Rourke (1931) to give credence to this black presence. Where we are now may serve the purposes of cultural recursive theory but, I hope, not at the expense of the Africanist presence. Minstrelsy's multilayered, skewed record is indeed a "highly faulted discourse."[13]

Kennard's statement is only one of many indicators that whites were aware of the black presence in the formation of American cultural constructs. Another quote that appears in several major works on minstrelsy and reflects the "field work" testimonials by white minstrels is the following anecdote about William W. Whitlock, one of the original members of Dan Emmett's Virginia Minstrels:

He made the banjo his study by day and by night. Every night during his journey South, when he was not playing, he would quietly steal off to some negro [*sic*] hut to hear the darkies sing and see them dance, taking with him a jug of whiskey to make them all the merrier. Thus he got his accurate knowledge of the peculiarities of plantation and cornfield negroes. (Brown 1912, 3)

Lott (50–52) makes one of his most important points in this regard
and locates the origin of the (American) bohemian trope at this site: The
white minstrel hangs out with disenfranchised blacks, is befriended by
them, and eventually appropriates (and alters) their cultural products.
As the Langston Hughes poem said, "You've taken my blues and gone."
Emmett is a good example. For most of his life, having been in close
contact with African Americans, he both acknowledged and denied his
liability, stating that he looked for inspiration in "'the habits and crude
ideas of the slaves of the South,' even though in the next breath he in-
sisted that the songs were of his own composition" (Rourke, 86).[14]   The
sad irony is that the white who may seem to be the friend of the black
cause may prove to be its sweetest abuser. He has stepped into black life
and taken from it without guilt or debt. The fact that the time was ripe
for these cultural products to be immediately channeled into a profit-
making leisure industry went hand in hand with the commodification
and industrialization of mid-century American society.

The Africanist products expropriated in minstrelsy were as obvious
as particular steps, songs, and phrases, and particular ways of holding
and moving the body or enunciating a sung phrase or note. They were
as subtle as the Africanist attitude, that high-affect yet balanced stance
between hot and cool.[15] Unbeknownst to them, the principle of ephebism
was another Africanist component that attracted the minstrels and stood
out as a markedly different attitude than anything from Europe. Thus,
old and handicapped African Americans—including Rice's model for
"Jump Jim Crow" and others representing "the lean, the fat, the tall, the
short, the hunchbacked, and the wooden-legged, all mixed in and hard at
it" (Winter 1948, 43)—were models of self-mocking yet self-aware humor
and youthful nimbleness, in spite of age or handicap. They represented
the radical juxtaposition and aesthetic redefinition that would stand
American performance on its head and permanently shift its values toward the Africanist. These models were a contradiction, in Europeanist
terms: old as young, awkward as effective, ugly as pleasing. Finally,
white minstrelsy robbed blacks of their visibility and substituted a blackface silhouette for the real thing. And the sexualized black body, the
dancing black body, was the crux of the matter, the most visible white
export from the subjugated culture.

But the minstrel stage was simply the site where the Euro-Afro-
American interactions became commodified; the exchanges date back to
the Colonial era.[16] As Dena Epstein points out (1977, 121), young colo-
nists were fond of participating in their servants' ceremonies, and the
descriptions of these events have an identifiably Africanist flavor. Couples and individuals take turns, compete with one another in challenging
and demonstrating their unique abilities, and dances last as long as the

energy of the participants will allow. In true Africanist fashion, individual improvisation was the norm and, rather than the form shaping the energy, it was the unbounded energy that directed the form. Epstein talks about "the African jig, a black-to-white exchange," (120) and corrects early accounts that talk about the Irish jig and English clog as though they were "pure" European retentions. (Similarly, folklorist-historian Roger Abrahams has found that what was assumed to be Irish-American fiddle music is highly inflected by the Africanist aesthetic.)[17] The Africanized jig cited by Epstein contains hop, tap, and shuffle steps. Likewise, Winter (40) points out that the "Juba" dance, brought to the plantation by enslaved Africans, "somewhat resembled a jig with elaborate variations, and occurs wherever the Negro settled, whether in the West Indies or South Carolina." Frequently a test of stamina as much as a show of virtuosity, this generic "Juba"-jig demanded energy and endurance beyond the parameters of Europeanist aesthetics, even for an Irish folk construct.[18] It is characterized by qualities and body postures (non-vertical alignment, exaggerations in the bend of knees and openness of the legs) that are, from a Europeanist standpoint, grotesque and awkward. It is open-ended in duration and improvisatory in vocabulary. Frequently it is characterized by patting, slapping, clapping, and otherwise rhythmically using body parts as musical instruments for percussion and syncopation, characteristics that were formalized in a dance called "Pattin' Juba." It is, as Epstein points out, an African jig. Or, to be more precise, it is a fused Afro-Irish jig in which the Irish influence was absorbed and transformed into an Africanist context, so much so that soon the jig became associated primarily with African Americans. As Stearns and Stearns (1979, 45) explain, William Henry Lane was known as a jig dancer at the moment when the original meaning of the term (namely, an Irish folk dance) was being amended to signify black dancing, in general. The jig became so closely associated with Africanist expressive forms that early twentieth-century white rural carnivals and small circuses—the descendants of the minstrel era—had a segregated section for African American performers called the jig top. An early form of piano ragtime music was known as "jig piano," and the epithet "jigaboo," for African American, surely comes from the same root.[19]

In the New World milieu of black–white exchange, not only dance but also the full performance environment took on a different cast. White audiences began to participate in call-and-response, humming, shouting, and signifying forms of expression that were alien to European culture, and to witness music and movement that were characterized by "syncopation, off-beats and contrapuntal harmony" (Todd 1950, 21). These rhythms had no Europeanist forerunners; they evidenced instead the complexities of Africanist polyrhythms (Toll 1974, 46). The song

styles were characterized by tones, timbres, and pitches that were unknown in the Europeanist music canon and that were best characterized,
in Europeanist vocabulary, as slides and runs (Nathan 1962, 129). A
measure of the Afro-Euro binary relationship is the fact that the two primary forerunners of minstrelsy were black and white, respectively—
William Henry Lane, or "Master Juba," and Thomas "Daddy" Rice. Rice
created and mastered a "darky" stereotype that would be elaborated
upon and embellished to expanded levels of grotesquerie as minstrelsy
progressed.[20] Lane's Africanist rhythms and syncopation, speed and
delay tactics, and torso articulation indelibly influenced popular dance
forms. He was the forerunner of tap dance as it is known today. He
used the extant Africanist transformation of the Europeanist jig to his
professional advantage and made this Africanized jig a popular American stage form.

The account of Rice's most famous routine, "Jump Jim Crow," is a
microcosm of the white minstrel trope. To make a long story short, Rice
observed on a street in one town a handicapped African American beg-
gar performing an eccentric, limping dance accompanied by a peculiar
song in which the chorus advised, "Wheel about, turn about, do just so,
and every time I wheel about I jump Jim Crow" (which was, supposedly,
the man's name). Whether he acquired this "act" by observation and
memory or by inviting the man to teach it to him varies with different
versions of the story. Then, while on a booking in another town, Rice
encountered another African American male, this time a stable worker
named Cuff, and another "found" performance. He decides to meld the
two characters into a new stage routine. He drags Cuff into his dressing
room, "borrows" his clothes for authenticity, and proceeds—with actions, costume, and, finally, by blacking up his face (as a final assurance
that no one would miss his message)—to do the first African American
cover act on the proto-minstrel stage, "Jump Jim Crow." Rice and the
long line of white minstrels who followed him were doing what is quin-
tessentially American—taking something and commodifying it. Whether
it was Jim Crow, Cuff the stableman, "Picayune Butler," or "Old Corn
Meal" (whom Rice imitated in a skit titled "Corn Meal," which he performed in New Orleans, where this African American vendor sold wares
and entertained on the street) (Kmen 1966, 244–45), African American
males provided the impetus and inspiration for white male performative
fantasy. And, ironically, the "Jim Crow" that meant white male liberation on the minstrel stage later designated the "Jim Crow" discrimination
laws that successfully kept blacks in a state of de facto slavery.

There is an extant, full-body rendering of William Henry Lane, re-
produced in several texts, including Emery (1988, 187). His pose is Africanist. The vertical torso deconstructs, the standing leg's right hip is

articulated backward and sideward of center, thus giving a forward, opposing dip to the upper torso and causing the left shoulder to hang front
of center. Both knees are deeply bent, and the knee of the gesturing leg is
lifted slightly above the hip. To top it off and to balance the "hot" lower
body, Juba has his hands placed coolly in his jacket pockets, his almost
straight arms pulling the jacket open, away from and behind his torso. It
is a pose that prefigures one of the characteristic gestures of today's hip
hop artists as they strut across the world's stages. As Winter (53) explains, Master Juba and his descendants introduced a new form of acro-
batics and "slapstick" — or manically absurd — characteristics to the white
minstrel stage as well as to the European clown tradition (this, through
Juba's smashingly successful European appearances, which is a further
illustration of Dehn's contention that the black Other brought new blood
to European popular entertainment forms). One contemporary reviewer
said of him: "[T]his youth is the delight and astonishment of all who witness his extraordinary dancing: to our mind he dances demisemi, semi,
and quavers, as well as the slower steps" (quoted in Winter, 52). Another described his work as "an ideality... that makes his efforts at once
grotesque and poetical" (quoted in Winter, 50). Unconsciously, they
were sensing his embracing of opposites, his balance between hot and
cool.

   In one of the extant renderings of Rice as Jim Crow (see, for example,
Nathan 1962, 51), we see some similarity to Juba's pose, but there is more
of the grotesque and exaggerated, and less of the cool. In particular, the
right hip juts outward, sideward and backward, even farther than Master
Juba's, thus breaking and twisting the angle of the torso, tipping the pelvis, and arching the spine. White minstrels played with Africanist characteristics and, like Rice, omitted the elegance inherent in them and
exaggerated them to the point of the grotesque.

   One of Dan Emmett's specialties involved an interesting, unwitting
combination of hot and cool, something so foreign to the traditional Europeanist aesthetic that it stood out as strikingly unique. According to
Nathan (1962, 62), with a relaxed (read "cool") body Emmett would lean
forward, let his hands droop, turn his head sideways, and sidle-slither
across the stage, his feet performing highly expressive (read "hot")
movements that involved manipulating the heel of one foot and the toe
of the other simultaneously to tread ground and move forward. Another
"delineator," while keeping his legs spread open and knees apart, kicked
up his heels, raised his arms aloft and waved his hands overhead, a
stereotyped imitation of African American religious fervor (Nathan, 62).
These white men aped the challenging, acrobatic, exhibition dances performed by African Americans on the plantation and in Northern en-

claves. Descriptions tell of physical exertion, angular steps, and strenuous twists of body (Nathan, 64–65).

The "Essence" dances were an early white minstrel stage form that illustrated perfectly the paradox of minstrelsy as both black and nonblack. This invention was a synthesis of authentic-but-transformed Africanist elements made famous by Billy Newcomb, one of the four original Virginia Minstrels. The "Essence" capitalized on Africanist shuffle steps and their many improvised variations. One variation survived through early vaudeville and involved the dancer moving his feet so as to suggest that he was sliding, or skating, as in the description of the Dan Emmett specialty. If we think about the "Moonwalk" of the hip hop generation, we get an idea of what this variation of the "Essence" was about. Another variant evolved into the vaudeville-era softshoe. The irony is layered further when real African Americans enter minstrelsy and people like Billy Kersands become known as masters of this white-inflected, Africanist synthesis. Another case of "yes and no" (that is, black and nonblack) is the climax of the minstrel show. Known as the "walkaround," it was a throwback to Africanist plantation dances in which individuals stepped forth out of a moving, walking, or dancing circle in order to improvise several bars of solo dancing. Capitalizing on the melodic and textual organization of African American spirituals, white minstrels incorporated into the minstrel "walkaround" elements of the "Ring Shout"—the Africanist plantation response to Christianity—and, as mentioned, were likely to throw their arms above their heads in simulation of Africanist religious expression and accompany the soloists by improvised vocal shouts. All these demonstrations were, of course, stripped of their religious connotations. Emery (1988, 192) points out that the "walkaround" also included "breakdown" elements from the plantation "Juba," which allowed the dancers to flaunt their individual specialties.[21] In the "Ole Virginy [sic] Breakdown" illustration, the deep, bended-knee, get-down position of the supporting leg balanced against the sharply flexed foot (with angularly raised toes and heel extended forward) is known as "cutting the long J bow" (Nathan 1962, 90). It was probably arrived at by sliding the foot forward, sinking into, and moving through the position—another variation on an Africanist shuffle—rather than by hopping into this position and holding it, which is a conclusion that could be drawn from a different reading of the static pose. The raised knee, flexed foot position of the dancer on the far left is a variation of Master Juba's classic pose, with knee lifted above the hip and legs rotated open from the pelvis. The shadowy figure in the center performs another variation of a jigging step and is balanced on the toe of the standing leg as he is about to move through this position. Again, the raised, waving arms were a convention lifted from African American religious practice. The style of dance depicted here — a modification from and potpourri of plantation-derived sources — became the norm for white minstrels and for black minstrels who followed, imitating the imitators, but adding their own individual and culturally specific quirks.

Let me point out how misinterpreted these Africanist characteristics were, which is why the white minstrel was able to use them as the basis for a form of grotesque-burlesque theater. Should these same characteristics have been read from an Africanist perspective, instead of measured up as a faulted Europeanist aesthetic, the course of American history and the fate of Africans in America may have been mightily altered. What Africans presented was not a ludicrous or primitive aesthetic, but an Africanist aesthetic, which held different criteria for line, form, and beauty and integrally conjoined the ludic and the tragic as elements in a continuum. Unfortunately, most white Americans, unsophisticated in dealing with difference and schooled in the doctrine of white superiority, knew only the Europeanist code as a measure of worth. They had no coordinates from their own culture for acknowledging that much of the expressive dance and music they witnessed were the sacred practices of danced religions. Still, those seductive, forceful (yet, simultaneously repulsive and frightening) Africanist forms were inescapably etched in the white American landscape. What to do? According to Nathan (1962, 81):

An eighteenth-century observer already noticed what appeared to him "most violent" about Negro dances in Virginia and he disapproved of it by calling them "so irregular and grotesque." Soon, however, one learned how to interpret the tribal ecstasy which was so alien to European or Europeanized culture. Fanny Kemble. . . found the slaves' complete lack of self-consciousness and their sultry concentration most impressive. She was fascinated by what "these people did with their bodies, and, above all, with their faces, the whites of their eyes, and the whites of their teeth, and certain outlines which. . . they bring into prominent and most ludicrous display,". . . the "languishing elegance of some — the painstaking laboriousness of others." And when we read about the "indescribable 'frills' of foot motion" of a Negro dancer in our own time, we know that the vast physical energy of the race is far from being exhausted.

What one did was to "disapprove" of these endeavors by characterizing them as Other, alien, primitive. Next, as Nathan proudly and patronizingly points out, the white American "learns" a suitable way to "interpret" (read "use, abuse, and excuse") these presences. Fanny Kemble's diary is a source frequently called upon in the literature on slave culture. As an actress, she was about the business of observing human behavior. She regarded the expressive body language and facial representation of African Americans as both labored and elegant, forceful and ludicrous. In other words, she saw the simultaneous conflict and embracing of opposites, was in awe of it, and didn't know what to do with it, where to place it, or how to measure and interpret it. In addressing elements such as "certain outlines which. . . they bring into prominent. . . display," she indicates that African Americans had a sense of line and form that fell outside the ken of the Europeanist aesthetic. Kemble knew there was something powerful and even intimidating here, but the only way she could deal with it was to disempower it and label it "ludicrous." Nathan, writing in the twentieth century, cannot acknowledge the worth and validity of this presence and ends this account by attributing Africanist invention to mere "physical energy." Earlier, Nathan cited virtuosity in performance, organizational ability, and the ability to burlesque as the "non-Negro" contributions to minstrel dance (72). Like many cultural historians and performance critics of our own era, he opined that it is the European touch, the white finesse, that brings validity and credibility, formalism and order, to Africanist forms. Indeed, we are dealing with a highly faulted discourse of power and control.

It is interesting that some of the Africanisms imported to the white minstrel stage foreshadow the Africanist presence in modern and jazz dance. Nathan (75) describes the minstrel dancing body as constantly in contorted or distorted positions, with legs spread wide. Arms and hands were particularly expressive; frequently fingers were splayed. A common position involved placing elbows near hips and extending the forearms at right angles to the torso, with palms facing down. The arm position described is common to most tap dancing and is frequently the cool component to balance hot, fast steps in a jazz routine (thus serving the same function as the hands-in-pockets position of Master Juba). Positions such as these, amended for the concert stage, became part of the twentieth-century avant-garde dance canon, itself a rebellion against classical European ballet, and characterized the work of most modern dancers.

The comments by Nathan and Kemble help set the stage for a discussion of the minstrel stereotype and its relation to issues of agency and control. Enlightenment-inspired race theory and the burgeoning discipline of anthropology, combined with Darwinism and new social and scientific theories, undergirded the efficacy of African stereotypes in Europe and America and indirectly helped to reinforce the white power politics of minstrelsy. As a public amusement, minstrelsy also helped school new immigrants in antiblack bias. As Toll points out (67–69), the structure of early minstrelsy was designed to show that, rich or poor, whites were superior to blacks. The early shows began with a "serious" concert performed without blackface. The black sections, performed in burnt cork, consisted of skits with titles like "Plantation Darkies" or "Northern Dandies," and were comic travesties. By this simple device, the stereotype of the black buffoon was reinforced and contrasted with whites, who were the "real" American citizens—serious, intelligent, and capable of performing "highbrow" art forms. Handbills depicted two renderings of the white performer: in street clothes, as the normal citizen, and in blackface, thus making a clear distinction between the man and the role. The Northern black dandy was a particularly mean stereotype and necessarily so, from the needs of a white supremacist perspective. Since poor whites and blacks lived side by side in New York, which was the center of the nineteenth-century minstrel stage, it was important for the lower-class white consumer to believe that his black peer was, in fact, his inferior. Given the physical grotesqueries and deformities of the minstrel make-up and the outlandish character of the costumes, white laborers could participate in a common sentiment of white superiority when measured against the black dandy, who was so dumb as to think himself smart and good-looking. And, to top it off, the dandy had no command of the only valid spoken word, the English language. (To take away the power of the word means taking away the power of selfhood.) He spoke in malapropisms and conundrums and used his imbecilic language to expostulate on science, politics, and current events—all to the delight of the white, male, largely working-class audience, who had every right to feel superior to these bumbling idiots and secure in the belief that the power of the word was not the domain of the black man. This black character considered himself "consumquencial" and "edjumakated" because he won the lottery; his conversations were "boldiggating." He might pompously philosophize on a current subject such as transcendentalism, concluding on a note about "de circumambulatin commotion ob ambiloquous voluminiousness" (Toll, 71). Anyone who has heard a stump speech or witnessed a performance that contains malapropisms knows that these forms are very amusing. They are also staples in the American canon of humor, providing a vehicle for lampooning book knowledge and elitism, on the one hand, and for political satire, on the other. The problem, however, was that these gross characterizations, when linked to blackface representation of an indigenous American population, *were assumed by the audiences to be true-to-life representations of authentic African American "types."* White spectators forgot that they were watching white actors and conflated the stage mask with the real-life black man. Some whites were so convinced of minstrelsy's authenticity that there are accounts of their mistaking whites in blackface for African Americans, even though the antebellum minstrel stage was an all-white affair. Thus, white minstrels began the practice of showing themselves on programs and handbills in blackface character as well as in whiteface original. Accounts not only by the working class but by audience members such as Mark Twain and Walt Whitman—sophisticated segments of the American white population—addressed the minstrel stereotype as though it were the real black article.[22]

What emerges from examination of these characters, in tandem with nineteenth-century newspaper articles on African Americans, is a portentously malign portrayal of blacks. The realpolitik of power is situated here. These depictions become a rationale for justifying slavery, and much of the minstrel material was proslavery. In this regard it is important to remember that another form of popular literature of this era was the proslavery novel, works written as responses to *Uncle Tom's Cabin* that emphasized the happy, carefree, dancing, singing, plantation "darky." Hardly does the minstrel stage seem innocent. It is raw and calculating in its use of ridicule and hatred. As much as a boxer in the ring, a street fighter, or a marksman at the target, the purveyor of the minstrel trope aimed and fired at his black scapegoat-stereotype, repeatedly shooting it down and nurturing its resurrection in order to fire again. Blacks—and whites—are still stuck in these stereotypes, updated as they have been from one generation to the next. The habit is so ingrained that it has become the norm. Mintrelsy reminds us that African Americans are limited to narrow confines that control their entry into mainstream American life and prosperity.

After reading descriptions of the Virginia Minstrels' act, one wonders how white Americans could have assumed that these antics were a genuine picture of anyone and how white delineators and their audiences could designate these stereotypes as the property of an alien culture when it was they—through the vehicle of their own bodies—who created and enacted this stock repertory of black Others. Whites were not acting out blacks in minstrelsy, but their fantasies of *themselves* as blacks—the sexy, lazy, scared, childish, pompous, happy-go-lucky, emotional, stupid, ugly sides of themselves. Again, in another permutation, we touch upon minstrelsy's central paradox. As Rourke (104) so eloquently put it: "The young American Narcissus had looked at himself in the narrow rocky pools of New England and by the waters of the Mississippi; he also gazed long at a darker image." Like Allan Jabbour or Ernie Smith copying the African American "Lindyhop" (see Chapter 3), like Elvis Presley (see Chapter 3), like white rapper Vanilla Ice, like the New Kids on The Block (see Chapter 7), white American males from minstrelsy to today take on the black style and forms as a badge that reads "freedom, defiance, and illicit, sexy fun." Yet, the white minstrel could not own up to the black part of himself. He treated it like a prostitute—bought, used, and denied.

The Virginia Minstrels—Billy Whitlock, Frank Pelham, Dan Emmett, and Frank Brower—in the 1842–43 season brought their separate black-

face acts together and created the first minstrel troupe, which institutionalized the character and structure of minstrelsy thereafter:

They were boisterous to the point of grotesqueness. . . . [T]hey would stretch out
their legs toward their audience in rowdy fashion and bend their feet and their
toes at the sharpest possible angles, . . . sputtering uncouth sayings, shouts, and
hoarse laughter. Pelham exhibited "looks and movements comic beyond conception. He seemed animated by a savage energy. . . . His white eyes rolled in a
curious frenzy. . . . [H]is hiccupping chuckles were unsurpassable." (Nathan
123–25)

The black male body, the black dancing body—as the Nathan quote indicates, the seat of difference is strongly centered in minstrel body language. In dancing, standing, moving, or seated postures, the body is the
thing—legs spread wide, distorted torsos, eccentric steps, vigorous foot
tapping. Europe and its formalities seem far away. Nathan excuses the
sinister effects that these shenanigans might have had on African Americans and states that the white minstrel imbued his "art" (Nathan's usage)
with the ribald, merry qualities that were, indeed, authentic attributes of
the "lower" social group (70). He goes further and asserts that the
stereotype is justified:

As was the plantation type, "Zip Coon" and "Dandy Jim" were close to reality.
Merely compare them with the colored dandy in Boston who was observed
"lounging down the street. He was a sable Count d'Orsay. His toilet was the
most elaborately recherché you can imagine. He seemed intensely and harm-
lessly happy in his coat and waistcoat, of the finest possible materials; and the
careful carelessness of the adjustment of the wool and hat was not readily to be
surpassed." (59)

I see little comparison between this description by an Englishwoman
traveling in the United States (Lady Emmeline Stuart Wortley, *Travels in
the United States. . . During 1849-1850*, as quoted in Nathan) and the bias-
driven, grossly eccentric exaggerations of the American white minstrel.
Granted, the woman's account is patronizing and condescending and is
based upon her amusement (and, perhaps, concealed anger or disgust) at
the idea of an African male assuming the posture and appearance of a
European fop, but it falls far short of the minstrel descriptions in Nathan
and other accounts. Nathan's interpretation—that her account justifies
the minstrel stereotype—makes one wonder about the blinding power of
ethnocentricity which allowed him, writing in 1962, to block out evidence
to the contrary and justify the white minstrel stereotype as a true-to-life
photograph of the African American male. His attitude reflects the bizarre influence that the minstrel trope continues to exert over white per-
ceptions of a black Other, a power that condones the simultaneous

appropriation and rejection of Africanist peoples, processes, and products, as well as the positing of ownership and agency in white hands. White ethnocentricity is the overweening power that shaped the central, "is/isn't black" paradox of minstrelsy.

A similar patronizing attitude is reflected in the writing of a late-1830s New Orleans journalist who encouraged any (white) man who wanted to make a fortune to package, produce, and capitalize on Old Corn Meal, the African American street vendor and performer (Kmen 1966, 243). There is no guilt, no blame on the part of the whites who sanctioned these thefts. This disposition became meaner and more rigid as minstrelsy matured and as the nation became involved in civil war. For example, many white Northerners made it clear that they were not against slavery. They went to war for a variety of reasons, but they were not, invariably, pro-abolition. With acquisitive eyes alert at the windows through which they observed black life and the doors through which they entered black culture, the nineteenth-century white American enjoyed counterfeit black experiences through the *mirror* and *mask* of minstrelsy, and regarded the real life of blacks as an imitation of minstrelsy. Here is an account from the "City Summary" section of the *New York Clipper* (1861, 206):

There's no end to the fun of the Nigger Minstrels, and for ridiculousness, we know of nothing that equals them except a real old darky meeting. The earnestness of the darks at some of their meetings, at the same time that their arguments are so destitute of common sense, makes them savor more of minstrelsy than anything else we can compare them to. We recently attended one of these "Nigger meetings". . . . held at the house of one of the brethren, in an out of the way place, and in addition to the colored community present, there was quite a sprinkling of "white trash," who had been led there by curiosity. Some of the very self-same plantation airs we had so often listened to at Bryant's were here given in all their purity by the assemblage present. In giving out the opening hymn, the officiating brother said, "Never mind de page of der book, brudderen," and he gave out . . . a tune somewhat resembling "Down in old K-Y—K-Y." Oh! but it was rich. Bryant's could make a fortune out of this famed black band. The text was on the creation, and the preacher, in announcing it, said, "De subjec of my discourse dis ebenin', you will find widin the lids of dis preshus book," at the same time giving the "preshus book" a tremendous slap with his open palm. "My bruddern," said he, "When de Lord make Adam and Ebe, he put 'em in a big apple orchard—took 'em to de middle of de orchard, and told 'em to eat as many apples as dey wanted off of all de trees except de middle tree—he didn't want dat one teched at all."

The condescending, dialect-ridden account continues at length, with the journalist's total "transcription" of the African American minister's sermon. In conclusion, this urbane Manhattanite advises, "Our minstrel

friends can get many a rich idea by attending these 'brack gatherings.'"
Lest we forget, this was an era in which, even in the city of New York,
white voyeurs such as those in the anecdote had the license to enter the
home of an African American who was holding a small religious cere-
mony, simply because they were white. No matter that the occasion was
sacred—the acquisitive white intruder saw it as fodder for a most secu-
larized form of commercial exploitation. Indeed, Africanist religious
practice was totally misunderstood by these whites and was perceived as
a poor relative to white practice, suitable for mockery on the minstrel
stage.

Typically, a white minstrel would leave a plantation no better informed than
when arriving. The idea that slave dance might be sacred appears to have been
beyond the minstrel's powers of imagination. Ignorant of the substance, the few
that ventured onto plantations took the shell of dance, and probably slave music
as well, with them when leaving.[23]

Slavery was certainly the operative principle here, with the supposedly
free African American community as chattel, and its cultural expression
as viable products on the open market. One issue of this paper in the
previous year (1860, 230) revealed an even more depressingly racist tone:

We hear of nothing now-a-days but the almighty Nigger, where formerly we
had a chance at the almighty dollar. The latter isn't a circumstance now—there's
nothing like the Nigger, the irrepressible Nigger, the Nigger dyed in the
wool. . . . It's Bell-Everett and the "infernal blacks" here—it's Breckenridge and
the "d----d" black rascals" there—Douglass and the "cussed Nigger," and Lincoln and Horrible Hamlin and the irrepressible darkey everywhere. Go to a
place of amusement, and what do you hear? Nothing but Niggerisms. If the
Nigger question don't make a breach in the Union the present year, united we'll
stand for all future time.

As if to add to the Nigger excitement, our "eminent American tragedian" must
needs shelve old King Lear, and present us with the "Inevitable Nigger," in the
shape of Othello. This is only adding fuel to the already burning shame now
agitating the country. . . .

What was the cause of the last failure of the Old Bowery Theatre? The Nigger
question without doubt. . . . Politics and Niggers did it, no doubt. . . .

Now just look how the Nigger Minstrels take. Go into Bryants' Hall any evening. . . and what do you see! A densely packed crowd in attendance to witness
and hear the irrepressible Nigger. No matter whether it's the real Nig, or only
mock turtle, it's all the same. . . . It's the black shade that makes them so attractive. A rose by any other name might smell as sweet, but a Nig in any other
color but black, never! So continued success to the Bryant Brothers, and their

famed black band. . . . They. . . don't meddle with common Niggers, and in that way have no cause for a trip on the underground railroad.

This lengthy, bitter tirade, longer than the section quoted here, represents the woes of a white New York theater aficionado who is disillusioned that "his" Broadway season is spoiled by the politics of war. Clearly, he is unsympathetic to the abolition issue, does not see it as a serious concern, and is highly incensed that it has become an issue and upset Broadway's economic apple cart. In addition, he is vindictive about the fact that there is a black presence infusing and pervading the American stage. He ridicules the white minstrels who black up and sardonically paints them as co-conspirators in a black takeover of white theater. His outcry about the white minstrel as "mock turtle soup" was surely echoed by other white spectators, once blacks were allowed entry on the minstrel stage (mid to late 1850s). These attitudes worked in favor of pushing whites into nonblack, prevaudeville material, while it forced blacks to sink into the stereotypes left vacant by whites. (Yet, it also insured blacks a means of employment.) On the brink of the Civil War, we hear the antiblack bias of a theater critic who was widely read and whose opinions were a rather accurate barometer of a prevalent urban, Northern point of view.

Another measure of the extreme antipathy and alienation by Northern whites from the African American cause is exhibited in the "Dark Artillery" illustration. Besides the overall evil character of this rendering (it is not quite a cartoon), the original newspaper print, in color, made it clear how much minstrelsy influenced white representation of blacks. The faces of the "contraband" are corked up, black, minstrel faces, complete with exaggerated red lips and whitened eyes. In this rendering and in the Clipper comment about the Underground Railroad, we see that the pro-slavery, capitalist-minded Northerner was particularly upset by the idea of African Americans escaping from bondage. If we look at the illustration captioned "Contraband Ball at Vicksburg, Miss.," we see again the way in which the minstrel stereotype pervades depictions of African Americans and how minstrelsy might serve as an adjunct, or kissing cousin, to slavery. The male dancing figure on the left is in a position reminiscent of Master Juba. He seems to be performing a step called the double shuffle. The eyes, lips, and facial expressions (glazed, staring, empty, dumb) are the stereotypical faces of minstrels. The term "contraband" refers to goods or merchandise whose importation, exportation, or possession is outlawed or forbidden. During the Civil War the meaning of the word was extended. It no longer meant only things that are stolen but also people who have escaped. The implication was that black people are things, objects. And so they were, in the slavery system and on the minstrel stage.

How little agency African Americans had in this. From the white minstrel era through the period of black minstrelsy, this genre remained a white-controlled monopoly. African American entrepreneurial efforts failed unless they were managed and produced by whites, because white theater owners refused to deal with black entrepreneurs. (Similarly, pre-minstrelsy nineteenth-century efforts of African Americans to create their own New York theater and produce Shakespearean dramas were undermined and, finally, overwhelmed by white hecklers and arsonists.) Before the advent of blacks on the minstrel stage, the white New York powers-that-be dictated that African Americans be confined to performing on the streets or in the cheapest dance halls, with an occasional African American programmed on the otherwise white minstrel format. The Africanist presence was, in effect, marginalized. It was to white advantage—and a measure of social control—to use black material but keep black bodies at bay. The white dancer John Diamond, known for his skill at "Negro dancing," advertised that he would publicly challenge any white man in contests to judge the best dancer. It was savvy—and an insidious means of social oppression—to refuse to contend with a black man, particularly the likes of a Master Juba, his contemporary. Likewise, an early black minstrel like James Bland, who represented the challenge of being a "real darky" to his white counterparts (and who composed some 700 songs; since most were not copyrighted, many were stolen) was so frequently unemployed in the United States during the white minstrel period that, at one point, he gave up and relocated to London. It is only when white minstrels move away from African American content that African Americans had permission to enter the field, and, even then, only within the limitations of the established stereotype. To be clear, it was not a case of whites moving away from black material simply because blacks entered the field. Instead, as whites brought new material to the minstrel format in response to national shifts of interest after the Civil War, they distanced themselves from plantation and urban black material, and African Americans were left to fill the gap. Whites in the black-dominated minstrel era are billed as "megatherian," "mammoth," and "mastodon" minstrels and perform routines such as clog dances, pedestal dances, and the softshoe. Blacks are billed as "genuine colored minstrels," often with the name "Georgia" or "Alabama" as part of their title. The plantation is their domain, and jigging and buck dancing are their style.

It is unfortunate that various historians fault the black minstrel for stepping into the stereotype. What else was there to do? The white power structure dictated the terms of entry. We could even perceive the convention of black minstrels blacking up as an ironic and rather snide comment on this power play. It makes sense for blacks to black up for minstrelsy, to parody these alien stereotypes. By the act of masking they, like whites in blackface, are taking on a role and creating for themselves some measure of distance from the stereotype. Like African Americans doing the "Cakewalk" and simultaneously imitating and parodying whites, it is a way of changing the joke to slip the yoke. Paradoxically, the burnt cork was a monolithic mask that could impart an anonymity — if not a measure of freedom — to the black minstrel. (Thus, as mentioned earlier, Bert Williams and many other African American male performers continued to perform in blackface after they left the minstrel stage.) Most important, it offered him a salary, which is, in the end, what being a minstrel was all about. African Americans tried to adjust that image in any way possible. They quoted from reviews that compared them favorably to white minstrels; they billed themselves as "the real thing." They tried, in a severely hostile context, to save their jobs and their skins, with saving their dignity as a third runner-up — although it was still in the running. As Winter (55) points out, the black minstrel would be out of work if he failed to fit in to the mold already cast for him. African Americans accepted this role and wore the mask so as to move in the white theater world "with safety and profit" (Huggins 1971, 261). Thus, if they helped to enforce the stereotype, blacks did so from very different motives than whites. For example, blacks may have emphasized their links to the plantation as a way of attracting audiences. However, it was the white backers who then took this starting point and advertised these largely Northern, largely free, and frequently middle-class men, like Bland, not as performing artists, but as plantation "darkies" demonstrating, on the minstrel stage, who they were and how they had lived just a short time ago when they were happily enslaved. With white managers at the helm and white minstrels moving away from plantation material, black minstrels stereotyped the stereotype by imitating the imitation. Minstrelsy was the vise that locked the image in place. It is most demeaning for any performer to have one's talents unrecognized as skills, but packaged and sold as natural behavior. It may be at this point in American history that the stereotype of the African American as possessor of "inborn" talent and rhythm — genes, not genius[24] — takes hold.

AFRICAN AMERICAN MINSTRELS

In reviewing 1870s and 1880s issues of the *New York Clipper*, it becomes evident that by the time African Americans were firmly ensconced as minstrels, this important theatrical publication (the nineteenth-century equivalent of *Variety*, as far as its theatrical function was concerned) no longer took a major interest in the form. In earlier days, from the 1840s to the Civil War era, feature articles and long obituaries on white minstrels appeared in the "City Summary" and other sections of the paper. By the 1870s, minstrel activity was reported principally in a special column on "Negro Minstrelsy," and seldom was an individual African American minstrel given more than a sentence or two. It was as though they didn't count as individuals. (This attitude may result from the assumption that black talent was inborn and thus unindividuated.) In 1879 the publication began a special feature, in addition to the less frequent "Negro Minstrelsy" columns, titled "Minstrelsy's Mementoes." White minstrels were "mementoed" with front-page photographs, feature articles, biographies, and career highlights. African Americans made their way to the minstrel stage without the recognition and panache accorded their white peers. According to Toll's chronology, the year that slavery was abolished marked the formation of five African American minstrel troupes (Simond 1974, 44). White theater owners refused to work with black managers or booking agents.[25] Thus, the only way for a group of black minstrels to get work was to be produced and run by whites. It was not uncommon for white theater personnel who were working with a black troupe to pull rank on the basis of racial superiority and allow no criticism or suggestions from the black performers. This situation meant that the black minstrel was not necessarily in control of his theatrical product. Frequently, whites simply refused to work with blacks at all. And, of course, onstage the shows remained strictly segregated. Sometimes a shrewd manager would book two large minstrel troupes in the same show, a black group and a white group, but keep them separated. There existed some black-managed troupes, but they functioned as filler for the small-time, out-of-the-way locations left unclaimed by white entrepreneurs. (A striking example of this syndrome is the fact that Charles Hicks, the most persistent of the black entrepreneurs, died in 1902 in Surabaya, Java, while touring an African American minstrel troupe; see Toll, 215). Black minstrel managers lacked the capital and the connections that would afford them the scope and fame of white-run companies. One of the arenas allotted to them was the rural, Southern circuit of gillies and carnivals where the audiences might be all black or where minstrels might perform under the jig top for black and white spectators in segregated seating. Even these small-time venues were, with few exceptions, owned, managed, and operated by whites.

A good example of how the black presence in minstrelsy amended the stereotype and moved the genre in the direction of vaudeville is described in the following excerpt from a pamphlet published by the Flushing (Queens) Historical Society (Haywood 1944, n.p.):

Encouraged by his success of the Mastodon Troupe which played London in the summer of 1880, Haverly brought his All Coloured Troupe to England the next year. They opened at Her Majesty's Theatre, London in July 1881. Harry Reynolds has left us a vivid description of his impressions of the first performance of this amazing troupe of all coloured artists: "When the curtain went up on opening night it disclosed on the stage about 65 real Negroes, both male and female, ranging in shades of complexions from the coal black Negro to the light brown mulatto or octaroon. They were of all ages, from the ancient Uncle Toms and Aunt Chloes, smart young coons and wenches, down to the little Piccaninny a few months old nestling in its mother's lap. Their costumes were of the plantation, in a picturesque plantation setting, somewhat reminiscent of the Jubilee Festival Scene from 'Uncle Tom's Cabin,' there were 16 corner men in all: eight bones and eight tambourines arranged in two rows on the stage. A particular feature of their business was the smart manner that they worked together, making a most picturesque display in unison with their bones and tambourines. Jubilee quartettes, and spirituals, interspersed with comic ditties and witticisms by the comedians."

Haverly, the white manager, has expanded and amended the traditional format by including women. The minstrel show described here is more of the "good, clean family entertainment" variety than the risqué male form of earlier days. And, at least in the curtain-raiser, the African American performers are not blacked up.

The advent of the African American minstrel also meant a new audience — African Americans, who responded quite differently to black performers than did white audiences. Blacks — working-class people, by and large, but certainly some of the bourgeoisie as well — turned out in droves. Always ready to change rules, even Jim Crow segregation, if there was a dollar to be made, white theater owners occasionally responded to the huge African American turnout by revoking their racially driven seating restrictions and allowing blacks to sit in the orchestra. The fact that blacks could perform for blacks was one of the conditioning circumstances that allowed the black minstrel to humanize the stereotype and to add Africanist cultural inflections to the standard material. Most important, they were also able to inject their own sardonic, mocking humor into the representations. Both they and their black audiences recognized the mask, knew who had constructed it, and knew how to live outside of it while appearing to live within it — which is what masking is all about. Blacks didn't need to be told that the distorted minstrel characters were not representative of real black people, they knew that. They also knew and experienced racism firsthand, on a daily basis. They had an intimate understanding of the necessity of living in two worlds and utilizing the mask as a survival mechanism. Thus, black laughter at blacks in blackface cannot simply be written off as black self-hatred; it is as much an affirmation and confirmation of common roots and familiar foes. In the context of the black minstrel playing to black audiences, this laughter slipped the yoke, mocked, and thus dominated the master, and exhibited black agency over and above white racism. The irony here is that minstrelsy by blacks and for blacks could be used as an act of defiance, empowerment, or liberation.

The areas in which the black minstrel could exert some agency were in his mode of representation and in the addition of black material to the repertory. By introducing genuine African American religious music into the minstrel format (in the 1870s), the black minstrel changed the course of its development. Both the antebellum white minstrel and the black minstrel expropriated black religious music and dance and created bastardized, burlesque forms for the minstrel stage, but the black minstrel also introduced authentic religious songs. In the paradoxical way that minstrelsy works, this cultural insertion also worked against African Americans. It fed directly into the white stereotype of the superstitious, emotional, childlike, uninhibited black. Like the Clipper description of the African American religious service, the white population — predominantly Protestant, and definitely not of a danced, geocentric religious tradition — regarded Africanist religion as loud, secular and, literally, "far out." Since these practices did not appear sacred in the Europeanist sense, white minstrels had no qualms about appropriating and lampooning them.

African Americans made subtle but important modifications in the traditional plantation material, which was now their exclusive domain (Toll, 234–69). Their plantation scenes and songs did not long for the good old days of slavery and white masters. Instead, the black plantation materials focused on the memories of friends, family, and youth. They continued to draw on earlier emancipation and anti-slavery material that had long been excised from white repertories. Lincoln was praised for freeing the enslaved. Freedom was the difference, and freedom was the theme inserted in the black minstrel's plantation material. Blacks also were instrumental in evolving the military burlesques of earlier minstrelsy into the uniformed marching unit act. Originally a form that lampooned the Civil War black soldier, these routines became a way to combine brass bands, marching units, and virtuosic strutting in a comedic setting. Finally, by developing unique and individual directions in their specialty acts, blacks inserted innovative material in the tired minstrel format, even while they reinforced the stereotype. Billy Kersands exaggerated the large size of his mouth to place in it a cup and saucer simultaneously. James Bland wrote a repertory of songs full of stereotyped, nostalgic "darkies" and strutting Northern dandies that neatly fit the stereotype without challenging it, and made him the most popular African American composer in white-controlled minstrelsy. For

Alex Hunter, billed as the "Old Alabama Slave," the specialty was imitating the sounds of industrial equipment and musical instruments (Toll 251–54). As we review these acts through a late-twentieth-century lens, they look obsequious and ingratiatingly stereotypical. But they paved the way toward blacks exiting minstrelsy altogether and entering a new form of "variety" entertainment known as vaudeville:

Because so many gifted men were able to acquire this experience [minstrelsy] they were able to contribute, directly or indirectly, to the development of musical comedy and the new music called "jazz" in a later era. Moreover, black minstrel stars served as models for black youngsters to emulate. (Southern 269–70)

One of the most important contributions to minstrelsy by African Americans was the insertion of the "Cakewalk" finale during the late minstrel era. This was the first African American dance to gain popularity both as a stage form and a ballroom dance. (Many other black-based dance crazes followed in the twentieth century.) Originally a competition dance performed on the plantation with a corncake as the prize, the dance exemplifies the Africanist tradition of masking, this time, through body language. The black Cakewalkers were mocking the pompous, strutting mannerisms of their masters and mistresses in this dance, but the plantation owners did not catch the gibing drift of their renditions. The body attitudes of the "Cakewalk" are decidedly Africanist and high-affect. The dancer may bend deeply forward or lean far backward, moving from low positions to high kicks. Like all Africanist social dances, it offers ample opportunity for individual idiosyncrasies and improvisations. There is probably some "Can-Can" influence in it, too. The female Cakewalker will occasionally raise the hem of her skirt and use it in an Africanized version of the French dancers' cheesecake style. The dance required a new music and heralded yet another innovation brought about by black minstrelsy—the introduction of ragtime. Just as the "Cakewalk" was a syncopated, stop-time, high-kicking, strutting dance (and it was the syncopation that made it so very different from a dance like the "Can-Can"), the new music was characterized by a syncopated, slow-yet-fast rhythm. This dance, and ragtime music, are representative emblems for the white-black American exchange and the recursive nature of that interaction.

The "Cakewalk" also marks an important addition to the minstrel audience, one that will become a significant, permanent feature in supporting black performers—the white elite. It is the elite who have first license to try the "wild," new Africanist dances, from "Cakewalk" through "Turkey Trot," from "Charleston" to "Lindy" to "Twist." In the black minstrel-vaudeville transition era, this class frequents exclusive black hangouts, like New York's Hotel Marshall, to rub shoulders with black artists. (In a later generation, it will be the white upper crust who come up to Harlem to frequent the Cotton Club and other such spots.) And it is the European elite—of England and France, in particular—who are the first to embrace the African American performers as artists and to take a serious interest in their work. The Josephine Bakers and Freddie Washingtons of the 1920s (Washington is the dancer-actress who supposedly taught the "Black Bottom" to the Prince of Wales) were preceded, as early as the 1870s, by the Fisk Jubilee singers, who performed for the English royal family, as did Bert Williams and George Walker at the turn of the century. By the 1930s and 1940s, the African American entertainer, after decades of initiation, had become a staple in respected European performance milieus. Many African Americans expatriated to cities such as London and Paris. Some assimilated into the native populations.

In his biography of a life in minstrelsy and vaudeville, Tom Fletcher describes several occasions between 1900 and 1910 during which he and his colleagues were invited to play at private, white socials in Manhattan:

One night, in the 1900 period, while entertaining at the home of Mr. T. Suffern Tailor, who then lived on Madison Avenue near 30th Street, and whose guests included Mr. and Mrs. William K. Vanderbilt and Mr. and Mrs. Philip Lydig, my dancing was such a hit that I was engaged by Mr. Vanderbilt to teach him and his wife, the former Miss Virginia Fair. (Fletcher 1954, 123)

The following summer he and his group were invited during the high social season at Newport to the estate of Pembroke Jones to organize a "Cakewalk" contest, with black entertainment, for the guests. With numerous other African American performers, Fletcher worked at private parties in top New York restaurants and hotels, the town houses and summer estates of the elite, and yacht parties on Cape Cod and the then-fashionable Sheepshead Bay.

"Cakewalk" contests became a regular feature in American life at private parties, on the theatrical stage, and in large arenas like New York's Madison Square Garden:

The inside of Madison Square Garden on such occasions was arranged like a race track. The space for the Cake Walkers ran alongside the boxes and loges. Chairs were placed on the floor to mark off the space for the contestants. When the contest music started, first would appear a drum major who would go through a routine with his baton then return to his place as leader. Then the curtain would part and 50 or 60 couples would come from behind the stage on to the floor, prancing and dancing to the tempo of the music. It was very reminiscent of the grand entry at a circus.

The girls' dresses were of all colors. The men wore full dress, clown clothes or comedy costumes with the big checks. When all the walkers were on the floor, then the 50 or 60 couples could all be seen doing different prances and dance steps ranging from buck-and-wing to toe dancing and, in fact, practically everything known to the terpsichorean art. (Fletcher, 105)

The dance was famous and infamous from the 1890s until the advent of World War I and served also as a bridge between black minstrelsy and the transition musicals that led to early black vaudeville. The change from minstrelsy to vaudeville is represented in a group of crossover musical comedies that were composed and produced between the late 1880s and the early 1900s by African American composers-producers such as Bob Cole, Sam T. Jack, J. Rosamund Johnson, Will Marion Cook, Bert Williams, and George Walker. As Fletcher points out, "The Creole Show" (1889) was instrumental in forging the break with minstrelsy. Women had already been introduced in some black minstrel troupes, as had the "Cakewalk." By combining these two elements, the door was open for all sorts of attendant innovations. Jack's production "had a minstrel, first part, with all women in the circle and a woman for the interlocutor. Men were used on the ends to tell the jokes and use the bones and tambos. In the finale of the show they did the Cakewalk" (Fletcher, 103). Including women in the "Cakewalk" finale offered a new potential. Male-female, couple dance improvisations became possible, and "Cakewalk" teams, like the renowned Dean and Johnson, created exhibition specialty forms of the dance. In addition, the introduction of females working the "Cakewalk" together in unison may well have been the origin of the precision chorus line, an invention that was refined and perfected by African American choreographers of the 1900s and the teens[26] (see Chapter 3).

In its final decade of popularity, the "Cakewalk" functioned as a conduit for African Americans to white show business. For an African American to get a job as a Cakewalker in a white circus was a move up the rungs of the entertainment ladder. Around this time (1900–10) a number of African Americans were engaged as Cakewalkers in white carnivals and circuses. This dance also marked a return to American forms after a period of decline. Imported European operettas and variety spectacles had grabbed public attention, filling in the space left by white minstrelsy's decline. The "Cakewalk" craze (followed by the "Turkey Trot," "Black Bottom," "Charleston," and so on) marked a return to popularity of American forms. Now in black hands—even though influenced by minstrelsy's stereotypes and delimited by racial discrimination—Africanist-inflected dance and music forms became (and have remained, into the late twentieth century) the dominant influence on white American popular culture. They replaced the waltz-and-operetta borrowings from Europe with grassroots, Euro-Afro-American fusion forms that, in turn, found their way to Europe and gained popularity there as well.

The "Cakewalk" exhibited the improvisation aesthetic that characterizes so much of Africanist endeavor. It foreshadowed the high-affect, virtuosic style of later fad dances like the "Lindy" and the "Charleston." Improvisation was wide open, as long as one began and ended with the defining steps of the dance. As Cakewalker Willie Glenn explained, steps as varied as tap or Russian dance could be inserted, as long as the dancing couple came together at the finish to strut and prance offstage (Stearns and Stearns 1979, 124). The Russian reference is significant and indicates a new area of appropriation for African American artists. The expressive form of Russian folk dance, with its high-affect shifts from standing high to crouching low and from moving fast to slow—as epitomized in the *kazotsky*, those leg-challenging gestures done in the deep knee-bend pose—corresponded to a similar high-affect, acrobatic, virtuosic style in Africanist dance. Borrowings are most likely to occur when there is some aesthetic correspondence between two traditions.

Bert Williams and George Walker are credited with spreading the popularity of the "Cakewalk." This famous team began as minstrel men. They were instrumental in moving black popular theater beyond minstrelsy into the early vaudeville format through a series of transition musicals they composed, produced, and starred in, with titles like "In Dahomey" (1902), "Abyssinia" (1906), and "Bandanna Land" (1908). In 1903 "In Dahomey" was featured on London stages for seven months. It helped make the "Cakewalk" an international fad. In an article published in London, titled "King Edward and the Negro Opera," we learn that the "Dahomey" company was engaged for a command performance of the musical on the occasion of the Prince of Wales' ninth birthday. (Small wonder that the prince grew up to be a lover of African American performance and, as an adult, was taught the "Black Bottom" by an African American dancer.) The prince's friends, sons and daughters of royalty, were treated to an abridged version of the musical, "to suit the requirements of a children's garden party": "The children were immensely pleased with the funny darkies, the first that most of them had ever seen, but the king and queen were still more amused. The king was especially entertained and laughed until he shook at some of the songs and the cake walk." (n.a., n.p., ca. 1903)

What is particularly interesting, as the account continues, is the level of innovation and social commentary manifested in the show's content. One number satirized European royalty while uplifting African American ethnic consciousness and self-identity. The author of the article comments that those familiar with the song, "Evah Dahkey is a King"

were surprised that George Walker had "the audacity" to sing it before
this "real" king:

> Evah dahkey has a lineage
> Dat de white fo'ks can't compete wid,
> An' a title, such as duke or earl,
> Why we wouldn't wipe our feet wid;
> Fo' a kingdom is our station,
> An' we's each a rightful ruler.
>
> When we's crowned we don't wear satin
> Kase de way we's dressed is cooler. Ho!
> But our power's just as mighty,
> Nevah judge kings by deir clo'es;
>
> (Chorus)
> Scriptures say dat Ham was de first black man,
> Ham's de father of our nation; . . . .
> Ham he was a king, in ancient days, ...

Although today we may react with disdain at the casual use of the
epithet and the exoticized exaggerations in spelling, we would do well to
pay attention to the content of the song, in spite of its objectionable form.
Such material was entirely new to any stage, presented a fresh spin on
African American heritage, and put the cap on the African American
transition from minstrelsy to vaudeville. The daring critique clearly put
blacks and whites, the elite and the disenfranchised, on equal ground.
This is a quintessential example of "slipping the yoke" and amending the
stereotype on the part of the African American minstrel.

The article then discusses the women in the company and recounts
an incident that happened to Walker's wife before she came to London.
It gives us a clue as to why black performers welcomed opportunities to
leave America to perform (and sometimes reside) in Europe:

The Williams and Walker company has a great number of attractive girls of all
shades of color. The leading lady is Ada Overton Walker, the wife of George
Walker. Mrs. Walker is an extremely pretty, graceful, slender woman, whose
dancing was highly appreciated in New York society. It will be recalled that Mr.
Robert Hargous waltzed with Mrs. Walker after a dinner given in honor of Mrs.
Arthur Paget at Delmonico's [a posh New York restaurant]. Some adverse
comment was excited in New York among people who are inclined to draw the
color line severely. Mrs. Walker has no occasion to feel puffed up over that epi-
sode now, for she has been admired and complimented by the King and Queen
of England.

Bert Williams' rendition of the song, "The Jonah Man," was the hit
number for the children. It was so pleasing to little Prince Edward, the

heir-apparent, that he memorized the chorus and amused everyone by singing along in his newly acquired "Negro" accent. Ironically, this "children's favorite" was a proto-blues. Full of innuendo and tongue-in-cheek humor, the Jonah man is "Mr. Bad Luck and Trouble walking on two legs," so to speak:

> For I'm a Jonah, I'm a Jonah man.
> It sounds just like that old, old tale,
> But sometimes I feel like a whale,
> Why am I dis Jonah I sho' can't understand.
> But I'm a good, substantial, full-fledged, real, first-class Jonah man.

Just as the blues is beyond happy or sad, but an indescribable fusion of the two, so also was Bert Williams. In his interpretation of this song and his most famous number, "Nobody," lies the quintessence of the ludic-tragic trope of the Africanist aesthetic: "Whatever character he assumed, left us trembling between hysterical laughter and sudden tears" (Van Vechten 1974, 35).

Danced by four couples in the cast, the "Cakewalk" finale was the climax of the afternoon gala. Although they would look outdated and stereotyped to our eyes, the Williams-Walker musicals depicted African Americans as agents of their own fate and helped crack the minstrel mask (even though, as mentioned earlier, Williams continued to perform in blackface throughout his career). As the Stearnses point out (1979, 121), even the distasteful-sounding early billing that the team used, "Two Real Coons," was not exactly what it seems like today. "Real," not "coons," was where the emphasis was placed. Their title was an effort to make a distinction between themselves and the more demeaning, downright humiliating "coon" characterizations of their white minstrel counterparts. On one occasion, dressed with their usual, impeccable flair, they stopped at the Fifth Avenue home of a renowned, wealthy family, left their calling card, and challenged the residents to a "Cakewalk" contest—a lovely publicity stunt. They performed as a "class act," that is, in dress clothes rather than plantation dungarees. And they were a class act, from start to finish.

There is a wealth of important information to be read from the "Annual Concert, Ball and Cake Walk" illustration. The year is 1898.[27] In examining the illustration, we see an African American couple, not in minstrel garb, but formally attired for a fancy, late-Victorian soirée. Their apparel announces to potential patrons that this will be an evening of high-class, black entertainment. Yet minstrelsy's influence persists. Their facial features, lips in particular, are modified caricatures, and their body stances are exaggerated. The male's hyperextended knees and exaggerated lift of chest emphasize his off-centeredness and increase the arch in his upper and lower spine. Everything in his body language is open and extended. His partner's posture is the opposite: smaller, rounded, and slightly tipped forward from the waist. Theirs is a contained black stereotype, again a possible indication that the evening's fare will be of a more refined nature than that offered at white working-class venues. The location of the event is a Harlem River casino. Harlem was originally an exclusive New York suburb for the white upper crust in flight from the congested, lower-class, immigrant neighborhoods of downtown Manhattan. (African Americans did not begin to inhabit Harlem until about 1910.) Sulzer is a German name. In the Creolized (by cultural borrowings) but polarized (by race, class, caste) mix that was and is Manhattan, Germans like Sulzer and the more renowned Pabst were frequently the landlord class—owners of the clubs, variety theaters, or casinos where whites or blacks were the performers. In addition, the event is sponsored by the Pocahontas Sporting Club. In this era, exclusive white male clubs frequently had sports and/or hunting as their focus. The fact that the *New York Clipper* was a "sporting and theatre" weekly and devoted its issues exclusively to those two leisure activities indicates the intersection of performance, the sporting life, and the upper classes. Often, as in this example, such clubs assumed a Native American name as their title. They also sponsored annual events. The Pocahontas Club may have set aside Easter Monday as the date for its yearly social affair. Thus, these two pieces of information—"Sulzer's Harlem River Casino" and "Pocahontas Sporting Club"—tell us that, most probably, this was a white-sponsored event for a select white audience. (At this stage of history a black bourgeois group would not engage a minstrel show for one of its socials.) Of course, all the entertainers would be black. This convention—all-black performances for all-white audiences—became the norm for the most costly and prestigious forms of African American vaudeville. For example, the Cotton Clubs and Plantation Clubs that cropped up in the 1920s and during the Swing Era of the 1930s and 1940s in American cities, coast to coast, maintained this unique etiquette of segregation. Thus, we see that a white, upper-class private club has hired a pick-up group of African American performers to do a minstrel show for them and to end it with a "Cakewalk" contest.

Continuing our examination and looking at the lineup of acts, we see the mixing of genres that was mentioned at the beginning of this chapter. A pianist billed as the "Black Paderewski" represents the classical repertory, just as "Black Patti" might have done. Also on the lineup are the sentimental songs characteristic of both black and white minstrelsy, including one by James Bland, "Carry Me Back to Old Virginia." There is also a "coon" song and one by Stephen Foster. "Pickaninnies," the staples of early white vaudeville, are included. Choruses of African American children, from ages four or five up to the early teens, these "picks" were generally used as the background chorus for solo, adult acts and wore their hair in little braids or wrapped in bandannas. They were excellent singers and dancers. Many African American performers (including tap artist Bill "Bojangles" Robinson) began their careers as "picks." We see that there will be buck dancing (an early style of full-footed, shuffling dance that was one of the forerunners of modern tap dancing and was a staple in African American minstrelsy). Just as jig dancing was associated with blacks earlier in the nineteenth century, so was buck dancing, a generic name for Africanist dance styles. This, too, became a staple in African American minstrelsy. Some of the day's "Cakewalk" champions are listed on the right side. Like the later "Lindy Hop" contestants in Manhattan's annual Harvest Moon Balls, these dancers enjoyed a moment of fame while they held their titles, and they also had a shot at a professional career. When we look at the bottom of the flyer and see the times posted, we realize that entertainment was indeed a serious industry. Guests had the option of being entertained for longer than an eight-hour workday, if they so desired. This extended, all-night format prevailed right through the Swing Era, when patrons left the Cotton Club or the Savoy Ballroom and had breakfast at dawn before going home to sleep all day. (That custom was cheered on in one of the lines of the song "Lullaby of Broadway," which states that, when Broadwayites say "goodnight," it's actually morning, and the milkman is on the way.)

Finally, we see that this performance includes women. This is a significant point that distinguishes black minstrelsy from its white counterpart. By the time blacks became major contenders in the minstrel field, other forms of variety entertainment that featured females competed with minstrelsy for mainstream attention. The French revue and English music hall traditions were imported to America in the post-Civil War era. Women brought a new dimension to the stage and increased profits. Black minstrelsy readily incorporated women in its format. Their inclusion laid the groundwork for the black transition from minstrelsy to vaudeville. This program, like the "Greatest Colored Aggregation" flyer, is an example of a transitional genre. The minstrel format, personnel, and content show a definite influence by and move toward the vaudeville-variety form.

Now, let us take a brief look at the "Greatest Colored Aggregation" flyer. Here is a typical late minstrelsy-early vaudeville African American show. In an effort to imbue the role of the African American performer with a sense of dignity and to adjust the negative stereotype, the phrase, "Making People Laugh is a Worthy Occupation" is added. A further effort in this direction is the phrase on the right side of the "Sunflower

Coons" depiction, "Most Elegantly Conducted." With jubilee singers
and other "cultured" acts (including opera singers and concert musicians) on its stages, black minstrelsy often functioned as the only available theatrical tool of racial dignity. The "Famous Colored Lady
Sextette" pictured at the bottom probably sang spirituals and other
sweet, uplifting songs. In looking at the names of the performers, we see
that there is a Marie McGee at the bottom and a Garfield McGee in the
minstrel show, probably husband and wife. It is noteworthy that these
females are billed as "colored ladies," a far cry from the common ways of
referring to African American women in that era. This is a program of
"clean," family entertainment with calculated elements of uplift for its
black audiences.

At the other end of the spectrum is one of the last, and biggest, of the
minstrel shows, an 1894–95 Goliath titled "Black America." Not so much
a minstrel show as a human circus (with African Americans as the
"animals" on display), the production billed its players as blacks who
were from the plantation and came up North, not as performers, but as
anthropological artifacts of real plantation life. They did not perform.
Instead, they simply replicated the inborn, natural things they did down
South. The obsession with authenticity was so strong that newspaper
descriptions like the following were not unusual:

The contestants [in the obligatory "Cakewalk" finale] always dressed in the cast-
off refinery of their masters and mistresses, and many humorous features were
introduced. In the performance at the Grand Opera House there will be seen
many costumes which have graced the persons of former slaveowners and
which only have been preserved by the most careful handling by the families of
the present owners. In addition to the features already mentioned, there will be
introduced many of the plantation pastimes never before seen in the North, and
which would never be attempted by other than the original people of the former
land of slavery. (*Black America Scrapbook* II)

Need I point out that we are in the era of the Bill Cody Wild West
Show and other such gigantic spectacles, all of which were based on the
lie of "authenticity?" The African Americans who answered the call and
were cast in this production were New York performers looking for a
legitimate job. Many eccentric and novelty acts were also a part of this
traveling production.

According to a *New York Herald* review (*Scrapbook* I),

George Wilson led the cakewalk last evening, and was master of ceremonies.
The march was across the main floor and up an incline to the stage, where 30
couples danced and pranced about a monster cake to the tune of "Mamie," until
the audience decided which couple was entitled to the reward of merit. . . . Other
grotesque features of "Black America" are buck and wing dancing, illustrative of

a type characteristic in the Southern states before the war; acrobatic evolutions by Slim Davis and others; and an assault-at-arms, with the participants incased in open-end barrels.

Although the African American vaudeville circuit was a viable quotient by the 1920s, black minstrelsy—always small in comparison to its white counterpart—continued as part of Southern and rural medicine shows, circuses, and carnivals into the post-World War II era. Even in the 1920s, when white minstrelsy as a theatrical genre was pretty much dead, most African American performers in minstrelsy and vaudeville, excluded from mainstream white vaudeville circuits (just as they had been excluded from white minstrelsy in the 1830s and 1840s), continued to be managed by whites. Many African Americans who went on to become vaudeville and early jazz or blues artists began in minstrelsy and confirmed what comedian Dewey "Pigmeat" Markham said, about his beginnings (in the minstrel show sections of rural, Southern gillies and carnivals in the early twentieth century): "Everybody was colored except the boss" (Stearns and Stearns 1979, 73).

The minstrel trope and stereotype were carried by American minstrels, black and white, to the far reaches of the globe, where they took hold and endured, particularly in English-speaking regions like England and Australia. In those two places it was the actual blackface minstrel show that persisted and had a life of its own, with native players feeding into the tradition. Both stateside and abroad, audiences tended to regard the minstrel show as representative of authentic African American life. The assumption was widespread and continued, in varying degrees, through the decades of the twentieth century. The power of the stereotype is such that Carl Van Vechten (1974, 37), the sophisticated, urbane New York man-about-town (and the first dance critic for the *New York Times*), who was an advocate of African American culture, did not think twice about writing the following excerpt in 1920:

In *My friend from Kentucky* [sic] some attempt was made to present the Negro as he really is and not as he wants to be on the stage. The first act on a Virginia plantation diffused a general atmosphere of black joy. How the darkies danced, sang, and cavorted. Real nigger stuff, this, done with spontaneity and joy in the doing. A ballet in ebony and ivory and rose. Nine out of ten, nay ten out of ten, of those delightful niggers, those inexhaustible Ethiopians, those husky lanky blacks, those bronze bucks and yellow girls would have liked to have danced and sung like that every night of their lives and they showed it.

It is not so much the racial epithets that rankle. They were the common currency of the day and may help put in perspective the importance of naming, and self-naming, for African Americans. The point is that even a man like Van Vechten could conflate the role assumed by the African American performer with African American values, aims, and outlooks in quotidian life. In doing so he, too, intimates that blacks are dancers and performers by nature, not by work, training, and cultivation of talent.

By the time that Hollywood entered the picture, the minstrel stereotype as the true picture of black offstage life was firmly ensconced in the American psyche. Beginning with the 1927 Warner Brothers release of "The Jazz Singer" (which featured Al Jolson as the Jewish, blackface performer singing the song, "Mammy,"), there were a substantial number of large studio musical productions that featured minstrel numbers, and some of our favorite Hollywood stars blacked up. Films that included blackface minstrel scenes in the spirit of the nineteenth-century stage form (of the cleaned-up, family variety) included "The Hollywood Revue of 1929" (MGM); "Happy Days" (Fox, 1930); "Mammy" (Warner, 1930); "Kid Millions" (MGM, 1935); "Babes in Arms" (MGM, 1939); "Dixie" (Paramount, 1943); "The Jolson Story" (Columbia, 1946); and "Walking My Baby Back Home" (Universal, 1953). These films included stars like Judy Garland, Mickey Rooney, Bing Crosby, and other favorites of the era. There were also a number of films that included blackface acts, even though they were not placed in the context of a minstrel show. Such films included the 1936 "Swing Time" (RKO), supposedly the one time Fred Astaire blacked up; the 1942 "Holiday Inn" (Paramount), with Bing Crosby blacked up as an elderly "Negro"; the 1945 "Dolly Sisters" (Fox), in which Betty Grable and June Haver are made up as pickaninnies for one number, and the Folies Bergère chorines are in blackface. These are just a few samples from a long list of Hollywood examples.[28]

At the same time, across America amateur recreational, social, and theater groups staged minstrel show reconstructions, sometimes as yearly events, for family and friends. Any number of white fraternities staged minstrel shows well into the 1960s as their annual variety performance. How-to books on the finer points of blacking up, plus books of stump speeches and jokebooks were religiously followed by amateurs in nostalgic recreation of "the good old days."

However, what has proven to be the most insidious level of minstrelization, from the Africanist perspective, is the way in which that influence has persisted in nonminstrel cultural forms. Let us close this chapter with only a few such examples from our century. Proceeding chronologically, one of the most significant markers of this syndrome is D. W. Griffith's 1914 pre-Hollywood film, "Birth of a Nation," a paean to racism and white Southern supremacy, in which the villain, and all the black characters, lowly and subservient, are grotesquely played by whites in blackface. Another example, this one cast in the cosmopolitan dressing of Jazz Age Paris, is the 1925 poster for the Revue Nègre at the fanciest of French vaudeville houses, the Théâtre des Champs-Élysées. The modified female stereotype in the illustration is based on Josephine Baker, who was featured in the program. Like the minstrels who came before her, Baker made no bones about mocking the role and the mold that had been cast for her—that of savage sex goddess. She lampooned both the role and herself as she played it, just as the minstrel men ridiculed themselves and the stereotypes in which they were cast. However, despite the Art Deco allure of the poster, the minstrel taint remains.

The Third Reich made ostentatious use of the stereotype in their anti-African, anti-Semitic cover for the "Degenerate Music" (*Entartete Musik*) section of their larger exhibition, "Degenerate Art" (*Entartete Kunst*) which traveled through Nazi Germany from 1936 through 1939. This exhibit was seen by several million Germans and was the most-attended exhibit in history. The conflation of Jews and Africans as minstrels was disseminated throughout Germany. Let us remember that those assumptions are not limited to the Germans, or to the Third Reich.

It feels fitting to bring us close to our own era with a final recollection, this one from the late 1970s avant-garde theater movement in Manhattan. A downtown ensemble, the Wooster Group, launched a minstrel show, a satirical blackface production meant to be on the cutting edge of confrontational theater. A hue and cry went up from local African American stage professionals that this white group, regardless of its politics, put on the black. Why? Because none of us, as Americans, are distanced enough from the minstrel stereotype, or sophisticated enough in our understanding of racial politics and our own internalizations of racism, to pull minstrelsy out of the hat as though we know how to wield it. It was and is an explosive. That we are not free of it, black or white, was the point and focus of the African American protest. And still we are not free. With or without burnt cork, onstage and in life, in America and in Europe, minstrelization of the black image persists.

NOTES

1.   I use the term "minstrelsy" (or, on occasion, "blackface minstrelsy") to denote the popular nineteenth-century American entertainment form in which the performers, black or white, used burnt cork to blacken faces and hands (and, generally, red, exaggerated make-up to enlarge and emphasize the lips). The terms "white minstrel(sy)" or "black minstrel(sy)" refer specifically to white or black eras in the genre.

2.   The Amos and Andy phenomenon is one of the clearest examples of minstrelsy's convoluted legacy. This stereotyped "black" duo was originally depicted by whites in blackface. When they gave up the roles, two African Americans stepped into their shoes — blacks playing whites playing blacks.

3.   Toll (1974, 40) quotes a typical white minstrel joke: "'Why am I like a young widow?' a comedian asked. After the line was slowly repeated, he fired back, 'Because I do not stay long in black.'"

4.   Rourke (1931, 79–80) recounts a bizarre anecdote about the American stage actor Edwin Forrest who, in Cincinnati in the 1820s, "made up for the part" of a Southern plantation black. He strolled the streets this way. Supposedly, an aged black woman mistook him for a (black) acquaintance and, as the legend goes, he invited her to join him onstage that evening "in an impromptu scene."

5.   The following biographical data are taken from the Lincoln Center Library Dance Collection holdings:

Mura Dehn, born in 1902 in Odessa, Russia, is most widely known for her study and documentation of African American social dances in the United States, epitomized by her film, "The Spirit Moves." While studying and performing modern dance in Europe in the 1920s she was exposed to jazz dance and moved to New York in 1930 to pursue her interest. . . . and eventually formed a company with James Berry [outstanding African American tap artist who, with his two brothers, formed the popular Swing Era flash tap act, the Berry Brothers] to promote jazz dancing [the Jazz Dance Theatre or Traditional Jazz Dance Company].

6.   A noteworthy New World inversion-parallel to this trend is cited by Stuckey (1994, 65). He points out that the Pinkster king—the chief celebrant in the eighteenth- and early nineteenth-century African American celebration known as Pinkster (a term probably derived from the Dutch name for Pentecost)—"by the [American] revolutionary period had donned the attire of the harlequin."

7.   Here Dehn is describing Europe as a Creolized culture, a condition that Europeans and European Americans may attribute to other cultures but rarely their own (Correspondence with Lawrence Levine, May 1995).

8.   See the introductory note to Ellison's essay, "Change the Joke and Slip the Yoke," which was written in response to an essay by Hyman on the relationship between African American literature and folklore. (Stanley Edgar Hyman, "American Negro Literature and Folk Tradition" [1958]. In *The Promised End: Essays and Reviews, 1942–1962*. Cleveland, O.: World Publishing, 1963, 295–315.)

9.   In the same breath and on the same note, I would also mention Sterling Stuckey's (1994, 61–63) challenge to Shane White's interpretation of the Pinkster celebration in Albany, New York.

10.   Both Jews and the Irish (and, for a time, Germans) were considered not of the white race at various times in English and American history. See Szwed (1975, 254–55) and Hentoff (1987).

11.   See, for example, Dena Epstein (1977) and Eileen Southern (1971).

12.   The "where is Egypt," and "who is Africa" debates are longstanding. Egypt is on the African continent and has deep roots in African culture, through its Kemetic, Nubian history. As an entity, Egypt itself is a microcosm of the vast degree of difference represented on its mother continent.

13. This phrase was used by historian Bernt Ostendorf in discussing minstrelsy with the author, January 1995.

14. A controversy has developed around Emmett's claim (and the world's assumption, for over a century) to authorship of the song "Dixie," the implication being that it was written by African Americans. See Howard L. Sacks and Judith Rose Sacks, *Way Up North in Dixie: A Black Family's Claim to the Confederate Anthem*. Washington, D.C.: Smithsonian Press, 1993.

15. Winter (1948, 54) suggests, "after Botkin," that the *danse aux chansons* of American play-party games had "songs often sung by the nondancing part of the party to mark the rhythms—much, it might be added, after the fashion of patting out the rhythm in Negro dances."

16. See also Eileen Southern's fine documentation of the Africanist influence in the antebellum South (1971). She gives a sense of the ineluctable way in which this influence shaped and changed the American landscape.

17. Abrahams, in conversation with the author, October 1992. A description by Southern (1971, 168) sets a precedent for Abrahams' contention and illustrates how Africanist rhythm, percussion, and syncopation were introduced into playing the fiddle, once blacks appropriated this instrument: "'The fiddler sang and stomped his feet as he played, the boy handling the needles all the while.' An expert fiddler 'could stomp the left heel and the right forefoot and alternate this with the right heel and the left forefoot, making four beats to the bar.'" (Knitting needles were used like drumsticks to beat out a rhythm on the violin strings.)

18. Southern (1971, 169) quotes a nineteenth-century source who states that the enslaved Africans danced as though "they had steam engines inside of them, to jerk them about with so much power; for they go through with more motions in a minute, than you could shake two sticks at in a month." And, according to Southern:

Slaves were very proud of their dancing prowess, and generally considered the "measured, listless and snail-like steps" of the society cotillions much inferior to their lively reels and jigs. . . . Holiday dances were generally all-night affairs. When the fiddler grew tired, the slaves provided a different kind of dance music by "pattin' juba." Basically, this procedure involved foot tapping, hand clapping, and thigh slapping, all in precise rhythm (168).

19. Neil Hornick, an English colleague, informed me that the term "jigajig" was slang for sexual intercourse when he was growing up in London in the 1950s.

20. Stuckey (1994, 59) asserts that African Americans may have inadvertently had a hand in the creation of the minstrel stereotype. He contends that, during the Pinkster festivities and in their efforts to amuse white spectators, enslaved Africans may have strained and "faked mirth" to the point of grotesquerie: "There is no reason to think that whites thought otherwise [of blacks as anything but happy], *for slaves found it safe not to be viewed as unhappy, so why not wear the mask when going about serious business as when simply making merry?*" (emphasis added).

21. Breakdown (like the terms "jig" and "buck dancing") is a loosely applied generic term for vernacular black dance forms. It can be used to mean breaking out, in individual improvisation, from whatever pattern or step is on the floor at the moment. It indicates a process more than a particular step.

22. See Lott (1993, 20), quoting Twain on the "happy and accurate" characterizations of minstrelsy, and in a convincing argument that mentions Whitman's racism (characterized by Lott as "ambivalence") and his (early) regard for minstrelsy as representative of African American life (78–79).

23. Sterling Stuckey, in correspondence with the author, May 1995.

24. A phrase used by Lawrence Levine in conversation with the author, March 1995.

25. For a full treatment of the ups and downs of black efforts at ownership and management, see Toll, 202–15.

26. Instrumental in this invention was producer J. Leubrie Hill and the phenomenally talented cadre of African American dance artists whom he assembled to create the "Darktown Follies." This musical opened in 1913 at Harlem's Lafayette Theater. Versions of it played to both black and white audiences through the 1915–16 season (see Chapter 3).

27. Thanks to Kathy Peiss (History Department, University of Massachusetts, Amherst) for date confirmation.

28. Many thanks to Neil Hornick for researching this information.

7

DANCE AND THEATER IN A MULTICULTURAL CONTEXT: WHO STOLE THE SOUL, WHO TAKES THE "RAP," OR FREE TO BE YOU AND ME?

STRIPPING THE "MULTICULTURALISM" EMPEROR

Manhattan is remarkable. One day I arrive in the city from Philadelphia, leave Pennsylvania Station at Thirty-Fourth Street, take the Seventh Avenue subway to Forty-Second street, and proceed to take the old BMT line (now called the "N" and "R" trains) downtown as I head for the Museum for African Art in Soho. Walking in front of me is a young couple engaged in animated conversation. He is black. Attached to his fashionable leather knapsack are yellow beads (indicating worship to Oshun, a Yoruba female deity), a red Action-AIDS ribbon, and a black and red (Malcolm) X pin. She is white. They are emblematic of the urban mix. This decor sets the stage for the intercultural vignette that follows.

There is an itinerant musician installed on the platform, this time not the usual violinist, percussionist, or reed player, not even a master of electric guitar. The middle-aged, Afro-Latino man plays acoustic guitar and is singing a song that sounds like a Spanish love ballad. His rendition is truly beautiful. He pours himself into it. The passengers in transit listen in that tolerant, nonchalant, but friendly way that is characteristic of Manhattan where, in spite of endless reports to the contrary, people rub shoulders, live side by side with difference, and obviously enjoy the mix. As he rasps on and finishes in a deep, caressing croon, I am the only one who applauds, thus setting myself apart as a tourist, a role that I savor on these visits to my hometown. Nonetheless, others obviously appreciate the performance and drop their contributions in the open guitar case at his feet. A mellow mood now pervades the contact zone at this end of the platform.

After my applause, a woman standing next to me on the platform says, with a heavy accent, "It is Russian song he sings!" And I think,

How about that for intertextuality! The Russian woman and I sit next to each other on the downtown local. Instant and transient camaraderie is another occasional experience of mine in Manhattan. In spite of its reputation as tough and cold as steel, this city has provided me with more friendly, no-strings-attached interactions than many another American or European venue. I ask her about the song. She tells me its title, "Dark Eyes," and adds that it is a folk song or romance. Her final piece of information is that he sang it in a "very unorthodox" way.

This scene invites the question of what belongs to whom and what is Other. To use George C. Wolfe's marvelous phrase, it shows how much "we are all up in each other's Other" (quoted in Pottlitzer 1994, 8). But, then, this is Manhattan, and this island city is a world in and of itself, one that has an infectious potential for accepting and celebrating difference. It has never been a reliable barometer of America. Yet, at the same time that it invites magical contacts between its diverse populations, it fosters a host of racial problems. In my middle age I am acutely aware of how these public sites can be beautiful one moment or ugly the next due to chance encounters and random circumstances on this overpopulated, tight little island. I am always grateful to catch it at a good moment.

Growing up in Harlem in the 1950s, I was blissfully unaware of any racist incidents happening directly to me or my friends and family. In my young mind racism lived "Down South." The Emmett Till lynching, the white supremacists who made my mother unhappy with her Democratic Party, segregated public facilities—all these and much more belonged to the South, not to my beloved Borough of Manhattan. But there was, of course, a lot that happened to me that I simply wasn't aware of, and a lot that my mother did not discuss in order to protect her children.

I attended city public schools all the way through college (and I regarded my alma mater, City College, as another public school), and all my teachers were white. Most were Jewish. This was a time when Jewish holy days were not legal holidays; when Ethel and Julius Rosenberg were tried and executed as Communist spies (I went to junior high school with one of their sons, whose life cause has been the exoneration of his parents); when Herman Wouk wrote *Marjorie Morningstar*, and Jewish girls got nose jobs and straightened their hair. In other words, Jews were not an accepted and assimilated part of the American mainstream. An earlier generation of African American New Yorkers was in daily contact with the Irish. Margot Webb, the African American vaudeville dancer whose career was the centerpiece of my doctoral dissertation, went to Harlem public schools populated by black children and Irish faculty and lived, in her pre-Harlem early childhood, in the impoverished Irish/African American tenement neighborhoods of Manhattan's Lower West Side. This was also the Irish-black connection for Oliver W.

Harrington, the Bronx-bred African American who became the creator of "Bootsie," the comic strip that was famous from the 1930s through the 1960s and was carried by African American newspapers nationwide. Harrington and Webb had had openly racist experiences. And Harrington, as an African American male, was regarded as more of a threat than Webb or I:

The year was 1919, when one of Miss McCoy's students began drawing caricatures of her being devoured by ravenous tigers, run over by speeding trains on the New York Central Railroad tracks or rammed into a meat grinder at the local butcher shop. A seven-year-old student penciled the violent images of his South Bronx teacher's demise after being ordered to the front of the room with the only other Black child in the class. McCoy then pointed her finger at the boys and declared, "Never, never forget these two belong in the trash." (n.a. *Emerge* 1994, 14)

This quote gives a taste of Harrington's coming of age. He left the United States in 1951 and lived in Paris, Sweden, England, and finally in East Berlin, where he was when the Berlin Wall went up. After it came down, he chose to stay. In 1919 and in the 1990s, African American males are thought of as trash. Hip hop artists, perhaps the cartoonists of the music trade, are the current objects of disaffection. Many of them grew up in the same area where the seven-year-old Harrington received his first racial knocks. In 1919 and in the 1990s we Americans are in a dilemma. The way we name it may help us to resolve it, for there is power in naming and power in the word, power already in the assertion of naming—not only in *how* we name but in *who* does the naming. Some of the contact zones shared by our forebears, like slavery, have been as bad as their names. What about a name like "multiculturalism?" Does it help us? What's in a name? To create an operative, functional multicultural context would require the move from a universalist, Europeanist ideology to a pluriversal approach. It would mean accepting the fact that spheres of difference are real; that equality does not mean sameness; that people of color may be Other to Europeans, but white is Other to others. It would mean living with difference but understanding that difference does not have to breed hostility. As Molefi Asante stated (1991), our nation could be united by bona fide multiculturalism because the occasion for past grievances to continue to wound would be lessened, should African Americans have even some of their needs for power-sharing fulfilled.

It is remarkable how the multicultural discourse was so quickly diverted from politics and economics and limited to culture. The definition of the term has been whittled down and severed from its potential for political and economic change. It is cheaper and easier to discuss education and the arts than to look at the basic issues of property, jobs, and ownership. But there is no shying away from the fact that the multicultural question is a political time bomb whose moment will come, whether we like it or not, whether we accept it or not. Literal and figurative borders of all kinds have become contact zones where opposites are obliged to meet. The question is: Are we willing to share power? What happens if we assume that power is never shared, only wrested or otherwise acquired? Typically, the contact zones between Africans and Europeans (not even factoring in other peoples) in the Americas have been unequal meeting places, with one side of the equation submerged by strategies of invisibilization, misnaming, and/or erasure. The contact happens in many different arenas, as mundane as clothes, hair, and food, and as "highbrow" as art. Taking the television sound bite as our model, let us quickly glance at a pocketful of examples, all taken from the media in the 1990s, although some readers may assume that I made them up:

1. Take two guys as different as David Duke, white supremacist from Louisiana running for elected office in the 1990s, and Michael Jackson, black superstar, both undergoing plastic surgery and skin stripping, reinventing their noses and faces so as to fit the dominant, Europeanist image. Then take the flip side of this coin: the numbers of white youth sporting dreadlocks, braids, and wrapped hair. Factor in the persona of a rapper-turned-television star, Fresh Prince, cleaned up and "whitenized," if you will, to fit the homogeneous television sitcom formula—an added twist to the "if we are all equal, then we all must appear the same" mentality. Then include a group of white male rappers who look, act, and talk like black male rappers and name their group "The Young Black Teenagers." Add to this identity snafu the white female fad of surgical lip implantation to make lips fuller—or blackenized, if you will. Conclude this bite with the 1994 marriage of Michael Jackson and Lisa Marie Presley and title the whole package "Annals of American Identity: Free to Be You and Me?"

2. Flash back to the 1992 Democratic National Convention. In the instant feedback after Senator Bill Bradley's speech, one of the commentators declared that the senator had "missed the big issues" when, in fact, Bradley singled out race conflict as the big issue facing Americans.

3. Recall the videotape of the Rodney King beating, the two trials, the two juries—two policemen freed, and two planning appeals. On the flip side, imagine the other much-publicized video of four African Americans beating a white man, and the outcome of their trial.

4. Recall a cross-burning on the lawn of a home owned by African Americans in a white neighborhood in St. Paul, Minnesota. That act, considered a misdemeanor by city ordinance, was condoned by the Supreme Court, in a decision led by Justice Antonin Scalia, which ruled that punishment of this and similar deeds violates the First Amendment and thus is unconstitutional. Then recall the brouhaha raised by the then-presidential nominee Bill Clinton as he nationally denied rap artist, Sister Souljah, her freedom of speech

for her admittedly sharp but ironic words, which Clinton misrepresented and quoted out of context. (Souljah was not giving a personal opinion but ironically describing what she saw as the attitude of those involved in the Los Angeles uprising when she said, "Why not have a week and kill white people? [Mills 1992, 20]. Stereotyping of rap artists as societal outcasts and would-be cop-killers, plus distorted media reportage are the main culprits that prompted Clinton's miscalculation.) Next, picture the likes of Manhattan socialite-millionairess Brooke Astor describing Sister Souljah as "a lovely young woman." The improbable pair "really bonded" while seated next to each other at a literary panel discussion in New York. To wind up this one, think about adolescent hip hop enthusiast Jake Hoffman, son of Dustin, asking Salt-n-Pepa (risqué female rap artists) to perform at his bar mitzvah. The duo turned him down.

5. Now, jump-cut to the 1993 movie, "Batman Returns." Check out the scene in which Catwoman graffiti spray-paints her clothes and apartment, and the one in which Batman, like a perverse MC, scratch-grooves a record on the moving turntable as he "fakes out" the Penguin.[1]

6. Imagine a report on KYW-AM, Philadelphia's all-news radio station, around the time that Spike Lee's controversial film on Malcolm X opened at local movie houses. The reporter recounts the following incident: Someone driving by a video rental store in Lilly, Pennsylvania (read Small Town, USA), calls the police and reports that an armed (black) man is robbing the store. Six state policemen arrive with guns drawn and encounter at the entrance a life-sized, cardboard cut-out of actor Denzel Washington, holding a gun — a promotional gimmick for his film, "Ricochet." Police confiscated the paper doll "in order to prevent any future cases of such mistaken identity."

7. Think about a student in a deep-Dixie whistle stop called Wedowee, Alabama, being told by her high school principal that her parents, an interracial couple, had made a "mistake" by having her.

8. Finally — and this one comes from experience — think about a group of undergraduate students who, asked by their teacher at Temple University to divide into two groups, divide into one black and one white group.

Cultural expropriation, denial, insecurity, disenfranchisement, legislated inequality, anger, arrogance, stupidity, fear, hatred of self, hatred of others — these examples run the gamut and include all of the above. And they bring us back to the question of power: Who are the haves and the have nots, and how do they negotiate a contact zone or border meeting? When we strip the multicultural emperor of his elaborately worded, politically correct disguise, we find that, for African Americans, the naked issues of power and agency are the same old ones, now updated and masked in postmodern make-up.

POWER

If you piss in my face, I'm gonna call it piss. I'm not gonna call it rain (The Reverend Al Sharpton, quoted by Anna Deavere Smith, "Fires in the Mirror," 1992).

If the USA is a melting pot, either the Negro never got in or he never got melted down. (Thurgood Marshall, Liberty Medal acceptance speech, Independence Hall, Philadelphia, July 4, 1992)

This object in which power is inscribed from time immemorial is language. Or to be more precise, its necessary means of expression: the tongue we speak. Language is a sort of legislation, the tongue we speak a legal code based on it. We do not observe the power contained in our tongue, because we forget that any tongue is a form of ordering, and that ordering is oppressive. (Roland Barthes, quoted in Goodson 1987, 40)

Word. In the beginning was The Word. Words set to rhythm are like gravy on meat: The sum is greater than the parts. For two decades a host of performers like Afrika Bambaataa, Grand Master Flash, Public Enemy, De La Soul, Queen Latifah, Gangstars, Digable Planets, and others have looked at our American dilemma through the lens of a revolutionary form that unites words with rhythm. The name of their form is rap, or hip hop, and it is all about power and the use of the word: in deconstruction jargon, *la parole*; in Africanist aesthetic terms, *Nommo*. I begin this discussion with rap because this contemporary form of sociopolitical art song (which, I believe, Bertolt Brecht would appreciate) — misrepresented by the media and misunderstood by various class, ethnic, gender, and age groups — symbolizes, in form and content, the big issue raised by multiculturalism: Who's got the power? Hip hop's aggressive, youthful, Africanist, deconstructionist, postmodern form and its political, sexual, often derogatory content are equally anti-establishment and indicate a huge American population who know they are the underdog and do not give a damn about becoming a part of the mainstream. Country music uses conservatism and traditionalism as its marketing ploy; rap is best described by words like "radical" and "outlaw." "Country" and "rap" function as code words for "white" and "black" and tell us how far away we are from a multicultural context. Rap quickly caught on as a sexy topic for cultural scholars. I like it because of the direct way it challenges conventional agency. It is a vital form of protest theater and a good entry for opening up the politically charged question of power to other areas of onstage and in-life performance.

Rap attracts first by its rhythm and then by the word. Giving definition to poetry, music, drama, and song through the ages, word and rhythm are instruments of personal or group power and cultural identity. Word travels fast. Rap music quickly spread from its neighborhood roots and by the mid-1980s had crossed class, gender, and ethnic borders and seduced a generation of young Americans, vying with punk, rock, and country music for popular hegemony. When the big scandal arose in 1993 around the release of Ice T's rap, "Cop-Killer," it was clear why the record was such a threat. Suburban white Americans are the largest consumers of the commodity known as "Gangsta Rap." The trend for whites to become large-scale audiences for black entertainment dates back to the minstrel show era of the nineteenth century and peaked again in the Swing Era, when whites trekked to Harlem to attend cabaret parties, ballrooms, and Cotton Club revues, to dance the "Charleston" in one decade and the "Lindy" in the next. In the 1990s neighborhoods are polarized to such a degree that whites and blacks avoid one another's turf. Since whites can no longer come to "the 'hood," it has to come to them:

America has transformed into this one big hood. You can get carjacked anywhere. You can buy dope anywhere. You can buy a Mac-10 any motherfuckin' where. You get killed any motherfuckin' where. You understand what I'm sayin'? There are crack houses all over America. (Schooly D, quoted in Jackson 1994, 13)

If Gangsta Rap is a matter of art imitating life, then rapper Schooly D's statement points to the reverse as that style moved to the suburbs from its place of origin. However, Gangsta Rap is not the subject of this discussion; neither is it the most widespread, creative, or representative category of hip hop music. There are other more compelling varieties in the genre: Arrested Development's "life music"; the jazz-inspired positivism of A Tribe Called Quest; the Afrocentric style of Digable Planets, Brand Nubian, and Nefertiti; the politically radical work of Public Enemy; the womanist raps of Queen Latifah; the gospel-like paean to black womanhood and call to "keep on keepin' on" in Tupac Shakur's "Keep Ya Head Up." Digable Planets cogently quip that they "be" to rap as key "be" to lock. As a matter of fact, hip hop may be like liberation theology to a certain generation of Americans. Artists like Rappin' 4-Tay and B.I.G. (also known as Biggie Smalls) were diverted from crime in the streets by the intervention of rap in their lives. The former honed his skills by rapping all day in his cell at San Quentin State Prison while serving a sixteen-month term (Wilson 1995, 34). B.I.G. gave up drug dealing and, as soon as he was a contracted artist, brought his "crew" along with him to the legitimate world of the music industry: "We was all doin' illegal shit, but one person out of the crew got in here, so that's my job now—to drag everybody in" (Jamison 1995, 64). Long Islander Craig Mack (earlier known as MC EZ) was rescued from homelessness and a life on the streets by clinching a record deal.

Some hip hop artists are Sunni Muslim or belong to the Nation of Islam. For others, traditional African American spiritual values infuse their philosophies, if not their lifestyles or lyrics. One of the songs on Mack's album, "Project: Funk da World," is titled "When God Comes." About it he states, "It's like Jesus put his hand on the back of my head, and I just started writing" (Valdes 1995, 51). According to reggae toaster and rapper Jamalski, "I'm trying to get across all types of messages. . . . It's not like I get deep into like Biblical details or anything. I talk about how I don't need a 9, how I don't need an uzi. I have this spiritual magnum, a metaphysical gun to shoot down negativity" (Greenleigh 1994, 81). There are many examples of the transformative influence of rap on young black lives that can be presented to counter the negative image. Still, rappers are not saints. I do not condone the misogyny in some rap songs, but something needs to be understood. By definition, rappers are not model citizens. Their commodity is the opposite; they are outlaws. They are not better, but badder, in the hip sense of the word. They represent a generic rebellion against the powers that be, and outrageousness is integral to their identity. So far, this description is not unusual for twentieth-century American youth. The big difference is that they are black, and here is where the issue of power clicks in. Black rebels are destined to take more heat than whites. Rappers are perceived as outlaws not chiefly from their status as rebellious youth, but because they are vociferous representatives of the African American underclass. Masta Ace, Incorporated (1994) succinctly addresses this issue in a rhythmically brilliant rhyme sequence in "Born To Roll," a rap about an African American male behind the wheel who blasts his car stereo as he drives through city streets:

> I wonder if I blasted a little Elvis Presley
> Would they pull me over and attempt to arrest me
> I really doubt, doubt it, They'd probably start dancin'
> Jumpin' on my tip an' pissin' in their pants an'
> Wigg'lin' an' jigg'lin' an' grabbin' on they pelvis
> *But you know my name, so you'll never hear no Elvis.*[2] [emphasis added]

Punk rockers like Sid Vicious, Siouxie Sioux and Ron Asheton of the Stooges dared to wear Nazi uniforms onstage, but most Americans didn't hear a peep about it. Dave Marsh, the biographer of Marvin Gaye, had this to say about the insidious double standard:

An expression of racism doesn't always require a robe and hood; it often manifests itself as an ethnic double standard. Imagine how the rapper Ice Cube would be denounced for a song about drunkenly disrupting an old girlfriend's wedding and threatening the groom, then setting out on a bender with his crew.

That's exactly the story line of Garth Brooks's "I've Got Friends in Low Places," an anthem for country-loving teenagers. Yet Mr. Brooks isn't seen as a dangerous instigator of social irresponsibility. Unlike rappers, Mr. Brooks doesn't threaten. (1992, 20)

The many rap songs that address the need for social change are largely ignored by the powers-that-be who are outspoken in condemning the artists and their record labels, but may have little understanding of the social conditions and policies that rappers critique.

> Black Boy, Black Boy, turn that shit down
> You know that America don't wanna hear the sound
> Of the bass-drum-jungle-music — go back to Africa
> Nigger, I'll arrest you if you're holdin' up the traffic here.

These Masta Ace words go to the heart of the matter. It is not only rap's content that rankles; it is also the form. This genre is all about rhythm, a component that can inspire fear in a Europeanist culture that knew enough about the power of African rhythm to prohibit drumming by enslaved Africans: "The thing that frightened people about hiphop [sic] was that they heard people enjoying rhythm for rhythm's sake. Hiphop lives in the world — not the world of music — and that's why it's so revolutionary." So stated the great jazz percussionist, Max Roach (quoted in Tate 1988, 73). When composer and musician Cecil Taylor was asked what Europe will never understand about African culture, he responded with one word: "Rhythm" (quoted in Tate, 73). There is power in rhythm — Black Power in black rhythm. The Civil Rights protest movement of the 1960s did not use only African American spirituals for inspiration. Black chants like "Beep-Beep, Ungawa, Beep-Beep, Black Power" — a proto-rap, if you will — demonstrated the combination of rhythm and text with the ideology of power. And it is not only the rhythm that raises hackles. It is also the black male dancing body that inspires fear and longing, as it did in the minstrel era, the black Broadway jazz age, the Swing Era of the great black tap artists, and in the present era of dancing rappers.

Hip hoppers, contemporary minstrels if you will, are both "gangstas" and clowns. But they are considerably different than yesterday's minstrels. Indeed, they wear baggy clothes and look and act the fool. Their rhymes are frequently humorous nonsense lines. But they are not about scraping and bowing. They openly exalt the previous generation of African American radicals — Malcolm X and, importantly, their lesser-known brothers who did time in prison — as their role models. The big difference between them and their minstrel forebears is that they are not outwardly humbled by their ludicrousness. Instead, they transform the ludic into the virile. Their clownish, ill-fitting, baggy clothes — oversized "sneaks," layers of socks, and trousers that, in other circumstances, would resemble the clothes of a youngster in an older sibling's ill-fitting hand-me-downs — have become icons of male potency and intimidation. Even their funny-style hairdos — dreadlocks, twists, braids, cornrows — are a testimonial to their transformative powers. These coiffures were reserved for African American women and children. Yet, this cadre of adult males sports them, and they are metamorphosed into signatures of masculinity. What was feminine is made male; what was droll is daunting. In the same vein, rappers have gone far in extolling African American female physical attributes heretofore regarded as inferior, by Europeanist aesthetic standards. Chocolate-black skin, big buttocks, and heft have been redefined as values. (The other side of this coin makes for the paradox: While Africanist female attributes are praised, the black woman is frequently demeaned and objectified, if not abused, in the lyrics.) Hip hop culture reverses and redefines the rules of the game and, in doing so, reconfigures the Africanist aesthetic. This means, of course, that these mavericks are redrafting the Americanist aesthetic. They are moving the mountain of what is deemed beautiful, handsome, elegant, hip, funny, or frightening. The hip hopper is the latter-day incarnation of the trickster, that dangerous, inscrutable, enigmatic quotient in diasporic African religions. It may be that Billy Kersands or some other minstrel man fantasized doing exactly what the hip hopper does: outright and forceful defiance and disdain of the societal and performative boundaries to which he is expected to conform.

> I'll be damned if I listen
> So, cops, save your breath
> And write another ticket
> If you have any left.

Thus ends the "Black Boy" stanza, with Masta Ace declaring their commitment to rebellion. Pumping up the volume is their way of acquiring a power that cannot be wrested from them, regardless of police intervention.

It is important to remember a commonly overlooked fact: Rap and other African American forms of protest art are not solely or principally a reaction to or haven from Europeanist oppression. That assumption is one that cuts off African Americans from their African heritage. Rap's form — the rhythmic base, together with the characteristic signifying, or making ironic, double-edged social and personal commentary through rhymed stanzas or couplets — is African. The concept of *Nommo*, the power of the word, is alive and well in hip hop. Acknowledgment of the connection means opening the door to empowerment. The African heritage shows off its resilience and flexibility in the fact that it can be channeled in so many different ways. Music as a vehicle of power and identity is integral to understanding the Africanist aesthetic and its role in hip hop.

Word. The power of The Word. God as The Word Made Flesh. The Word is God. The power of the word and the power of language can make or break a people. When a speaker is orating powerfully, the African American audience urges her on by exclamations such as "Talk!"; "Tell it!"; "Tell it like it is!"; or, simply, "Word!" Language is an essential cultural reflector. It mirrors the world we live in and, reflexively, it molds our realities. People and systems are not different because of their language but because of their experiences in the world, which made different things important to different people. We can use language to build bridges or barriers. (As an aside I cite the devious language of dehumanization used in the Persian Gulf war: a "Patriot" missile surely has a noble mission; "collateral damage" gives "us" the right to decimate "them" without having to bear the guilt of acknowledging murder; and "friendly fire" exonerates us even when we attack ourselves.)

Let us leave hip hop culture and examine the disempowering potential of language by decoding a review that was published in an internationally distributed dance magazine and written by a European American male about a postmodern dance company whose artistic director and members are African American (from both the United States and the Caribbean). Here is his opening paragraph:

For dancerly directness, simplicity, cohesion, and strict kinetic pleasure, the most rewarding moment in a performance by Garth Fagan Dance occurs during the curtain calls. Neatly lined up across the stage, standing in recognizable First Positions [*sic*], the company bends forward into smooth and unaffected bows. The uncomplicated actions, clearly centered in consistently loose lower backs, give a potently elemental effect: They tell of plumb-line stretch, central force, and plastically easy articulation. (Greskovic 1991, 112)

This introduction, praising the company's post-performance bows, states that none of the criteria that the writer values appear in the performance and that virtually the only "rewarding moment" is after the performance proper is over. Then is the only time that the performers show a clear-cut, linear arrangement. Phrases like "neatly lined up across the stage," "clearly centered," and "plumb-line stretch" tell us that linearity and verticality matter a lot to this writer. He goes so far as to give the phrase "first position" initial capital letters. These value indicators, used to the detriment of Fagan's choreography, indicate that he perceives Fagan's work as though it were bad ballet. The writer uses the language of Europeanist ballet aesthetics (line, form) to discredit and disempower the all-important New York season of this major African American choreographer. But his assumption is a major categorical error ("Major," to adopt his emphatic style) and an example of comparing different languages. The critic or scholar who takes the time to study Fagan's choreography will understand that his work is not based primarily on ballet precepts. (Similarly, although Alvin Ailey's choreography is not founded on the principles of modern dance theorist Louis Horst (see Chapter 4), it has suffered by the skewed calculations of those who use traditional Horstian composition principles of "how to make a dance" as the measure of his work.)

Because Fagan's work consciously ignores the centered verticality of ballet, that standard will not be a value exhibited in his choreography. His canon represents a synthesis of African and European influences, with a strong emphasis on the fluid, articulated torso, which is a prime aesthetic value in African dance forms. It is a forceful, dynamic, and effective marriage of cross-cultural influences. This critic does not see the merger as the measure. Instead, he holds on to the European ballet side of the equation, implying that the African side is lesser because it doesn't uphold that standard. He reinforces this point of view in the next paragraph of the review: "Beyond a pervasive air of unaffected gentility, the company of fourteen tends to bypass the structural niceties of theatrical dancing for the quirky, hard-to-follow idiosyncrasies of Fagan's choreography."

What are the "niceties of theatrical dancing?" Who sets those criteria? Is the critic privy to them, but not the choreographer? Is theatrical dancing meant to be "nice?" The "unaffected gentility" line carries a bit of the "noble savage" trope as an innuendo, although it is updated and masked for a 1990s readership. The implication in these excerpts and, indeed, the rest of the review is that Fagan knows neither the rules nor how to abide by them, but the critic does. However, one can justifiably make a reverse assessment: It is this critic who doesn't know the criteria underlying Fagan's work. To simply characterize it as idiosyncratic is an ingenuous indication of his ignorance. The phrase, "hard-to-follow idiosyncrasies," reveals that the critic really does not know what is going on, how to look at it, or how to write about it. It veers from the only norm the writer knows and reveres, but which the choreography was never meant to obey.

I won't belabor the point. The review continues in this vein; it is demeaning and small-minded. No matter that the review dates back to 1991. Distortions and biases are perpetuated as old-school critics trained in one aesthetic perspective are faced with a panoply of dances that simply do not fit the mold. One of the easiest ways to disempower others is to measure them by a standard that ignores their chosen aesthetic frame of reference and its particular criteria. In examples such as this one, language is the Patriot missile that ensures that the object of scrutiny is demolished.

In Michael Kirby's excellent, thought-provoking article, "Criticism: Four Faults" (1974, 59–68), another kind of misnaming occurs. The point I want to make here was probably unnoticed by European American readers, male or female, and probably was unintentional on the part of the author. To prove that criticism is subjective but that there still exists some consensus regarding aesthetic values, Kirby states that it would be possible to take a poll and ascertain that Marilyn Monroe is considered a beautiful woman in our society. He explains his argument, using the term "woman" to refer to the (European) female who is characterized as beautiful. He states that "the beautiful woman that Rubens painted and the 'beautiful' woman photographed in the last century are quite different from the 'beautiful' woman of today" (61). So far this is okay, even though one would wish that he had not chosen such a sexist example to make his point about cultural and individual aesthetics. Then he claims that, in spite of the "subjective nature of experience," it is still possible to be objective in describing a performance. His choice and framing of an example are what interest me. He states: "If I say that there are three performers on stage, that one of them is a black girl, that none of them is speaking, and so forth, these statements are both value-free and objective" (67). In using the term "black girl," he has used the language of disempowerment in referring to the only African American female mentioned in his essay. All other females—all European—are described as women. His inconsistency shows that even the most innocent, supposedly simple and straightforward language is in fact subjective and value-laden. Mature African American women and men were pejoratively referred to by European Americans as boys and girls until recently. Dancers, too, have been subjugated to the less-than-full-person status of the boys-and-girls terminology. The use of that word undercuts Kirby's illustration of the objective aesthetic and instead points to his subjectivity.

I find this example noteworthy because it comes from a researcher and historian whose work has been about breaking stride with traditional currents. It shows that whether the label is avant-garde or traditional, liberal or conservative, when a Eurocentric standard is universalized as the norm, other values will be misnamed and possibly rated as inferior. Of course, there are examples throughout our culture that are more blatant than these two in illustrating the use of language as a tool that effectively ascribes an inferior rank to the Other. However, gentlemanly manifestations such as these are potentially more dangerous than their screaming counterparts. It is ironic that this seemingly tangential slip (after all, "black girls" were not the subject of the essay) is one of the points upon which one may justifiably hang a refutation of Kirby's thesis regarding objectivity.

Both of these examples involved the written word. Visual images are even more potent. Film and video are powerful languages that can shape the fate of both actors and spectators in a given situation. A good case in point is the near-legendary video of the Rodney King beating. "A picture is worth a thousand words," or so we thought, until the brutal, seemingly straightforward document that all America witnessed via television was deconstructed, reframed, and reinterpreted by clever trial lawyers defending apparently guilty policemen. Offstage and behind the scenes I hear the voice of 1980s Harvard-based critical legal theorists uttering The Word and telling us that legal systems do not represent objective truth, justice, or fairness but are the instruments of received power and hegemony wielded by and for privileged groups:

In the California case, the defense was able in a sense to shift captions on the videotape, to provide a different framework for the seemingly damning images. Defense attorneys not only undercut the stark emotional power of the videotape in question but also suggested a reading of it that shifted the jury's understanding of the scene from one of police brutality to one of self-defense and prudent procedures.

The jury was shown the tape more than 30 times in the course of the trial, projected at various speeds. The tape was even broken down into a series of still frames, each of which was then subjected to lengthy analysis by defense witnesses and attorneys. As a result the defense was apparently able to deaden the impact of the tape, separate it from its reference to reality. (Hagen 1992, 32H)

Two lessons may be learned from this example. First, no evidence is irrefutable; and second, the overweening power of the dominant culture is real. It should come as no surprise that conspiracy and genocide theories are alive and well amongst African Americans—and that a rapper produces a song called "Cop-Killer." This trial and the way in which the video was used provide another kind of evidence: namely, reason to dismiss the principles of analysis and objectivity as instruments of truth on the grounds that they are too frequently the misnamed, sophistic tools of the established power structure. Video manipulation goes hand-in-hand with the computerized maneuvers made possible by high-tech digital techniques as seen in films like "Jurassic Park" and "Forrest Gump." The fact that the jury was able to be convinced by the defense's interpretation indicates the depth of distrust between black and white Americans. The all-white jury sided with the white policemen, in spite of what the prosecution saw as indisputable evidence. Here and in other walks of life, whites side with whites, and blacks with blacks.

What is the antidote? Where is the balance? Can we perceive the world differently and make changes? What chance is there for sharing power? What choices are there? How do we take the first steps? There is little hope if African Americans are perceived as outsiders, and their Word goes unheeded. Where and how do cultural spheres — education, religion, and art — figure in creating a climate conducive to change or, at least, a climate that acknowledges the need for change? Let us look at a sampling of 1990s productions to see how performance artists have dealt with the dilemma.

COLLABORATION

I think that this play ["Angels in America"] is standing centerstage and saying, Oh, you thought America was this. Well, I'm here to tell you that America is this, this, this, this. I'm here to tell you that my story ultimately is your story. That the specifics of my story may require you to surrender your arrogance to go on the journey, but once you surrender your arrogance and go on this journey, you will find yourself in my story. Because we are now at a time in this country when we are all up in each other's Other. There is no "Other" anymore. We'd like to think that there is. We keep on trying to move out and out into the sub-urbs or further and further away, but there is no escape anymore. Everybody is up in each other's story. So it becomes very important that we know the other person's story, the other stories in America so that we can begin to negotiate sharing the watering hole of survival. (George C. Wolfe, quoted in Pottlitzer 1994, 8)

As I see it, the word "multiculturalism" means equality among peoples of diverse ethnic, cultural, gender, and class backgrounds based upon respect, acknowledgment, and the embracing of difference. It is more than a begrudging resignation to the fact that there is no going back to a one-track world. The word reaches beyond its etymological root to imply parity in diversity and proactive power to all parties involved. Given this definition, I do not see that there is much multiculturalism going on in our times. Where can we look for forms that might take us beyond what we know to what we can dream?

From traditional African aesthetics, the principle of call-and-response offers a fine model for coexistence and equal partnership. What is beautiful about this construct is the interdependence, the symbiotic relationship between caller and respondent. Taken together, the two are greater than either one alone — an observation that could go far in informing a multicultural philosophy. In the call-and-response interaction, it can be difficult to tell who is leading and who is following. In fact, the concepts of "lead" and "follow" lose much of the hierarchical connotations attached to them by traditional Europeanist usage. Maybe that is why most African American get-togethers—church services, parades, parties—look and sound so chaotic in comparison with their European American counterparts. When the call-and-response mode is in operation, orderliness and exactitude are lost, but the power of the people is gained. I think of the difference between, say, the Columbus Day parade marching down Manhattan's Fifth Avenue (a parade with lines of people marching in their designated places, with the paraders clearly differentiated from the onlookers, in a military sense of parade) and the Caribbean Day parade in Brooklyn, New York, in which spectators may become paraders at any time. There is virtually no spatial separation between paraders and onlookers in the latter; paraders do not necessarily remain in their assigned places, and participants dance, rather than march. The Caribbean Day parade looks disorderly, but it is a participatory event, as democracy is supposed to be. Call-and-response implies that every part of the community is important to its continuity and richness, that every one has a voice and, through it, the power to act, enact, react.

From the postmodern performance tradition, the movement form known as contact improvisation offers another model for parity (see Chapter 4). On an intimate, one-on-one level, two bodies meet and interact responsibly by conversing in the language of movement improvisation. Ideally, the two people involved in the contact moment have not chosen to work together on the basis of body similarity. The point is to find ways to be responsible for one another's weight, timing, dynamics—body language—in spite of the fact that each body is unique in size, shape, and impulse. The most fulfilling contact moments may occur when two radically dissimilar bodies negotiate the movement medium, improvising wordlessly to experience a mutually acceptable body language that they coinvent and in which they coexist. This act of improvised negotiation constitutes their performance. As in the call-and-response example, this one gives a model for equality-with-difference and living with and negotiating the process of existence. These lessons must be learned if we are to have a multicultural context. Both contact improvisation and call-and-response are forms that reside in the subjunctive world of improvisation. Yes, there is theory to ground them, but it hovers on the periphery and is complete only when realized and vitalized in practice. More than theories, we need practices to emulate as multicultural models.

I want to turn to some particular trends and productions that appeared in the performance arena in the early 1990s. Taking the lead from performance theorist Richard Schechner (1991, 28–31, 135–36), I use the term "intercultural" rather than multicultural. We have not yet reached the point of parity and equality implied by the word "multicultural." "Intercultural" designates performance genres that look at the tensions, frictions, and discontinuities that arise in the contemporary encounter and/or clash of different cultures. I have extended Schechner's definition to include a second category — those performances that are touted as multicultural but seem to perpetuate Eurocultural hegemony. Some performances succeed in what they set out to do; many do not. However, there is always something to learn, even from a failed attempt. We need examples of "how to" but also of "how not to." Although the focus of this study is American performance, I bring into the discussion several European examples, for the sake of comparison, as that continent struggles to come to terms with its particular issues of diversity.

The Native American pow-wow is an interesting example of intercultural collaboration. Tribes with past antipathies are united at these large, seasonal events for a coming-together that, like many intercultural collaborations, is based on necessity. It is a sublime example of cultural survival through adaptation. What had previously been small, sacred, monocultural gatherings have evolved into large-scale, secular, public events. In true intercultural spirit, the pow-wow does not exclude any ethnic group. Thus, non-Native Americans, particularly whites, are welcomed, and a group of European Americans known as "hobbyists" regularly attend these events. In spite of the pejorative sound of the term, these outsiders are not scorned, and those that I have observed take their "hobby" quite seriously. Frequently they are avid students of Native American life, lore, and culture and may actually appear at pow-wows in Native American garb. They may be allowed to perform in selected dances. What is important is that they are not the ones who are calling the shots. The pow-wows are run by intertribal councils and are solidly in Native American control. Native Americans, although nearly decimated by European colonization, brilliantly devised this way to not simply resurrect a cultural relic, but put the old, traditional form to a new use in the service of survival.

"If I could find a white man who had the Negro sound and the Negro feel, I could make a billion dollars," is the claim attributed to Sam Phillips, the man who became Elvis Presley's manager. By the time we reach the 1990s, the same proposition is still potent but, at least in one case, the tables are turned in a significant way. It is a black manager who succeeds in pulling it off. Maurice Starr, an African American, created and produced the all-white, male, singing and dancing pop group, New Kids on the Block. There are a host of interesting aspects to this collaboration. First, New Kid Donnie Wahlberg would dispute the fact that African American culture is not his:

"I don't say that I'm taking from anybody's culture," said Mr. Wahlberg, the Kids' leader and at 20 hardly a kid. "It's what I grew up on. I'm a hip-hop dude. If Maurice [Starr] hadn't done this, I'd probably be making house records" — electronic dance-club music. "Because that's what I like, house and rap. Rap was what I listened to, from the Sugar Hill Gang's 'Rapper's Delight' on; I was in the fourth grade. So I'm just being me." (Watrous 1990, 34)

Certainly Wahlberg and people like postmodern dance choreographer Doug Elkins (also white and who, as a teenager in New York, had been a breakdancer with his African American and Latino buddies) grew up living, loving, and breathing African American culture. Yes, it is theirs. To repeat the driving premise of Chapter 1, African American culture is locked into the fabric of American life and belongs to all of us — white, black, and brown. Wahlberg and Elkins are open about their indebtedness to African American culture. Others don't know it or deny it. Regardless of which camp they are in, European Americans must realize the contradictions and conflicts inherent in the fact that they "own" a culture whose creators were enslaved and are still subjugated by the dominant Europeanist culture of which they are members. As individuals they may not be culprits, but collectively their culture was and is. African American culture is perceived as theirs for the taking. Well, it is, and it isn't. And the same, tired question rears its head again: Who's got the power? This is the intercultural moment, when Wahlberg, a white kid from Boston, one of the most racially polarized cities in the United States, sees himself as an honorary black. This is the intercultural moment, when a white group, schooled by a black producer, imitates black music and dance in order to perform in middle America for mainstream white audiences who would not be interested in seeing black groups perform the same songs and dances.

What about Starr? He is one of a new generation of shrewd but "fresh" African Americans in the highly lucrative pop music business. The means of production, distribution, and management have eluded black control since the minstrel era, with very few exceptions; this trend persists even in the hip hop era. The few who finally have some access to white markets base their techniques on those established by Motown, the black-owned company that produced soul music in the 1960s primarily for African American audiences. Before managing New Kids, Starr produced New Edition, a black group that was very successful on black radio. A savvy businessman, Starr had this to say about his next move: "Given the demographics of the country and the history of the music business, I figured that five white kids could be very big. If New Edition was as big as they were, I could imagine what would happen if white kids were doing the same thing" (Watrous, 34).

Watrous explains how Starr not only wrote all the material for the white group but also chose the choreographers and even went so far as to have his "Kids" rehearse at a community center for African American youth in Dorchester, a black Boston enclave:

I put the band there to see the black talent, to feel the vibe. . . . Singing, they had to have a certain tone. When Joe [McIntyre, one of the Kids] first came in he had an operatic voice. So I got him a Michael Jackson album and told him to listen to the way he phrases, the way he handles the vibrato. From when to open or close their mouths, when to sing or not to sing vibrato, from A to Z, I went over it all." (Watrous, 34)

Wahlberg addresses the issue of audiences:

People don't take us seriously, and it gets me really angry. . . . When you go out to Nebraska or South Dakota where there's a small black population and the audience and the fans see us casually hanging out with our tour people and manager, who are all black, and it's obvious that we have a tight relationship with them, it subtly teaches them. They might start to examine themselves some. That's teaching them, too. (34)

Wahlberg also asserts that "every white person in America should read *The Autobiography of Malcolm X."* The intercultural moment is when, through their contact with African Americans, a group of young white performers undergo a change of consciousness that reaches beyond the music industry.

An excellent example of intercultural theater are the one-woman performances pieces created by Anna Deavere Smith dealing with 1990s social crises. "Fires in the Mirror" explores the African American and Jewish sides of the Crown Heights, New York, tragedy in which a black child was killed by a Hasidic Jewish limousine driver and an uninvolved Jewish scholar was subsequently murdered in retaliation by a group of blacks. Smith portrays nearly thirty characters who were directly or tangentially involved in the incident. According to an article in *American Theatre* magazine:

As the performer evoked one speaker after another to persuade us of the rightness of his or her point of view, any preconceptions about the controversial incident quickly crumbled, and we were left wanting to know more, ask more, hear more about the extraordinarily complicated emotions and beliefs of the people caught in the middle of longstanding cultural fears. (Robinson 1992, 20)

"Fires in the Mirror" and "Twilight," Smith's piece on the Los Angeles uprising of 1992, are part of her developing series entitled "On The Road: A Search For American Character." For these event-specific shows Smith interviews and then portrays "a diverse collection of women, men and youths with varied points of view about current issues" (Smith 1992). Her talent is in posing the questions and exposing the dilemma.

Less publicized but as effective are the theater pieces created and performed by New York-based experimental theater actress Robbie McCauley, who frequently works in collaboration with other performers. The piece I am particularly interested in is one she created with Jeannie Hutchins, an Irish-American woman. Called "Sally's Rape," it is named after McCauley's great-great-grandmother, who was a young mother when slavery officially ended. The leitmotif is the power of language: McCauley's fear of saying the wrong thing and jeopardizing the possibility of moving up in the white world; her ancestors' founding of one-room schoolhouses to pass on the written word to the next generation. Then the question arises as to what words mean, in different ethnocultural contexts. Hutchins' word "free" means something light and airy, as in "free as a butterfly," while the word takes on a different character when associated with McCauley's heritage. The two women then reverse roles. Hutchins is put on an auction block, made to strip, and sold off to the highest bidder as the audience participates in this role reversal, with McCauley as auctioneer. I am reminded of a line from another McCauley piece, "Indian Blood," in which she states: "Our Holocaust was worse: We were forced to survive it."

One of those great sounding "multicultural" productions that did not work for me played in Berlin in 1992. It was a collaboration called "Kathakali King Lear," a cross-cultural attempt to interpret the Shakespearean tragedy in Kathakali (Southern Indian dance theater) style. What does it mean to merge Hindu mythology with Shakespearean tragedy? That we are all alike? That Lear is universal? That Shakespeare is timeless? That Kathakali or Shakespeare needs new blood? What does it mean to universalize? If Shakespeare is universal, then what about Rama or Siva? Is the situation different if a native of the culture directs the universalizing? Is it the right thing to do because collaboration sounds good and attracts grant money? And what does it mean that the program listed two Europeans as directors, a title that places them in control and posits the Indians as actors? But wait. Isn't it the Indian cast members who own the Kathakali repertory by dint of having created it? Even though they superimposed the Lear narrative on the Kathakali characters, the Europeans could not possibly *direct* this Indian company that was born and bred in the tradition. They *staged* the production, and there is a big difference between the two functions. The deed must be named by its rightful name, because naming is important and naming is power. Who is directing what? What is the "exchange rate" in the transaction? Who reaps the profits and the credits? Where does the buck stop? Who gets the bucks and the future grants? In this case, I felt the production added nothing to Kathakali or to King Lear.

One of the production's two "directors" was a woman named Annette Leday. In a London newspaper article she is credited with "creating the first contemporary Kathakali performance":

This, "La Sensitive," offers a parallel of two cultures and two sources—Shelley's poem, "The Sensitive Plant," which dramatises the creation and destruction of a garden, and an Indian ritual in which a floral design is made on the earth and then destroyed in a demonic trance. (Haider 1993, 22)

Leday, a choreographer of French origin, spent ten years studying Kathakali. It seems that she specializes in the Europeanization of this ancient Indian form. Ten years of study represents more than a casual commitment to the form. One would expect a level of humility and respect for the Other culture. (I am reminded of a statement by Paul Bowles, the American expatriate writer and composer who, after living in Morocco for fifty years, said that no European can fully fathom that culture.) We can tell by the wording of the newspaper article that the English-Indian comparison is not multicultural and democratic, but hierarchical. The English garden is merely created and destroyed; the Indian counterpart involves "ritual" (not belief or religion) and destruction through "demonic trance."

Is our task to prove that we are all the same, even down to our myths and symbols? Can we acknowledge and embrace our differences and our frictions and make theater about that? I am neither a purist nor an essentialist. I have no qualms about authenticity or the lack of it. My gripe with Leday and the English-Indian collaborations she has created with Shakespeare, Shelley, and Kathakali is that a universal aesthetic, not a multicultural one, is represented here, and the collaboration is one-sided. The universal component, in each case, is the European text, and the power of the written word stands out as the leading edge against the oral tradition of Kathakali.

Besides her Kathakali King Lear venture, Leday is also the driving force behind Compagnie Keli, a group of dancers from Kerala who performed "La Sensitive." (One can guess who gave them their French name.) The stories in Shelley's poem and Shakespeare's play are used as the organizing principle, or form, to shape, contain, and modernize the content—the Kathakali vocabulary. It is Kathakali that is being Europeanized. Why? Such a move clearly places the power and the last word in the seat of European forms and in the hands of a European woman. Who has the power? And what is presumed to be the universal measure? I am not questioning Leday's intentions or insinuating that she is forcing her will upon the Kathakali dancers. The reins of power and the universal assumptions of Europe as the model for the rest of the planet have been in place for so long — at least since the Age of Enlightenment — that even good intentions are shaped by superiority complexes, on the European side, and inferiority complexes, on the indigenous culture's side. These productions seem to shout: "Look! Our Shakespeare, our Shelley, and our modern dance can update and improve upon even the staid tradition of Kathakali and make it belong to all cultures!" And it may very well be that the Indians involved in these collaborations, victims of their own internalizations of colonialist values, invited and welcomed the opportunity to "modernize" and Europeanize their traditional forms.

The way cultural interchange is played out in a black-white American context is very different from these Euro-Indian examples. Take American concert dance, where the Africanist presence is already a basic integer, although it has been invisibilized. In "Revelations," one of Alvin Ailey's masterpieces, the movement vocabulary is a lucid example of agentic African American entry into the European-American-dominated arena of concert dance. The power of determination and choice is on Ailey's side. "Revelations" takes the African American forms of spiritual song and church service and gracefully integrates (rather than superimposes) them into a modern dance vocabulary that is itself already a fusion of Africanist and Europeanist languages. It would be difficult to equate the African American experience in modern dance with European efforts to bring Indian dance under the European concert dance umbrella. Whereas the Europeanist influence seeks to change the shape of Indian dance, the Africanist presence is already an equal (although unrecognized) partner in shaping European American modern dance. The Anglo-Indian example is forged unilaterally; the black-white American example is the result of centuries of Creolization. Diasporan African peoples are adept at embracing foreign cultural influences within their forms without losing the Africanist integrity of the original. This characteristic occurs in the African American tradition in American modern dance and in forms as diverse as jazz and blues music and African American religions such as Candomblè (Brazil) and Vodun (Haiti).

Earlier I asked the question: Is the situation any different if a native of the culture directs the universalizing? Let us pursue the question with two examples of Asian choreographers who have adopted the precepts of modern dance choreography. The first is the Lebanese Caracalla Dance Company (Craine 1993, 33). The group, which has performed internationally, was founded in 1970 by Abdul Halim Caracalla, described in Craine's article as "a wealthy Lebanese," after he studied at the London School of Contemporary Dance. One of the productions he brought to London was his version of — yes, Shakespeare — "A Midsummer

Night's Dream." This was the Caracalla Company's second Shakespeare production; it had earlier done "The Taming of The Shrew." Caracalla locates himself under the Euro-universalist rubric by some of his comments. He states: "The Arab world is very rich in petrol, yet very poor in culture. We [Caracalla Dance Company] represent culture for the Arab world" (Craine, 33). It is noteworthy that a wealthy, educated Lebanese would describe as "poor" a culture as old and rich as the Lebanese. Lest we forget, that cultural heritage goes back to ancient Phoenicia and was layered over by successive Roman, Arab, and Ottoman influences. In fact, it is an intercultural mecca of Asian—not European—persuasion. Further on, Caracalla states: "I am obsessed by Shakespeare. It's strange for an oriental [*sic*] man to adore such a mind. But for me Shakespeare illumines our spirit, he illumines our reality to ourself; for the whole human race not only for yesterday, but for today and tomorrow" (33). It may be my own skeptical nature, but I cannot believe that there are not excellent Arab and/or Lebanese sources that have a broad appeal, although the idea of appeal "for the whole human race" seems to be a Europeanist construct that in itself needs examination. It is interesting to note that this Europeanized Asian characterizes himself as Oriental. He seems to have swallowed Eurocentric categories hook, line, and sinker. I look for the day when Asia is considered Asia—not the Orient, not the Middle East, not the Near East. Then, we would talk about Israelis, Lebanese, Pakistanis, Chinese, and so on as Asian cultures and herald their differences. I also look forward to Africa being acknowledged and celebrated as Africa, in all its diversity—from Egypt, Morocco, and other North African nations, through the West, East, and South African nations that are now given the separatist, Eurocentric title of "Black Africa." Of course, the continental ascriptions and designations that I suggest represent a revisionist perspective. Only in revising our point of view and revising cultural canons can we begin to shape a multicultural context.

A final note on Caracalla's latest production (at the time the report was written) perhaps tells more than any critique I might offer about his efforts: "His latest production is a hotch-potch of styles: modern, folk and oriental, all delivered at a frenetic pace by two dozen dancers in elaborately colourful costumes. The score is an equally exotic brew: a bit of "William Tell," "Frère Jacques," string quartets, even a tango" (Craine, 33).

A more complex case is that of Hindu choreographer Shobana Jeyasingh who, on the one hand, is a trained dancer of Bharata Natyam (a traditional Southern Indian dance form), although not a guru (or master). On the other hand, Jeyasingh is a longtime resident of London. In a newspaper article (Meisner 1994, 33) this choreographer is presented as the modernizer of what is characterized as an "ancient, classical tradition." Apparently, she works in the Bharata Natyam vocabulary but uses Europeanist choreographic principles of space, rhythm, and dynamic, thus superimposing a Europeanist form on Asian content. Like the Annette Leday examples, the European form shapes and contains the Indian content. An interesting argument emerges from another indigenous perspective. According to Indian dancer-scholar Ananya Chatterjea, it is misleading for Jeyasingh to represent Bharata Natyam to European audiences as an ancient, classical form. Chatterjea asserts that such a statement ignores the history of the dance form. Because it was banned during the long period of English imperialism/colonialism, it had to be re-created in the 1940s. Thus, the form of Bharata Natyam that we now see is neoclassical, not classical. It is already modernized, in that sense.[3] The Caracalla and Jeyasingh examples are weighted on the European side of the scale; they are intercultural, in the second meaning assigned to the term, rather than multicultural.

An example of an Asian American performance artist highlights a different approach. In this case, the difference is that the specific quotient is the aim, not the universal. Ping Chong is a Chinese American who grew up in Manhattan's Chinatown. I had the opportunity to see the work-in-progress showing of his "Chinoiserie" in 1994. Through broad and fine sweeps the work examines contexts and relationships between Chinese and English, Chinese and European American, Chinese and Chinese. According to Chong, the form of this quasi-historical piece was influenced and inspired by the work of Latino writer Eduardo Galliano, particularly his *Memories of Fire*, a tome on the founding of the Americas. Thus, one of Chong's main sources is an intercultural text. Chong is about finding his own form, rather than adopting a Europeanist model. The music, composed and played by Guy Klucevsek, a Polish American, was performed by four actors, two of whom also performed Chinese martial arts movements. Cast members were Americans of African, Asian, European, and Native American descent. Chong and dramaturge Anna Seckinger did a thorough research job and brought out amazing bits and pieces of this largely unretrieved history. One performer, Michael Edo Keane, stood out particularly for me. He had a rich, baritone voice with a mellow, soulful timbre that played with vibrato and ritardando in a way that comes straight out of African American pop song style. I was glad to have the opportunity to talk with him at the reception following the performance. When I told him that I could close my eyes and believe, on hearing him, that he was black, he accepted this comment as high praise and mentioned his great regard for his mentors—black vocalists like Otis Redding and other rhythm-and-blues greats who, he said, had shaped his style and aspirations as he grew up. We talked a little longer, and he revealed that he is Eurasian American and grew up in an African American section of San Francisco — an Other shaped and nurtured by an Other.[4] The message in this man's experience — and in the fact of a performance like "Chinoiserie" — stands in radical contrast to the Euro-Asian examples from London. Of course, populations of color have been sizable in the United States for centuries, but they have constituted a critical mass in European cities only for the past fifty years or so. Thus, African, European, and Asian presences are more integrally interwoven in American society than in European culture; and the way in which intercultural transactions occur is culture-, locale-, and history-specific.

Take the Pan-African dance company Adzido, founded by Ghanaian George Dzikunu, a member of the Anlo culture of the Volta region. The troupe was formed in 1984 by this artist, who comes from a family of master drummers and dancers. He is now a Londoner. His company's repertory includes not only Ghanaian dances from several Ghanaian cultures, but also dances from South Africa, Nigeria, and Sierra Leone. It is surprising, for an African dance company, that his group is composed of both black and white dancers. He explains, "I feel that just as blacks should be welcomed into white dance circles, so we should accept people of any colour" (Pascal 1986, 70). A cleverly conceived inverse of this example comes from the realm of photography. Black Londoner Maud Sulter has photographed women of African heritage, including herself, posing as the classical muses of antiquity — and why not? Her collection of color photographs in gilded frames was displayed in a show titled "African Themes" at England's Victoria and Albert Museum in 1993. Sulter posed black women artists as the classical inspirations, including writer Alice Walker as Thalia and herself as Calliope. Terpsichore, the muse of dance, appears in baroque gown and a white wig, "referring to the way in which slavery ensured the riches of the West" (Talbot 1993, 45). Polyhymnia, the muse of storytelling, holds the sacred songs of the ancestors and wears the sacred scarab beetle of Egypt on her breast. These two examples are interesting in their indication that all of us are Creolized peoples and have shared heritages. Not only do we rub up against each other, but we also live within each other.

Still in London, the issue of mixed-ethnic casting in an originally monocultural play (Peter, 1993, 8.17) reminded me of the controversy over the same issue some years ago with regard to the musical "Miss Saigon" on Broadway. There the big issue was whether a white man should be cast as an Asian in the lead role. The fact that this argument occurred is a healthy sign that multicultural sweet-talk is being exposed as the intercultural conflict that it really is. In the past it has been acceptable for whites to yellow, red, or black up to play Asians, Native Americans, or Africans, in highbrow and lowbrow entertainments. How many times have we seen a production of Othello with the main character played by a white in blackface? European opera tradition didn't give a second thought to blacking up white singers in operas such as "Aida" and "The Love for Three Oranges." Thus, the "Miss Saigon" issue showed some forward movement even in posing the argument. Yet, the reverse situation—people of color playing whites—arouses controversy, even though it is not a matter of blacks in whiteface. What happens when an Asian or an African is cast in a white role, with or without make-up adjustment? In the present dispute we are back again to basic black-and-white. London was up in arms at the casting of black actor Clive Rowe as Mr. Snow in the National Theatre production of "Carousel." According to writer John Peter, "Integrated casting is operating at the boundaries of taste and aesthetic judgment, both of which are constantly changing" (1993, 8.17). Peter cites the potential shock value for the English public if some fifteen years earlier, a black were to be cast in a lead role in a Shakespearean play and states that this phenomenon is easily acceptable nowadays. He mentions "Othello" as the exception, in which ethnicity is crucial to the tale. (He does not discuss the European custom of blacking up for the role.) It might seem that only members of the conservative, white population would be against interethnic casting. However, there are African Americans who are of the same opinion, although they approach the issue from the other side. This group resists interethnic casting on the grounds that to ignore black ethnicity is to ignore the obvious and introduce a new, postmodern form of black invisibilization. They do not want their ethnicity overlooked or disregarded. On the one hand, I appreciate their perspective. A multicultural world is not about pretending that we are all the same. On the other hand, I also appreciate Peter's final comment on the "Carousel" debate: "The theatre is, after all, about impersonation; about people reaching out beyond their own lives and characters in order to live other lives, be other characters. The theatre is an on-going experiment: it is not a place for black and white judgments" (17).

Theater, television, video, and film performance may seem true to life, but even the most realistic theater is artifice. If willing suspension of disbelief allows us to accept as real what we know is performance, why should interethnic casting burden the spectator's imagination? There has been little complaint about middle-aged men and women—white, that is—playing the role of an adolescent Juliet or a young and wild Hamlet. With the issue of age, the message and rationale seem to be that we all have common experiences to draw upon in creating a role, whether we are young or old. What we actually are, or look like, is discounted in favor of who we become on stage. Is cross-ethnic casting any more taxing on the brain than cross-generational casting?

Back in the United States, Ping Chong is not alone. A slew of artists explore the frictions in ways that show the depth of their creativity and the complexity of the issues. Choreographer Bill T. Jones' work over the past decade has included metacommentary, both in movement and spoken language, on specific sociopolitical issues. I remember his presentation at one Dance Critics Association conference in New York in the mid-1980s. Jones "played the dozens" — that is, he critiqued the critics. He had been invited to give an informal solo performance that would then become part of the discussion by a panel of dance critics and scholars. He danced and spoke a caustic response to critical reception of his work (not necessarily by the critics who invited him to the conference), in no uncertain terms. Although his "critique" was not cast in racial terms, he embodied the conflict that exists between the performer who is both black and gay and the predominantly white, heterosexual, middle-aged, middle-class female critic writing for mainstream American publications.

Jones' "Last Supper at Uncle Tom's Cabin: The Promised Land" is an American epic (1991). He describes it as a multilayered work about race, sex, and class difference and the possibility for processing those differences in an effort to arrive at a new place. It is his own personal history, plus the particular stories of his company members as they intersect with social realities, cultural memories, spiritual strivings, and political stances. Jones' medium is a combination of modern dance, African American vernacular dance forms — tap, social, and earlier forms such as the Ring Shout — with mime, text, and narrative, all brought together in the concert dance arena. Using movement tropes of "darkies" dancing jigs and through fragmentation of phrases in such gestures as tipping the hat or bowing, he achieves broken lines that symbolically speak of his subject matter. Jones' dance company members are African American, Latino, Filipino, and white; gay and straight; male and female; young and not-so-young. It is, in many ways, a revisionist company that is re-defining what it means to be a concert dancer in America. Do you have to be white? Do you have to be black? Do you need a long, slim body? (Dancer Arthur Aviles' short, stocky muscularity defuses that one.) Do you need a youthful-looking, muscular body? (Dancer Laurence Gold-huber is round and large, but he is an agile, intelligent mover with a thinking body.)

The "Uncle Tom" text draws on African American preaching styles and includes Sojourner Truth's "Ain't I a Woman" speech. "The Last Supper" section deconstructs undercurrents of violence, sexuality, conflict, and anger that emerge while an inverted version of Dr. Martin Luther King Jr.'s "I Have a Dream" speech is used as dialogue. (Jones intended this section to pose the question: How much difference can be embraced by concepts such as "free at last" and "equality"?) At the same time, a guest company member named Justice recites a rap poem he wrote on the theme of justice. Julius Hemphill's extraordinary musical score—dry but dripping with irony, yet sometimes open and yearning—is played by his saxophone sextet. Jones used the Uncle Tom part of the title to explore the story beyond the stereotype. Who lives inside the insulting connotations that made this character Other in both black and white worlds? Tom and the other characters become vehicles for revealing specific gender, race, and class issues of the people who are performing—his company members. There are four Elizas—three women (African American, Jewish, and Filipino) and one gay male, who portrays her in white pumps. I felt an irrational sense of panic on seeing Jones' depiction of the dogs that chase Eliza: a menacing chorus of men in black T-shirts, jockey shorts, trooper boots, and gloves, with arms and legs naked, and black leather dog muzzles covering their jaws. They execute quasi storm trooper techniques, complete with jabbing fists, and fast, heavy, hard running in place while grunting and yelling.

The last part of the title, "The Promised Land," is Jones' vision for salvation. He explains that, for those who are not believers in an afterlife, hope rests in existing together in the here and now without killing each other. (This reminds me of Rodney King's plea, "Can we all get along?" at the height of the 1992 Los Angeles uprisings after the police attack on him.) As Jones puts it, "The commonality is the body." For this final section he requires the involvement of over forty members of the particular local community that has sponsored the performance. These volunteers must be willing to appear nude onstage. For him, the naked human body represents the site of reconciliation. Do we accept or reject it? The decision to appear nude or to condone nudity on their stages most often requires some degree of community "discussion and soul-searching." Thus, Jones has built into his piece a conflict mechanism that must be resolved for the performance to occur and that is emblematic of our larger problem of accepting difference (which is also a question of accepting self). Completion of the performance is contingent upon the process of solving and resolving this issue. The piece, then is about *getting* there, not getting *there*. Jones wants the spectators to ask themselves if they, too, would or could step into this naked landscape: "Am I that comfortable with myself, with him, with her?" He describes this ending not as art, but "an act of faith."

Jones appears as Job, whom he describes as "the paradigm of the man of faith." This role has a particular intersection with his personal story: He lost his mate to AIDS several years earlier. Job's trials were the result of a bet between God and Satan, a test of one man's faith, an arbitrary decision to strike a man down to see if his faith would waver.

AIDS-infected people are arbitrarily struck and die in their prime. Unlike Job, they cannot be resurrected.

Like the best creative minds of every era, Jones stands on the boundary, playing, teasing, and stretching the edges of his genre and, by his particular combination of the personal and social with the artistic, he is helping to expand the parameters of his discipline. He has been roundly criticized (again, by those old-school critics who would have their dance "over easy" or in their favorite cup, so to speak) for bringing such powerful issues to the concert stage as race, gender, and AIDS (in his 1994 premiere, "Still/Here"). But Jones, who, onstage and off, is an eloquent, cool, yet passionate wielder of the spoken word, warns of what he is about in words that are not flippant but bluntly honest:

Marcel Duchamp said art is primarily an intellectual activity, right? Well, that's not where I live. I want my art to be tender, brave, sexy, outrageous, seductive. Is that being fair, I ask myself? Yes, I say, yes it's fair because I'm the one who makes the rules. So — don't buy a ticket if you can't handle that. (Robertson 1994, 24)

The work of performers like Tim Miller and Holly Hughes (performance art), the late Reza Abdoh (theater), Yvonne Rainer and the late Marlon Riggs (film), and choreographers Blondell Cummings, David Rousseve, Jawole Willa Jo Zollar (Urban Bush Women), and Ron Brown (Evidence Dance Company) also comes to mind as potent examples of exploring similar conflicts.[5] The collaboration of musician-composer Pauline Oliveros and playwright-director Ione on "Njinga The Queen King" branches out in another direction and has a striking story line:

The play is based on the life of a seventeenth-century African regent Njinga Mbandi who ruled the kingdom of Ndongo (present-day Angola). When tribal custom forbade her to rule as queen after the deaths of her father and brother, she ascended to the throne as "king." She dressed as her father had, and following the prevailing custom for kings, took 40 concubines and dressed her male servants as women for the role. Njinga was a skilled diplomat and a fierce warrior who kept the Portugese slave traders at bay during the 40 years of her reign. Spanning five centuries, the play traces the diaspora of Njinga's people up to the present time, and ventures into the future as well. (Oliveros and Ione 1992, 4)

Although the plot sounds astonishing, equally interesting is the contact zone shared by the two collaborators. Oliveros asks Ione, in this interview, why Ione invited her, a white woman, to compose, because that could be interpreted as appropriation. Ione answers that she "never considered" Oliveros white. She explains that, in effect, she never regarded Oliveros as Other. She was attracted, first and foremost, to the quality of her music and then to her dark-skinned, Mediterranean appearance and the poetry and rhythm of her surname. Ione assures Oliveros that she is not appropriating African music and points out that people could complain about her own decision to take on this project since she, Ione, is not African but African American. To add to the chemistry of this interview, Oliveros mentions the fact that the burial ground of enslaved Africans that had recently been found in Manhattan is almost directly underneath Ione's Chambers Street loft. She states:

This is a very complex time. Bones of ancestors are being exposed and social or cultural forms are exposed. . . . There are so many appropriations without any real connection to spirit. So it's a very tight line that one walks to try to feel the subject matter in the manner of the ones who created the form, as a carrier of this tradition. But a lot is just breaking down, changing in preparation for a more unified culture of the spirit which is more delicate. (Oliveros and Ione 1992, 18)

Like Bill T. Jones and Urban Bush Women, Ione has structured her play to include members of the communities where it is performed and to create a new kind of performance—a subjunctive, processual, intercultural experience: "It's not just this play that I wrote, a finished product. It is happening and continuing to evolve each time that it's performed with new, additional communities. And that is a meaningful, living theater" (18).

Now, in the context and spirit of collaboration, let us return to hip hop culture and focus momentarily on dancer-choreographer Rennie (Lorenzo) Harris. In his breakdancing days with Philadelphia's Scanner Boys his tag, or name, was "Prince of the Ghetto." Earlier he had been a Philly-style step dancer, performing a genre that resembled tap dance without the taps.[6] Nowadays Harris is busy expanding the definition of dance as art by bringing hip hop suites to concert stages. His dance company is called Pure Movement, and its aesthetic domain is a potent mix of three elements. The basis of vocabulary is urban, African American dance (misleadingly termed "street dance"). With his particular genius and creativity and from his vantage point as an African American male who has performed and choreographed professionally since he was fifteen years old, his combination of recent forms such as "Breakdance," "Electric Boogie," hip hop, and house forms reflects the vital streams of three decades of vernacular dance. Second, as his command of the African American vernacular deepens, so, too, does his understanding of its African roots. His work with postmodern dancers and world musicians (including tabla player Lenny Seidman and percussionist Toshi Makihara) is the third major conditioning force in shaping his aesthetic. The result of these combined presences is a new energy on the concert dance stage.

Movementwise, Harris combines the freeze-frame angularity of "Electric Boogie" and the staccato, up-tempo vocabulary of house dancing with his own fluid style. For example, in a solo called "Endangered Species II," the stop-start, fragmented gestures—or "locking"—of "Electric Boogie" parallel the psychic fragmentation experienced by an African American male. "State of Mind," a duet for himself and Shalimar, his erstwhile Scanner Boy colleague, is a poignant personality portrait that combines the vocabularies of theatrical mime with vernacular dance. In "Students of the Asphalt Jungle," a group piece for his all-male company, these five young brothers come onstage with body attitudes and a movement style that tell us that they are the hip hop generation, weaned on breakdancing. Then, to a soundtrack of African-inspired hip hop music that belongs to a style known as "tribal house," the quintet explodes into samba-based African steps, to the surprise and exhilaration of the audience. It is remarkable and paradoxical that Harris infuses the stereotypically hard-edged hip hop dance vocabulary with a sensual, embracing presence. His work defuses the Eurocentric trope of the violent, nihilistic black man and shows a range of feeling in the movement vocabulary and the individual dancers, with rage as only one of its facets. The dancers expose their human frailties while celebrating and flaunting their strengths. In embracing the conflicts and accepting the contradictions, Harris imbues his work with love and spirit. His qualities of openness and giving act as pointers to a potentially multicultural world in which difference is celebrated.

Harris is highly sensitized to both the female performer as equal partner and to his own anima. His work with a woman, Asian performer Roko Kawai, one of his fellow founding members of Splinter Group (a Philadelphia-based postmodern music-dance improvisation company), spoke worlds about creating gender and culture bridges. At one point in "Endangered Species II" he allows himself to feign femininity, waving and shaking his hips at the audience in freeze-frame time. This moment is not about mocking the female but taking on the feminine in himself. In the true tradition of Africanist improvisation so basic to all the forms of dance that have shaped his aesthetic, Harris' performances of his repertory change with each airing. His aesthetic intention is to allow dance to be the connective tissue for bridging and embracing the seemingly contending opposites: black-white, male-female, self-Other. In his words, "I've decided to start a healing process that will enable me to face my deepest fears and by healing myself I'm healing my oppressors" (Harris 1994, 17).

This last batch of artists finds power in creating new forms to contain and express their voices. The old forms simply won't do. Likewise, an older member of another colonialized culture, V. S. Naipaul, said in 1994 that his earlier books had cost him "a lot of pain" and "they didn't come out well because I was a prisoner of a borrowed form. I wasn't writing my own kind of book" (quoted in Gussow 1994, 3). Once we begin to write our "own kind of book," the forms we create challenge the existence of traditional models, be they models in performance, scholarship, or everyday life.

STYLE

With mass misinformed media promoting out of ignorance what they did not understand, the karma of hip hop mutated into whatever was on the minds of those who embraced it, and most people were embracing it for all the wrong reasons. Now fools assume that all you need is a pair of baggy pants, a fancy book bag, backward baseball cap, and a blunt [a marijuana cigarette] in order to be identified as a "B-boy," but of course this is bogus. All you need is universal love in your heart, bona fide soul, and a genuine desire to create the unimaginable. Until you acquire these keys, the B-boogiefied level of pure hip hop funk will be forever unattainable. (Ghetto 1995, 42)

Lifestyle is a strong seat of power for African Americans, and one of its most obvious aspects is hair. According to Lisa Jones (1991, 47), "Everything I know about American history I learned from looking at black people's hair. It's the perfect metaphor for the African experiment here: The price of the ticket (for a journey no one elected to take), the toll of slavery, and the cost of remaining. It's all in the hair."

"What does she mean?" the non-African American reader might ask. Hair is a potent, visible icon for all cultures. But African American hair literally bears the weight of both black resistance and black resilience. A coiffure may represent oppression or liberation. Is it naturally kinky, curly, straight, or some combination of all of these generic characteristics (which is the case for most African Americans)? Is it straightened, processed, braided, dreaded, twisted, wrapped, dyed, or bleached? Is it long, short, or a combination of both? For African American women, like most other women, is it still used in the traditional way as a gendered, sexual tool, or is it a statement to the brothers that "This is who I am, whether you like it or not"? Regardless of style, black hair is generally strong, resistant, thick, heavy, or tough stuff. It is not about blowing in the wind. Unlike thin, straight hair, one of its virtues is that it can be sculpted and molded. Ironically, it *holds* the shape of change. Yet it can be stubborn and unyielding. It is a powerful medium, naturally and symbolically.

There was a wonderful and telling repartee between movie director Spike Lee, pop superstar Stevie Wonder, and an audience member on the Oprah Winfrey show (June 11, 1991):

Audience member: Stevie, can you tell whether people you meet are black or white?

Wonder: Not all the time, but I can usually tell when I touch their hair.

Lee: Not anymore you can't!

Lee was pointing out the enormous amount of informational exchange that now takes place between black and white hair styles. Since about the 1960s whites have imitated black hairdos as frequently as blacks have imitated whites. I am sure that the pseudo-kinky European American perm of the 1970s was a response to the full, frizzy African American "Afro" of the 1960s. The ironic black double take on this one was the "jerri curl," a coiffure that imitated the frizzy perm and created small, tight curls as a revisionist amendment to the Afro. One might call it the old "Cakewalk" syndrome in reverse—blacks copying whites copying blacks. Next, white entertainers and superstars began to experiment with braids and beads, African style. An interesting twist was the use of a coiffure tool called a bevel iron. This nifty machine crimps the hair so that it looks like braids unbraided. Thus, the origin of this white "do" and its relationship to an African American style are easily obscured.

Women of all ethnicities have been imprisoned by the imagined male preference for long, flowing hair. The 1920s flapper's bobbed hair was the first widespread Europeanist protest to this long-accepted tradition. African Americans jumped on the bandwagon then and pursued black versions, like Josephine Baker's, and revisited that look in the 1990s. The updated black bobs include the near-shaven natural look; the nappy-natural, close cropped look, so splendidly displayed by supermodel Roshumba; the short, permed, coiffed-to-a-tee look of vocalists like Anita Baker and Toni Braxton; and the amazing, skull-hugging cold wave look, an homage to "La Bakaire," once sported by the artist Salt of the rap duo, Salt 'n Pepa, as well as by countless black females in all walks of life.

Then there is the phenomenon of African Americans, male or female, who dye their hair blonde, and those on the fringe who take the next step and bleach it platinum, a practice which may have originated in the gay white community. Before launching into my comments on this trend (one, by the way, that has existed in the core black community since at least the post–World War II era amongst working people, entertainers, and those in the sporting life), let me relate an incident that occurred in conversation with a white female professor at Temple University some years ago. As we lunched together, she complained to me about the terrible bureaucracy bogging down a particular university office. She then zeroed in on one of its employees, against whom she had lodged a formal complaint. My colleague then added, "On top of it all, she had blonde hair; and I just can't stand it when black women dye their hair blonde." I wondered why this white, middle-aged, middle-class, liberal, elite-educated feminist professor should be offended by a young, high school-educated, African American female office worker who made the choice to dye her hair. What about white women? If it is ridiculous, then isn't it equally so on whites, and even more so on the old (the fact that old women no longer become gray, they become blonde)?

I think I know what my colleague was reacting to. Like most people, especially white liberals, she read this sign as black self-denial and an attempt to be white. But that is a monolithic reading of a complex matter. Black self-regard has changed its tenor through the generations and has moved ahead, urged on by the Black Power, black-is-beautiful, and Civil Rights movements, and recently by hip hop culture. Although eras pass, their effects are accumulations that we wear either closely, like second skins, or a bit more roomily, like overcoats. There have been enormous changes in the African American sense and presentation of self in each decade of this century, and those changes live in every present era. When New York politician the Reverend Al Sharpton wears his hair in long, wavy, processed locks, it is a quote from and homage to the legendary soul-funk artist James Brown, who was one of Sharpton's mentors, Similarly, the marcel wave is a reference to Josephine Baker, even if some of its wearers are unaware of its origins. These fashions are not in emulation of white role models.

Just as they did with hair-straightening processes—defining "straight" hair by a black standard, not a white one—blacks have taken the concept of "blonde" and redefined it in their own image. Of course, there are some African Americans whose natural hair color, like their skin, is some shade of blonde, red, or light brown. In earlier generations, both whites and blacks who dyed their hair tried to make the acquired shade look natural and blend in with skin tones. With postmodernism and the embrace of artifice above authenticity, the young, punk, hip hop, avant-garde, and daring of black, white, and brown persuasions are dyeing their hair for the fun of it, not to look as though they were born that way. Thus, we see African Americans with ebony black skin sporting platinum-dipped coifs. They may have closely cropped, near-shaven platinum-blonde pates or long, blond, Africanesque braids, for a particularly ironic comment on being simultaneously blond and black. A blonde extension, braid, fall, or tail may be added to a brunette head of hair for additional effect. People are getting a lot of mileage out of high-affect juxtapositions in novel and unexpected areas such as this. As Balanchine used and contrasted black against white in casting Arthur Mitchell in key roles with white ballerinas, so African American young people are playing black against white in contrasting their skin tones against shades of blonde tresses.

I have a hunch that the source of this new way of being a black blonde dates back to the 1960s era of Ike and Tina Turner. Tina was famous for sporting super-long, often blonde, wigs to balance her super-short, tight skirts. She used the wig, not as a substitute for "white" hair, but as a prop that set off and highlighted the rest of her costume. (By the way, her luscious skin was an important part of the costume, and much of it was on display.) I interpret this black-blonde syndrome as the opposite of my colleague's reading. In this instance I see blacks again "changing the joke to slip the yoke," as Ellison so aptly and eloquently phrased it. Like the minstrel who donned the mask and imitated the imitator, Tina Turner donned the blonde tresses, flipped and dipped them and made them dance with her, and deconstructed the blondes-have-more-fun trope—or reconstructed it, from a new vantage point. Following in her footsteps, the 1990s hip hop generation has taken blondeness to new heights.

There is a politic of power in taking the prized possession of the white Other and making it one's own, while also poking fun at it. The blonde mystique is thus taken off its pedestal. But, as in minstrelsy, poking fun at the Other is also a way of mocking oneself. There is an "in your face" sense in the way that I see blacks sporting blonde hair that says, "Hey, this is a role that I can play, and I can inhabit this role with elegance and with humor, see?" Blacks have absorbed, integrated, and redefined what it is to be blonde, or blonde in black skin. Finally, the point is that *it's just hair*. A lot of psychobabble surrounds the trope of black hair, and it seems an unfair weight to place on this wonderfully resistant yet flexible medium. A political reading is as useful as a psychological one.

As a result of the hip hop generation, the dizzying plethora of traditional, continental, African male cuts (called "fades") have been appropriated first by African Americans, male and female, and later by European Americans. It is exhilarating to see the different ways in which a fade, a half-shaved head, or a shaved-in logo sits in black hair or white. Some of the logos are not even shaved in but are bas-reliefs created by shaving all the hair around them. Carved symbols can be designed by customers and taken to stylists to be clean-shaven into the already shorn head of hair. Logos (in some circles called "tribal designs") have gone far beyond the "X" for brother Malcolm or the bearer's initials. They may be intricate designs taken from Kente cloth or replicas of the human form. It is disturbing to see white fashion writers talk about these "dos" as though their roots (excuse the pun) were European. For example, in a Sunday *New York Times* "Fashion" piece titled "Call It Hair, More or Less" (n.a., June 9, 1991, 54), the text accompanying a photo collage of these terraced hairdos on both black and white subjects describes them as "medieval bowl cut crossbred with Victorian Gothic braids. Top finials and flying buttresses of long hair sprout from a basic crew cut." The reporter's own anxiety of influence is on display, along with the haircuts. Their most immediate, nitty-gritty reference point is urban black invention based on age-old, Africanist ways of dealing with (black) hair, but no such reference appears in the author's flights of fancy. Allusions to things Victorian, gothic, medieval, and so on give an air of "class" and validation to something African by misnaming its authentic roots and stamping it with a European pedigree.

Hair and fingernails — these substances figure in Africanist traditions of medicine, healing, and power. They are elements that are supposedly dead but live and grow, even after death — or so we were told as children. There are many superstitions around hair. The cuttings should be kept from the hands of evildoers who may use them to wreak havoc upon the owner. Visual artist David Hammons exalts black hair. Many of his canvases include the thick, blacker-than-black clumps that the artist collects from the floors of barbershops in the neighborhood where he lives. Harlem's droppings are exhibited in faraway art galleries, giving visibility and stature to the culture and people they came from. As Lisa Jones (1991, 47) stated, "Black hair has a power about it, if only because it's been so forbidden."

The "forbidden" hip hop cuts go along with the baggy clothes. Hair and dress represent the Africanist irony and double meaning of being both tough and comic, sexy and silly — of embracing opposites and coming out with something entirely new. Baggy clothes and asymmetrical haircuts are not only amusing; they also defy conventional order and proclaim agency from the underground. Prison inmates were forced to wear oversized, poorly fitting clothes as part of the dehumanizing tactics of the American penal system. Hip hoppers do what African Americans have done since their beginnings on these shores: They take what was meant to harm them and reshape it to their advantage. Now it's hip, not humiliating, to wear clothes that don't fit. And what headgear goes with these outfits, besides the "phat" cuts?[7] How about a tube hat that is a cross between an African American stocking cap (which males of my father's generation slept in so as not to disturb their "dos") and a traditional, African head wrap? And how about the humor implicit in these crazy, cotton, striped or patterned pull-downs? There is power in taking something that looks silly or humble and wearing it with pride and style. To make the clownish chic gives status and strength to both the look and the wearer. Comedy is a means of proclaiming agency and power, control and cultural identity.

Another representation of power rests in the elevation of "naughty" above "nice." If African Americans have to change their image — hair,

clothes, way of speaking, and so on — to be considered "nice" in the white
mainstream (and, even then, run a high risk of rejection), then why not
make an art out of being nasty? In a noteworthy article (Morgan 1993,
20–21) an anthropologist contends that loudness in speech and manner of
dress is an assertion of power for some African American women. Silence may mean nothingness, either through not being heard or "read"
in the black community, or through repressing black style and manners
and adopting white middle-class norms to gain acceptance in the white
(academic) community. Stereotypically associated with "bad black
girls," these icons (loud talk; four-letter word vocabulary; gum-cracking;
large hoop earrings) enfranchise the black wearer by giving her specifically black-owned power and visibility, for she is both seen and feared.
It is remarkable that the bad-girl, black-girl behavior and dress gain
positive status when white women adopt these traits and styles, from
braiding their hair and having lip-enlarging implants to imitating the
stage mannerisms of Tina Turner from her "Ike and Tina" era. It brings
again the message that African Americans have heard for centuries:
Black physical attributes and inventions are acceptable, not in their own
right as created or owned by blacks, but only as they are adopted and
"refined" by the white touch.

In mid-July 1994 — one of the hottest on record for Philadelphia — the
"Styles" section of the Sunday *New York Times* (July 17) is smoking from
the heat generated by black presences. Did I or didn't I begin this chapter by talking about Manhattan as a Creolized city? Well, this fact of life
has definitely come out of the closet. African American hip language is
used in the title of the lead article on the cover page (31): "See Dick and
Jane Give *Attitude*" (emphasis added) reports on the use of parody and
double meaning in children's books for three- to eight-year-olds. The
African American usage of that word has taken hold and become common currency nationwide. It is accepted shorthand for a cool, sarcastic
stance. Running under this piece is one called "Where the Beat Goes On .
. . and On." This one made me smile at the irony of reversal. The time
was when blacks weren't allowed in downtown, white Manhattan clubs.
Now a new hangout, called Club Soda, is validated for the reporter only
when she revisits it to find that the previously bland atmosphere and
"almost entirely white" clientele is now "mixed, and the house music has
a furious, frantic beat. . . . Club Soda is a place for dancing. Very quickly,
and very well." A 1930s popular tune called "They Can't Take That
Away from Me" talks about the way we dance until three. In fact, not
only can't "they" take that away; on the contrary, they have joined it, en
masse. Page thirty-two shows society shots of the black bourgeoisie on a
cruise around lower Manhattan to benefit Support Network, a group that
raises funds for children of color to attend private elementary schools in

New York. Page thirty-four, where the "attitude" cover article continues, is topped by a photo collage of African American women leaving a Bible Way Church World Wide convention in Manhattan. This gathering was held at the Waldorf-Astoria Hotel, a venue that was unequivocally off-limits for blacks when I was a child. The women are striking and trend-setting in that inimitable Africanist way. They are looking sharp in a breathtaking variety of whimsical, silly-beautiful hats. Theirs are in the high-fashion tradition of designers like Chanel or Lily Daché. Be they fantastical for church ladies, turned backward or sideward for hip hop-pers, pulled down over one eye for bopsters, or puffed up for Rastas, black invention with headgear is a near-legendary presence in and influ-ence on European American style. That old standby, "They Can't Take That Away from Me," speaks not only about dancing until 3:00 A.M. but, significantly, points out another important characteristic of the serenaded love object—the way she wears her hat.

The "Styles" section, a combination of the former fashion and society sections, ends with that traditional staple, wedding announcements. This time the focus is on an interracial nuptial (36). Intercultural issues were highlighted by a good-sized article (for these pages) accompanying a large photograph. Points were raised not only about the fact of race but also religion: The black groom is Episcopalian; the white bride is Jewish. Furthermore, the groom, who was former Governor Cuomo's Deputy Director for Black Affairs, was founder and head coach of the North Park Hockey Association, which brings together "project kids" with "Park Avenue patricians" to play on the same team at the Central Park skating rink. Furthermore, the program is coeducational. Further-more, his Jewish bride is a fourth-grade teacher at the Cathedral School of St. John the Divine on Manhattan's Upper West Side. "What more 'furthermores' can there be?" one might ask. How about one more—the final words of the article, which sum up the tale. The bride describes the groom as "my best friend, and I get to legally hang out with him for the rest of my life."

Let me turn, once more, to that old pop standard, composed by George Gershwin, which is my refrain for this section of the newspaper on this particular Sunday. The ditty ends by enumerating all the special ways and habits of the love object, which have changed the life of the serenader who declares, once more, that "they can't take that away from me." As in the words of the song, there is a love affair going on between white and black America. African American attitudes, tastes, styles, and people are all up in the Other's face, reshaping and recoloring it. It is irreversible, and no one and nothing can take that away.

THE LAST WORD

Where does this leave us? Who has the power? What's in a name? What about the word "multiculturalism"? (And, to be clear, I do not mean the empty word bandied about in current usage.) Do we have it? Can we aspire to it? Can we make it happen by collectively naming, defining, and supporting it? I offer the reader a final conglomerate of quotes as food for thought:

History is a fable agreed upon. So too is identity, which is a story not only arrived at by the individual but conferred by the group. (Lahr 1990, 10)

Power — (1) The ability or capacity to act or perform effectively; (2) A specific capacity, faculty, or aptitude; (3) Strength or force exerted or capable of being exerted; might; (4) The ability or official capacity to exercise control; authority. (*American Heritage Dictionary 1980, 1027*)

You can't have the White House unless you have a Black House. (Sun Ra, the late composer-musician)

Whites must do more to eliminate their own prejudices. In principle, most whites abhor racism. But continued housing and social segregation proves that many whites say one thing and do another. As long as the current pattern of discrimination continues, blacks will never become fully integrated into the American economic mainstream — and both races will continue to pay the price for living in different worlds. (Updegrave 1989, 172)

I close with a personal story. The black family reunion movement is a way for African Americans to bridge the abyss and heal the wounds wrought by slavery. Informal get-togethers became regularly planned events and gained momentum as a result of Alex Haley's work on black roots. African Americans began tracing their genealogies through lines that were warped and shattered by slavery and discrimination but were nonetheless retrievable. Lost and unknown relatives have been found. Many reunions, like that of my mother's family, take place in the locale of the earliest known common relative and involve intricate planning to bring 100 to 200 relatives together in one place for a marathon, extended weekend. Our family's 1994 reunion concluded with a simultaneous naming and call-and-response process. Each of us was given a form labeled "Aspirations." We were directed to enter what we hoped to accomplish in the two years before our next biannual meeting. We were also invited and encouraged to stand and say aloud what we wrote. The forms were put in a grab bag from which each family member pulled a name. During the two-year interim until our next reunion we pledged to support and track the progress of the relative whose name we pulled. Why mention my family? And why focus on the aspirations questionnaire, which, after all, is not an Africanist technique but emanates from the self-help fervor of late-twentieth-century America? I do it because here is a metaphor for multiculturalism. In the first process, the rationale was that when we name the dream by giving voice to it and writing it down, we place the energy, commitment, and support for it out in the world and thus increase the possibility for its realization. In the second process, call-and-response—that flexible, give-and-take experience—was put to the task of encouraging fulfillment and completion. In our family unit, each person was made giver and receiver, caller and responder, with the idea that the well-being of all individuals will promote well-being in the family. The emphasis on process—of seeing an experience through, not as director, but as witness and supporter—is also significant; not to critique, judge, rank, and distance the other, but to support her in her chosen aim, while someone else does the same for you.

Is it possible to enlarge this concept to the nation? If we could conceive of multiculturalism this way, we could have an embracing, powerful practice. The process of finding and defining the practice together—and adding equally valued, equally weighted ingredients from other than white cultures—has not taken place. Multiculturalism—right now the term is weakened because it does not reflect a mutually agreed interethnic perspective. The family grab bag allowed us to take a name and hold a person responsible, not to our dream, but to hers (and our individual aspirations represented the range of our differences: to enter law school; to have a baby; for me, to have this book published).

Who is the holder of our aspirations in the world at large? Only those who are in power? Who has the right, and to what extent, to support, extend, amend, or squelch our aspirations? If being white means being in charge of setting the terms, even for defining and designing multiculturalism, there will be no multiculturalism, which can be built only out of power shared equally. But that share is not simply a matter of generosity. If the white invites the black into her house, it is still *her* house. The house—the space, the contact zone—is there, and it is also our hope, if we are able to rearrange it or even rebuild it so that white and black—and all—shape it and own it equally.

NOTES

1. "Fake out" is outdated slang meaning to outsmart, insult, or lord it over another.
2. The following anecdote that was told to me at a scholarly conference on popular culture may serve as a companion piece to the Masta Ace lyrics. Allen MacDougall, a middle-aged white American male who teaches at a high school in an affluent suburb of Boston and listens to hip hop as he rides the regional roads, noticed, while blasting his car stereo one evening, that he had attracted a

police escort. He stopped and pulled over. From his rear-view mirror he saw a policeman approaching, hand on pistol, with gun partly drawn from its holster. When the cop drew nearer, peered into the car window and, according to Mac-Dougall, "saw that I was white, he said, `Excuse me,' sort of waved me away with a backhanded gesture, put his gun away, and walked off."

Masta Ace's scathing reference to "Elvis" reflects the widespread disdain for Presley, by the black community, as a thief of black music. It is a sentiment that cuts across age and class barriers. Thus, to state "But you know my name" is to claim, acclaim, and reclaim one's black identity and black solidarity, through *Nommo* (here translated as the power of naming) by identifying a common foe.

3.   Ananya Chatterjea, in conversation with the author, June 1994.

4.   Michael Edo Keane, in conversation with the author, July 1994.

5.   Both Riggs and Abdoh have died of AIDS. Jones and Brown are both HIV-positive.

6.   This style of step dancing is not to be confused with the African American fraternity genre of the same name.

7.   "Phat" is the hip hop word for wonderful, fine, beautiful.

BIBLIOGRAPHY

Abrahams, Roger D. Lecture at Temple University, Philadelphia, October 1991.

Akbar, Naim. Interview on "Morning Edition," National Public Radio, August 1990.

Asante, Molefi Kete. *The Afrocentric Idea*. Philadelphia: Temple University Press, 1987.

————. Interview on "All Things Considered," National Public Radio, January 3, 1991.

Baker, Jean-Claude, and Chris Chase. [1993]. *Josephine: The Josephine Baker Story*. Holbrook, Mass.: Adams Publishing, 1993.

Banes, Sally. *Terpsichore in Sneakers*. Middletown, Conn.: Wesleyan University Press, 1987.

Barthes, Roland. "Bichon and the Blacks." *The Eiffel Tower and Other Mythologies*. Trans. Richard Howard. New York: Hill and Wang, 1979, 35–38.

Bernal, Martin. *Black Athena: The Afroasiatic Roots of Classical Civilization. Vol. I. The Fabrication of Ancient Greece, 1785–1985*. New Brunswick, N.J.: Rutgers University Press, 1987.

n.a. *Black America (Scrapbooks I and II)*. 1895. Theater Collection, New York Public Library at Lincoln Center.

Bloom, Harold. *The Anxiety of Influence: A Theory of Poetry*. New York: Oxford University Press, 1973.

Brathwaite, Edward. *The Development of Creole Society in Jamaica, 1770–1820*. Oxford, England: Clarendon Press, 1971.

Brown, T. Allston. "Early History of Negro Minstrelsy." *New York Clipper*, March 2, 1912, 3.

Brown, Trisha. "Beyond the Mainstream." Directed by Merrill Brockway. *Dance in America*. New York: WNET, 1980.

Broyard, Anatole. "Portrait of the Inauthentic Negro." *Commentary*, July 1950, 56–64.

Carter, Sandy. "An Interview with Johnny Otis." *Z Magazine*, April 1995, 52–57.

Cerwinske, Laura. *Tropical Deco: The Architecture and Design of Old Miami Beach.* New York: Rizzoli, 1981.

"City Summary." *New York Clipper*, October 12, 1861, 206.

―――. *New York Clipper*, November 3, 1860, 230.

Clinton, Catherine. *Tara Revisited: Women, War, & the Plantation Legend.* New York: Abbeville Press, 1995.

Cohen, Selma Jeanne. *Next Week, Swan Lake: Reflections on Dance and Dances.* Middletown, Conn.: Wesleyan University Press, 1982.

Craine, Debra. "Defying Darkness with Dance." (London) *Times*, March 18, 1993, 33.

Croyden, Margaret. "Jerzy Grotowski: The Experiment Continues." *American Theatre.* September 1992, 42–43.

Dehn, Mura. "American Minstrel Show—Black Face Minstrelsy and Its Heritage." *Unpublished Papers on African American Social Dance—1869–1987.* N.d., n.p., Dance Collection, New York Public Library at Lincoln Center.

Deren, Maya. *Divine Horsemen: The Living Gods of Haiti.* [1953]. Kingston, N.Y.: McPherson and Company, 1991.

―――. "Divine Horsemen: The Living Gods of Haiti" (videocassette), Kingston, N.Y.: McPherson and Company, 1991.

Dixon, Brenda. "Black Dance and Dancers and the White Public: A Prolegomenon to Problems of Definition." *Black American Literature Forum.* Spring 1990, 117–23.

Drewal, Margaret Thompson. *Yoruba Ritual: Performance, Play, Agency.* Bloomington, Ind.: Indiana University Press, 1992.

Du Bois, W. E. B. *The Souls of Black Folk.* [1903]. In *Three Negro Classics.* Ed. John Hope Franklin. New York: Avon, 1965, 207–389.

Ellison, Ralph. "Change the Joke and Slip the Yoke." [1958]. In *Shadow and Act.* New York: Vintage, 1972, 45–59.

Emery, Lynne Fauley. *Black Dance from 1619 to Today.* [1972]. Princeton, N.J.: Princeton Book Company, 1988.

Epstein, Dena. *Sinful Tunes and Spirituals: Black Folk Music to the Civil War.* Urbana, Ill.: University of Illinois Press, 1977.

Fletcher, Thomas. *One Hundred Years of the Negro in Show Business.* New York: Burdge and Company, 1954.

Foner, Eric. Interview on "Morning Edition," National Public Radio, August 1990.

Gay, Geneva, and Willie Baber, Eds. *Expressively Black: The Cultural Basis of Ethnic Identity.* New York: Praeger, 1987.

Ghetto. "Reflections of that Good Olde Hip Hop." *Vibe*, June/July 1995, 42.

Gillespie, Arthur. "Evolution of Minstrelsy." In *The Green Book Album.* October 1909. Theater Collection, New York Public Library at Lincoln Center.

Gilman, Sander L. "Black Bodies, White Bodies: Toward an Iconography of Female Sexuality in Late Nineteenth-Century Art, Medicine, and Literature." In *Race, Writing and Difference.* Ed. Henry Louis Gates, Jr. Chicago: University of Chicago Press, 1985, 223–61.

———. "Black Sexuality and Modern Consciousness." In *Blacks and German Culture*. Eds. Reinhold Grimm and Jost Hermand. Madison, Wis.: University of Wisconsin Press, 1986, 35–53.

———. "Degenerate Art." Directed by David Grubin. Los Angeles: KCET, 1993.

n.a. Glover, Savion. "Goings on About Town: Dance." *The New Yorker*, July 9, 1990, 6.

Gonzalez, Miguel. "A Deeper Shade of Blue." *Philadelphia City Paper*, February 10–17, 1995, 24–25.

Goodson, A. C. "Structuralism and Critical History in the Moment of Bakhtin." In *Tracing Literary Theory*. Ed. Joseph Natoli. Urbana, Ill.: University of Illinois Press, 1987, 27–53.

Gordon, David. "Beyond the Mainstream." Directed by Merrill Brockway. Dance in America. New York: WNET, 1980.

Graham, Martha. [1930]. Quoted in Juana de Laban, "What Tomorrow." *Dance Observer*, May 1945, 55–56.

Green, Chuck. "About Tap." Directed by George T. Nierenberg. Los Angeles: Direct Cinema Limited, 1985.

Greenleigh, Jill. "Fresh Faces." *Word Up*, July 1994, 81.

Greskovic, Robert. "Garth Fagan Dance." *Dancemagazine*, February 1991, 112–15.

Gussow, Mel. "V.S. Naipaul in Search of Himself: A Conversation." *New York Times Book Review*, April 24, 1994, 3, 29.

Gutman, Madeleine. "The Legacy of Bronislava Nijinska: Her Memoirs and Choreographic Art." Town of Greenburgh [N.Y.] Arts and Culture Committee *Newsletter*, n.d. [1983].

Hagen, Charles. "The Power of a Video Image Depends on the Caption." *New York Times*, May 10, 1992, 32H.

Haider, Amera. "Mix and Match." (London) *Sunday Times*. September 26, 1993, 9.22.

n.a. Harrington, Oliver W. "A Satirist Gets Reacquainted with America." *Emerge*, May 1994, 14.

Harris, Dale. "Stepping Over Boundaries." (London) *Guardian*, May 13, 1995, 28.

Harris, Rennie. "Notes from Rennie Harris of Pure Movement." "Festival of Four Worlds" program. Philadelphia, Spring 1994, 17.

Harrison, Paul Carter. *The Drama of Nommo: Theater and the African Continuum*. New York: Grove Press, 1972.

Haskell, Arnold. *Balletomania Then and Now*. [1934]. New York: Alfred A. Knopf, 1977.

Haywood, Charles. "James A. Bland, Prince of the Colored Songwriters: A Discourse Delivered Before the Flushing Historical Society." October 25, 1944. Schomburg Center, New York Public Library.

Heilbut, Anthony. *Exiled in Paradise: German Refugee Artists and Intellectuals in America from the 1930s to the Present*. Boston: Beacon Press, 1983.

Hentoff, Nat. "Semitic Solidarity." *Village Voice*, August 25, 1987, 23–25, 91.

Herskovits, Melville. *The Myth of the Negro Past*. [1941]. New York: Harper and Row, 1958.

Hodgson, Moira. "A Balanchine Ballet for Nureyev." *New York Times*, April 8, 1979, D1, D17.

Holloway, Joseph E. Ed. *Africanisms in American Culture.* Bloomington, Ind.: Indiana University Press, 1990.

hooks, bell, and Cornel West. *Breaking Bread: Insurgent Black Intellectual Life.* Boston: South End Press, 1991.

Horst, Louis. *Modern Dance Forms.* [1961]. Princeton, N.J. Princeton Book Company, 1987.

Huggins, Nathan Irvin. "White/Black Faces—Black Masks." In *Harlem Renaissance.* New York: Oxford University Press, 1971, 244–301.

Hughes, Langston. "Note on Commercial Theatre." *Selected Poems of Langston Hughes.* [1959]. New York: Vintage Books, 1974, 190.

Jabbour, Alan. Keynote panel discussion of Congress on Research in Dance Conference. Williamsburg, November 1989.

Jackson, Major. "American Gangsta." *Philadelphia City Paper,* January 28–February 4, 1994, 12–13.

Jamison, Laura. "Poppa Large." *Vibe,* June/July 1995, 64–65.

Johnson, James Weldon. *Black Manhattan.* New York: Knopf, 1930.

Johnston, Jill. "How Dance Artists and Critics Define Dance as Political." *Movement Research Performance Journal,* Fall 1991, 2–3.

Jones, Bill T. "Bill T. Jones/Arnie Zane Company." Directed by Mischa Scorer. *Dance in America.* PBS: 1991.

Jones, Lisa. "Hair Always and Forever." *Village Voice,* August 13, 1991, 47.

Jowitt, Deborah. "Looking Back from Tomorrow." *The Village Voice* (special dance section). April 21, 1987, 3–4.

————. *Time and the Dancing Image.* New York: William Morrow and Company, 1988.

Kagan, Andrew. "Improvisations: Notes on Jackson Pollock and the Black Contribution to American High Culture." *Arts,* March 1979, 96–99.

Kealiinohomoku, Joann. "An Anthropologist Looks at Ballet as a Form of Ethnic Dance." [1969–70] In *What Is Dance?* Eds. Roger Copeland and Marshall Cohen. New York: Oxford University Press, 1983, 533–549.

Kenner, Hugh. "Explosive Memories." *New York Times Book Review,* March 13, 1994, 12.

n.a., n.p., "King Edward and the Negro Opera." London, ca. 1903. Schomburg Center, New York Public Library.

Kirby, Michael. "Criticism: Four Faults." *The Drama Review,* September 1974, 59–68.

Kisselgoff, Anna. "Josephine Baker: Dancing Through the Jazz Age." *New York Times,* March 29, 1987, 14, 38.

Kmen, Henry. *Music in New Orleans.* Baton Rouge: Louisiana University Press, 1966.

Kochman, Thomas. "The Kinetic Element in Black Idiom." In *Rappin' and Stylin' Out: Communication in Black America.* Ed. Thomas Kochman. Urbana, Ill.: University of Illinois Press, 1972, 160–169.

Kramer, Jane. "Letter from Europe." *The New Yorker,* October 12, 1987, 130–144.

Lahr, John. "The World's Most Sensational Absence." *New York Times Book Review,* June 24, 1990, 10–11.

Leymarie, Jean. *Picasso—The Artist of the Century.* New York: Viking Press, 1972.

Long, Richard. *The Black Tradition in American Dance.* New York: Rizzoli, 1989.

Lott, Eric. *Love and Theft: Blackface Minstrelsy and the American Working Class.* New York: Oxford University Press, 1993.

Machlis, Joseph. *Introduction to Contemporary Music.* New York: W. W. Norton, 1961.

Marsh, Dave. "Just What's Being Sold in Country?" *New York Times*, May 24, 1992, 2, 20.

Martinez, Elizabeth. "Seeing More than Black and White." *Z Magazine*, May 1994, 56–59.

Mason, Francis. *I Remember Balanchine.* New York: Doubleday, 1991.

Mazo, Joseph H. "A Little Offbeat." *Dancemagazine*, August 1991, 54.

Mazrui, Ali A. *The Africans: A Triple Heritage.* Boston: Little, Brown and Company, 1986.

McDonagh, Don. *George Balanchine.* Boston: Twayne Publishers, 1983.

Meisner, Nadine. "Taking Dance Down a Passage from India." (London) *Times*, March 23, 1994, 33.

Mills, David. "Rap as Politics." *Emerge*, September 1992, 20–21.

n.a. Arthur Mitchell. "Talk of the Town." *The New Yorker*, December 28, 1987, 36.

Morgan, Joan. "Professor Studies 'Those Loud Black Girls.' " *Black Issues in Higher Education*, June 3, 1993, 20–21.

Morrison, Toni. "The Pain of Being Black." *Time*, May 22, 1989, 120–22.

————. "Unspeakable Things Unspoken: The Afro-American Presence in American Literature." *Michigan Quarterly Review*, Winter, 1989, 1–33.

————. *Playing in the Dark: Whiteness and the Literary Imagination.* Cambridge, Mass.: Harvard University Press, 1992.

Muller, Hedwig. "Parlez-Moi d'Amour: On the Tenth Anniversary of the Death of Josephine Baker." *Ballett International*, April 1985, 20–25.

Nathan, Hans. *Dan Emmett and the Rise of Negro Minstrelsy.* Norman, Okla.: University of Oklahoma Press, 1962.

n.a. Nicholas Brothers. "Goings on About Town: Dance." *The New Yorker*, July 8, 1991, 6.

Nixon, Will. "George C. Wolfe Creates Visions of Black Culture." *American Visions*, April 1991, 50–52.

Novack, Cynthia. *Sharing the Dance: Contact Improvisation and American Culture.* Madison, Wis.: University of Wisconsin Press, 1990.

O'Connor, Francis V. *Jackson Pollock.* New York: Museum of Modern Art, 1967.

O'Connor, Patrick. "Josephine." (London) *Observer* (Sunday magazine), January 19, 1986, 20–29.

Oliveros, Pauline, and Ione. "A Dialogue." *Movement Research Performance Journal*, Fall/Winter 1992, 4, 18.

Otis, Johnny. Interview on "Fresh Air," National Public Radio. November 21, 1989.

Palmer, Brian, et al. "Culture, Politics, and the N.Y. Times." *Lies of Our Times*, December 1990, 3–7.

Pascal, Julia. "Dance Culture." (London) *Observer*, September 14, 1986, 70.

Paskman, Dailey, and Sigmund Spaeth. *"Gentlemen, Be Seated!": A Parade of the Old-Time Minstrels.* Garden City, N.Y.: Doubleday, Doran, 1928.

Pasteur, Alfred B., and Ivory Toldson. *Roots of Soul: The Psychology of Black Expressiveness.* Garden City, N.Y.: Anchor Press, 1982.

Paul, Angus. "New Research Center in Chicago Strives to Preserve and Promote the Legacy of Black Music." *Chronicle of Higher Education,* January 28, 1987, 6, 7, 10.

Peter, John. "Not a Case of Black or White." (London) *Times,* February 14, 1993, 8.17.

Pottlitzer, Joanne. "Cultural Diversity in U.S. Theatre." *International Theatre Institute of the United States Newsletter,* Fall–Winter 1994, 1, 3, 7, 8.

Powell, Richard. "The Blues Aesthetic: Black Culture and Modernism." In *The Blues Aesthetic: Black Culture and Modernism.* Ed. Richard Powell. Washington, D.C.: Washington Project for the Arts, 1989, 18-35.

Reagon, Bernice. Lecture at Temple University, Philadelphia, March 1992.

Reed, Ishmael. *New and Collected Poems.* New York: Atheneum, 1988.

Rice, Edward LeRoy. *Monarchs of Minstrelsy from "Daddy" Rice to Date.* New York: Kenny, 1911.

Rich, Adrienne. "Split at the Root." In *Fathers: Reflections by Daughters.* Ed. Ursula Owen. London: Virago Press, 1983, 170-86.

Riggs, Marlon. "Ruminations of a What Time." *Outlook,* Spring 1991, 12-19.

Robertson, Allen. "Kiss and Tell." *Time Out* (London), April 13-20, 1994, 24.

Robinson, Louie. "The Blackening of White America." *Ebony,* May 1980, 158-60, 162.

Robinson, Marc. "Rights & Passage." *American Theatre,* September 1992, 18-25.

Roman, Robert C. Obituary for Hermes Pan. *Dancemagazine,* January 1991, 30, 32.

Rourke, Constance. *American Humor.* New York: Harcourt, Brace, and Company, 1931.

Rubin, William, Helene Seckel, and Judith Cousins. *Les Demoiselles d'Avignon.* Quoted in Julia Frey, "Anatomy of a Masterpiece." *New York Times Book Review,* April 30, 1995:,18.

Schechner, Richard. *Environmental Theater.* New York: Hawthorn Books, 1973.

———. *The End of Humanism.* New York: Performing Arts Journal Publications, 1982.

———. "An Intercultural Primer." *American Theatre,* October 1991, 28-31, 135-36.

———. Keynote panel discussion. Congress on Research in Dance Conference, Atlanta, August 1992.

Shipman, Pat. *The Evolution of Racism: Human Difference and the Use and Abuse of Science.* Quoted in Robert Wright, "The Perversion of Darwinism." *New York Times Book Review,* July 31, 1994, 7-8.

Simond, Ike. *Old Slack's Reminiscence and Pocket History of the Colored Profession from 1865 to 1891.* Chicago, ca. 1892. Bowling Green, Ohio: Popular Press, 1974.

Slyde, Jimmy. "About Tap." Directed by George T. Nierenberg. Los Angeles: Direct Cinema Limited, 1985.

Smith, Anna Deavere. "About 'On the Road: A Search for American Character.'" "Fires in the Mirror." *Playbill.* New York: Summer 1992.

Southern, Eileen. *The Music of Black Americans: A History.* New York: W. W. Norton, 1971.

Stearns, Marshall, and Jean Stearns. *Jazz Dance: The Story of American Vernacular Dance* [1968]. New York: Schirmer, 1979.

Stuckey, Sterling. "The Skies of Consciousness: African Dance at Pinkster in New York, 1750-1840." In *Going Through the Storm: The Influence of African American Art in History*. New York: Oxford University Press, 1994, 53–80.

Supree, Burt. "Doug Elkins and Carlota Santana." *Village Voice*, July 30, 1991, 98.

Szwed, John F. "Race and the Embodiment of Culture." In *The Body as a Medium of Expression*. Eds. J. Benthall and T. R. Polhemus. New York: Dutton, 1975, 253–70.

Szwed, John F. and Roger D Abrahams. "After the Myth: Studying Afro-American Cultural Patterns in the Plantation Literature." In *African Folklore in the New World*. Ed. Daniel J. Crowley. Austin, Tex.: University of Texas Press, 1977, 65–86.

Szwed, John F. and Morton Marks. "The Afro-American Transformation of European Set Dances and Dance Suites." *Dance Research Journal*, Summer 1988, 29–36.

Talbot, Linda. "Ancient Muses Reborn in the Women of Africa." (London) *Hampstead and Highgate Express*, March 26, 1993, 45.

Tate, Greg. "Diary of a Bug." *Village Voice*, November 22, 1988, 73.

———. "Brown Sound." *Vibe*, November 1994, 38.

n.a. Richard Thomas. "Goings on About Town: Dance." *The New Yorker*, September 2, 1991, 8.

Thompson, Robert Farris. *African Art in Motion*. Berkeley: University of California Press, 1974.

———. "An Aesthetic of the Cool. West African Dance." In *The Theater of Black Americans*. Ed. Errol Hill. Englewood Cliffs, N.J.: Prentice-Hall, 1980, 99–111.

———. "Afro-Modernism." *ArtForum*, September 1991, 91–94.

Todd, Arthur. "Negro-American Theatre Dance." *Dance Magazine*, November 1950, 20–21, 33–34.

Toll, Robert. *Blacking Up: The Minstrel Show in Nineteenth-Century America*. New York: Oxford University Press, 1974.

Torgovnick, Marianna. *Gone Primitive: Savage Intellects, Modern Lives*. Chicago: University of Chicago Press, 1990.

Updegrave, Walter L. "Race and Money." *Money*, December 1989, 152–72.

Valdes, Mimi. "Mack Daddy." *Vibe*, February 1995, 50–51.

Van Vechten, Carl. "The Lindy Hop" [1930] and "The Negro Theatre" [1920]. In *The Dance Writings of Carl Van Vechten*. Ed. Paul Padgette. New York: Dance Horizons, 1974, 34–40.

Vaughan, David. "About Ballet, in Black and White." *New York Times*, January 23, 1988, 27.

Vogel, Susan. *Aesthetics of African Art*. New York: Center for African Art, 1986.

Walker, Sheila. "New Worlds, New Forms." *Dancing*, Part 5. Directed by Orlando Bagwell. New York: Thirteen-WNET, 1993.

Washington, Mary Helen. "Rising up with 'I'll Fly Away.'" *Emerge*, September 1992, 35.

Watrous, Peter. "White Singers + Black Style = Pop Bonanza." *New York Times*, March 11, 1990, 2.1, 34.

Welch, Sharon D. *Communities of Resistance and Solidarity: A Feminist Theology of Liberation.* Maryknoll, N.Y.: Orbis Books, 1985.

Welsh Asante, Kariamu. "Commonalities in African Dance." In *African Culture: The Rhythms of Unity,* Eds. Molefi Kete Asante and Kariamu Welsh Asante. Westport, Conn.: Greenwood Press, 1986, 71–82.

n.a. Williams, Dudley, and Ves Harper. "Goings on About Town: Dance." *The New Yorker,* June 1, 1992, 5.

Wilson, Elliott. "Jailhouse Rock." *Vibe,* March 1995, 34.

Winter, Marian Hannah. "Juba and American Minstrelsy." In *Chronicles of the American Dance.* Ed. Paul Magriel. New York: Henry Holt, 1948, 39–63.

Wittke, Carl. *Tambo and Bones: A History of the American Minstrel Stage.* Durham, N.C.: Duke University Press, 1930.

Wright, Robert. "The Perversion of Darwinism." *New York Times Book Review,* July 31, 1994, 7.

Zwerin, Mike. "A Brubeck Credo: Never Give Up Jazz." *International Herald Tribune,* June 3, 1994, 20.

INDEX

Abdoh, Reza, 157
"About Tap," 52, 53, 55
Abrahams, Roger, 2, 12, 97
"Abyssinia," 117
Adams, Diana, 64
Adolescents: attraction to black life-style, 22, 25, 104, 135; identification with "other," 26, 28
Adzido, 153
Aesop's fables, 83
Aesthetic of the cool. *See* Cool (aesthetic)
Africa: association with promiscuity, 9, 37–38, 41, 45n.18; as single entity, 46n.21, 151
African Americans: and "attitude," 16–17, 83, 96; class status among, 86; as expatriates, 109, 115, 131; family reunion movement, 167; hairstyles, 24–25, 26, 43n.6, 138, 160–64; lifestyles, 22, 25, 138, 160–66; and masking, 85, 112, 114; performance styles, 31, 88, 98. *See also* Hip hop culture; Racial stereotypes; Racism; Segregation; Slavery
African Art in Motion, 12, 16
Africanist aesthetic: characteristics, 12, 19n.2, 51, 85; as cultural im-perative, 23–25, 47–49; improvi-sation in, 31, 49, 117; invisibilization of, 2–3, 5, 23, 32–33, 41, 50–60, 86–87; ludic-tragic trope in, 13, 119; misinterpreta-tion of, 101–2; potency of, 4–5, 9; principles, 7–10, 12–19, 101; tex-tuality in, 3–4, 12; and Thompson's canons, 12; value of movement in, 11. *See also name of specific aesthetic principle*
Africanist art: appropriation of, 39–41, 48–49; motion in, 12
Africanist dance: aesthetic principles, 8–9, 57; compared to ballet, 12–17, 64; contrariety in, 13; criticism of, 9, 53, 139–41; high-affect jux-taposition in, 50; movement in, 11–12, 49, 54, 57, 67–68; planta-tion-derived, 83, 97, 99–101; re-ligion and, 9; speed and density in, 67; styles of, 57, 121; urban, 158–59. *See also name of specific dance*
Africanist drama, 11
Africanist music, 8, 13. *See also* Blues music; Jazz music; Rap music
African masks, 39, 40, 45n.18
African religions: dancing deities in,

About the Author

BRENDA DIXON GOTTSCHILD is Professor of Dance at Temple University where she teaches performance history, theory, and criticism. Formerly a professional dancer and actress, she is the Philadelphia critic for *Dancemagazine* and has published articles in *The Drama Review*, *Dance Research Journal*, *Design for Arts in Education*, and *The Black American Literature Forum.* She is coauthor of the third and most recent edition of *The History of Dance in Art and Education.*